JAN -- 2005

Praise for *The New Laws of the Stock Market Jungle*

"A sophisticated trip through the ever-changing jungle."

—Barton Biggs, Managing Partner, Traxis Partners

"Michael Panzner, an experienced investment professional, has written a great book! It contains so many interesting observations supported by well-selected figures that every investor will gain insights that will serve him well for the rest of his life!"

—Marc Faber, Managing Director, Marc Faber Limited,
Editor, *Gloom, Boom & Doom Report*

"'This time is different' may be the most dangerous phrase in the investment lexicon, but sometimes things really are different. In this valuable book, Michael Panzner applies his encyclopedic knowledge of the markets over the last three decades to analyzing the many crucial ways in which investing today is, indeed, different than ever before."

—Mark Hulbert, Editor, *Hulbert Financial Digest*,
Columnist, *CBS Marketwatch*

"*The New Laws of the Stock Market Jungle* is definitely not for dummies. This sophisticated but lively book is for serious investors who want an insider's perspective on making money in uncertain markets."

—Jon Markman, Contributing Editor, *CNBC* on *MSN Money*,
and Senior Investment Strategist and Portfolio Manager,
Pinnacle Investment Advisors

"Stock market speculation is both an art and a science and with this book, Michael Panzner explains just why this is so in a way practical and thorough enough to actually help you invest and trade more intelligently. What more could anyone ask?"

—Peter Navarro, author of *If It's Raining in Brazil, Buy Starbucks*
and *When the Market Moves, Will You Be Ready?*

"Over the last decade, important changes in technology and trading rules have transformed the way that Wall Street operates, while new incentives for institutional investors have altered their behavior and our markets. Panzner's book identifies new opportunities and threats and offers insights that can help investors to profit in the years ahead."

—John Nofsinger, author of *Investment Madness* and *Infectious Greed*

"Panzner's book reveals many of the tools and tricks we professionals use every day to make money. If you wonder why the 'little guys' are always at a disadvantage and why many commentators and academics can't seem to explain these markets, it is because they are unaware of these factors. Honestly, I wish he had not said a thing."

—Robert Jafek, principal, Torrey Pines Capital Management, and former partner, Nicholas-Applegate Capital Management

"As an equity dealer for a fund group managing nearly $30 billion, I have used Michael Panzner's market insights and expertise on a daily basis to help me trade effectively. Now, through this book, his 20 years of market experience are available to everyone. From the seasoned investment professional to the casual investor, anyone looking to gain a better understanding of how new market forces are changing the dynamics of investing today, will benefit from reading this book."

—Ronald J. Lysek, Jr., International Equity Trader, Franklin Mutual Advisers, Inc.

"This 'bible' on trading and markets is packed with the most up-to-date information. I recommend this book to anyone who wants to understand the intricacies of today's stock market environment."

—Peter Tropaitis, Vice President, Senior Global Equity Trader, Federated Investors

The New Laws of the Stock Market Jungle

An Insider's Guide to Successful Investing in a Changing World

Michael J. Panzner

FT Prentice Hall

FINANCIAL TIMES

An Imprint of PEARSON EDUCATION
Upper Saddle River, NJ • New York • London • San Francisco • Toronto • Sydney
Tokyo • Singapore • Hong Kong • Cape Town • Madrid
Paris • Milan • Munich • Amsterdam

www.ft-ph.com

Library of Congress Cataloging-in-Publication Data
Panzner, Michael J.
  The new laws of the stock market jungle : an insider's guide to successful investing in a
changing world / Michael J. Panzner.
  p. cm.
  Includes bibliographical references and index.
  ISBN 0-321-24785-X
  1. Investments. 2. Stocks. 3. Stock exchanges. I. Title.
HG4521.P26 2005
332.63'22--dc22   2004050519

Editorial/Production Supervision: *Donna Cullen-Dolce*
Cover Design Director: *Jerry Votta*
Cover Design: *Nina Scuderi*
Art Director: *Gail Cocker-Bogusz*
Manufacturing Buyer: *Maura Zaldivar*
Executive Editor: *Jim Boyd*
Marketing Manager: *John Pierce*
Editorial Assistant: *Richard Winkler*

This book is sold with the understanding that neither the author nor the publisher is engaged in rendering legal, accounting or other professional services or advice by publishing this book. Each individual situation is unique. Thus, if legal or financial advice or other expert assistance is required in a specific situation, the services of a competent professional should be sought to ensure that the situation has been evaluated carefully and appropriately. The author and the publisher disclaim any liability, loss or risk resulting, directly or indirectly, from the use or application of any of the contents of this book.

© 2005 Michael J. Panzner
Published by Pearson Education, Inc.
Publishing as Financial Times Prentice Hall
Upper Saddle River, New Jersey 07458

Financial Times Prentice Hall offers excellent discounts on this book when ordered in quantity for bulk purchases or special sales. For more information, please contact: U.S. Corporate and Government Sales, 1-800-382-3419, corpsales@pearsontechgroup.com.
For sales outside of the U.S., please contact: International Sales, 1-317-581-3793, international@pearsontechgroup.com.

Printed in the United States of America
1st Printing   ISBN 0-321-24785-X

Pearson Education Ltd.
Pearson Education Australia Pty, Limited
Pearson Education Singapore, Pte. Ltd.
Pearson Education North Asia Ltd.
Pearson Education Canada, Ltd.
Pearson Educación de Mexico, S.A. de C.V.
Pearson Education—Japan
Pearson Education Malaysia, Pte. Ltd

To Catherine,
Girl of my dreams,
Love of my life,
My best friend.

In an increasingly competitive world, it is quality
of thinking that gives an edge—an idea that opens new
doors, a technique that solves a problem, or an insight
that simply helps make sense of it all.

We work with leading authors in the various arenas
of business and finance to bring cutting-edge thinking
and best learning practice to a global market.

It is our goal to create world-class print publications
and electronic products that give readers
knowledge and understanding which can then be
applied, whether studying or at work.

To find out more about our business
products, you can visit us at www.ft-ph.com

FINANCIAL TIMES PRENTICE HALL BOOKS

For more information, please go to www.ft-ph.com

Business and Society

Douglas K. Smith
On Value and Values: Thinking Differently About We in an Age of Me

Current Events

Alan Elsner
Gates of Injustice: The Crisis in America's Prisons

John R. Talbott
Where America Went Wrong: And How to Regain Her Democratic Ideals

Economics

David Dranove
What's Your Life Worth? Health Care Rationing...Who Lives? Who Dies? Who Decides?

Entrepreneurship

Dr. Candida Brush, Dr. Nancy M. Carter, Dr. Elizabeth Gatewood, Dr. Patricia G. Greene, and Dr. Myra M. Hart
Clearing the Hurdles: Women Building High Growth Businesses

Oren Fuerst and Uri Geiger
From Concept to Wall Street: A Complete Guide to Entrepreneurship and Venture Capital

David Gladstone and Laura Gladstone
Venture Capital Handbook: An Entrepreneur's Guide to Raising Venture Capital, Revised and Updated

Thomas K. McKnight
Will It Fly? How to Know if Your New Business Idea Has Wings... Before You Take the Leap

Stephen Spinelli, Jr., Robert M. Rosenberg, and Sue Birley
Franchising: Pathway to Wealth Creation

Executive Skills

Cyndi Maxey and Jill Bremer
It's Your Move: Dealing Yourself the Best Cards in Life and Work

John Putzier
Weirdos in the Workplace

Finance

Aswath Damodaran
The Dark Side of Valuation: Valuing Old Tech, New Tech, and New Economy Companies

Kenneth R. Ferris and Barbara S. Pécherot Petitt
Valuation: Avoiding the Winner's Curse

International Business and Globalization

John C. Edmunds
Brave New Wealthy World: Winning the Struggle for World Prosperity

Robert A. Isaak
The Globalization Gap: How the Rich Get Richer and the Poor Get Left Further Behind

Johny K. Johansson
In Your Face: How American Marketing Excess Fuels Anti-Americanism

Peter Marber
Money Changes Everything: How Global Prosperity Is Reshaping Our Needs, Values, and Lifestyles

Fernando Robles, Françoise Simon, and Jerry Haar
Winning Strategies for the New Latin Markets

Investments

Zvi Bodie and Michael J. Clowes
Worry-Free Investing: A Safe Approach to Achieving Your Lifetime Goals

Michael Covel
Trend Following: How Great Traders Make Millions in Up or Down Markets

Aswath Damodaran
Investment Fables: Exposing the Myths of "Can't Miss" Investment Strategies

Harry Domash
Fire Your Stock Analyst! Analyzing Stocks on Your Own

David Gladstone and Laura Gladstone
Venture Capital Investing: The Complete Handbook for Investing in Businesses for Outstanding Profits

D. Quinn Mills
Buy, Lie, and Sell High: How Investors Lost Out on Enron and the Internet Bubble

D. Quinn Mills
Wheel, Deal, and Steal: Deceptive Accounting, Deceitful CEOs, and Ineffective Reforms

Michael J. Panzner
The New Laws of the Stock Market Jungle: An Insider's Guide to Successful Investing in a Changing World

H. David Sherman, S. David Young, and Harris Collingwood
Profits You Can Trust: Spotting & Surviving Accounting Landmines

Michael Thomsett
Stock Profits: Getting to the Core—New Fundamentals for a New Age

Leadership

Jim Despain and Jane Bodman Converse
And Dignity for All: Unlocking Greatness through Values-Based Leadership

Marshall Goldsmith, Cathy Greenberg, Alastair Robertson, and Maya Hu-Chan
Global Leadership: The Next Generation

Management

Rob Austin and Lee Devin
Artful Making: What Managers Need to Know About How Artists Work

J. Stewart Black and Hal B. Gregersen
Leading Strategic Change: Breaking Through the Brain Barrier

Contents

Acknowledgments

One of the first—and hardest—lessons that individuals must learn if they want to be successful traders or investors is how little they know—and how much they actually need to understand—about the complex and often illogical world of financial markets. For a lucky few, sometimes all it takes is the bruising and battering resulting from some early, but less-than-catastrophic, mistakes and misjudgments that sets them on the path to fast-track enlightenment. For most people, though, it is a combination of years of hard-knocks experience and volumes of second-hand wisdom—passed down from astute observers and seasoned veterans—that eventually turns the light bulb on. In my case, it is the latter that applies.

Nonetheless, I consider myself fortunate, because the journey thus far has been both interesting and enlightening, and often fun. During the past two decades, I have had many ongoing personal and professional relationships with colleagues, clients, and others who have constantly opened my eyes to the many mysteries of the markets, often on a real-time basis. In doing so, those individuals have helped me to reach a point where I better understand why people buy and sell, and otherwise act they way they do once trading gets underway. They have also given me the confidence to set my ideas down on paper, so that I might share my knowledge with others.

I am especially indebted to John Liang and Bill Siegel, who have been a major part of my life going all the way back to our days at Columbia University. I thank them as much for their enduring friendship as for their words of wisdom and their phenomenal understanding of people and markets.

I am also grateful to the following individuals for their interesting insights, valuable advice, and helpful support through the years: Howard Appleby, Mike Bellaro, David Bhonslay, Fred Bond, Bill Dalton, Christian Derold, Brian Doherty, Louis Florentin-Lee, Doug Foulsham, Kate Gallagher, Joe Greco, Justin Haque, Rob Jafek, Tom Kalaris, David Learned, Chung Lew, Alan Lewis, Jeff Lovelock, Ron Lysek, Eric Marx, Kevin Melly, Brian Monahan, George Noble, Jonathan Perkin, Chas Player, George Ross, Emma Shear, Steve Siegel, Mary Ellen Smith, Philip Sofaer, Benn Spiers, Chris Spurlock, Erin St. John, Brian Staub, Ulrik Trampe, Peter Tropaitis, Chris Tucker, Harry Tyser, Derek Wallis, and Jeff Weishaar.

"Hats off" as well to those fine people at Bloomberg LP, who have done their best to provide information and technology resources that make life so easy for anyone who wants to get to the bottom of what is going on in any of the markets around the world.

I also want to thank my sister Paige, for her ongoing support and infectious enthusiasm, especially when the book was nothing more than a dream; Danielle Sessa, for her valuable insights and for pointing me in the right direction when it really mattered most; my editor at Financial Times Prentice Hall, Jim Boyd, for believing in the project and for setting forth a vision of what I was capable of that surprised even me; my production editor, Donna Cullen-Dolce, for all her hard work in ably overseeing the evolution of raw material into finished product; and, my agent, John Willig, of Literary Services, Inc., for his essential advice and for being the voice of calm and understanding.

Undoubtedly, I would not have gotten through this effort at all without the support and understanding of my children, Sophie, Emily, Mollie and Nellie, and my wife, Catherine, who really make it all worthwhile.

Preface

In the forest, there are small creatures that move almost effortlessly beneath the ghostly pall of a moonless night, slipping through dense vegetation, a jumble of hazards and traps, and a menacing cabal of hungry predators poised to pounce on the weak and the unwary. Instinctively, they remain attuned to the threats posed by those who are bigger, stronger, or more ruthless than they are. In true Darwinian fashion, they manage to survive and thrive, despite seemingly poor odds. Why? Because like successful investors in today's stock market, they understand the laws of the jungle—as well as the sights, sounds, and subtle nuances that signal danger and opportunity—and they act accordingly, making the most of their unique individual strengths and evolutionary advantages.

The New Laws of the Stock Market Jungle is designed to help you improve your investment performance by giving you an insider's perspective on how equity investing has changed in recent years—and by showing you how to capitalize on these changes. This will enable you to reduce risk and avoid pitfalls, to take advantage of market volatility and short-term price anomalies, and to formulate a winning strategy with a professional edge. Written for those who have at least some measure of experience, the book explores how a broad range of coincident and convergent influences—including the dramatic boom and bust of the past decade—has affected time horizons, speculative behavior, investor psychology, risk preferences, price patterns and relationships, performance metrics, and other aspects that have made the stock market more treacherous than before.

Admittedly, there are some who might argue that the accounting and other scandals that have come to light during the past few years are evidence that circumstances have only recently changed or, perhaps, that the turmoil is fleeting—like a summer squall that will soon blow over. In reality, these developments are but one small part of a much more widespread pattern of upheaval that has been taking place over the course of two decades or so. In many respects, they are symptoms of the shift, rather than the shift itself. Unfortunately, such headline-grabbing revelations often end up directing investors' attentions away from what they need to focus on to come out ahead in the modern share-trading arena. As with crimes of violence, the horrors of war, and the various natural forces wreaking havoc around the world, these events, while terrible for those involved, often have little direct impact on most people's lives.

Part 1 of *The New Laws of the Stock Market Jungle* reviews many of the significant developments that have affected equity—and other—markets in recent years, including advances in technology, improvements in electronic communications networks, the rise of powerful new players, the increased use of leverage, infrastructure changes, the globalization and democratization of finance, burgeoning information flows, falling transaction costs, and the dramatic growth of "alternative" investing.

Part 2 contains Chapters 1 through 10, which explore and dissect each of the 10 New Laws of the Stock Market Jungle. Each chapter sets forth a description of the core issues, pertinent factors behind the modern developments, the potential consequences for investors, and tactics and strategies for counteracting or capitalizing on current circumstances. Throughout, these chapters highlight situations where the unexpected seems to be occurring more often, and where the "Old Laws" have changed dramatically—or have otherwise been completely replaced—as outlined in Table P.1. There are also valuable resources to tap in to, tough questions to ask, and important signs to look—and watch out—for in yourself and others when contemplating a buying or selling decision. Although a number of potential investing approaches are touched upon, the emphasis is on providing you with critical intelligence that complements and strengthens your own investment plan.

Part 3 offers a brief conclusion and looks at the potential implications for investors of a continuation of recent developments, as well as other factors that might impact stock market investing in the years ahead. The Additional References and Resources section provides supplemental background material for those who would like to know more about some of the key issues and themes that are affecting the modern day share-trading environment.

While many books on investing seem to offer nirvana in the form of a "silver bullet," or even a black box method for garnering outsize returns in nearly all market conditions—with little in the way of subjective input—

Table P.1 New Laws of the Stock Market Jungle...and What They Have Replaced

	New Law	Old Law
1	**INTRADAY VOLATILITY**	
	Intraday share price volatility is on the rise.	In the past, wide intraday share price swings were less common, and when they did occur they were often associated with unexpected geopolitical or economic developments.
2	**TRADING LIKE COMMODITIES**	
	Stocks are increasingly being bought and sold like commodities.	In the past, institutions generally bought and sold stocks based on traditional methods of investment analysis, often with a longer-term perspective in mind.
3	**APPROACHES AND ATTITUDES**	
	Investing and reason frequently give way to speculation and emotion.	In the past, institutional buying and selling was primarily driven by logic and measured analysis (although emotions have always influenced investor behavior).
4	**INFORMATION AND COMMUNICATIONS**	
	More information and faster communications often have unexpected consequences.	In the past, information tended to circulate around the marketplace in a slower and more orderly fashion, and the telephone was the primary means of communication.
5	**DERIVATIVES**	
	Derivatives are exerting a growing influence on share prices.	In the past, the action in the derivatives market was generally secondary to what took place in the underlying cash markets (except on certain occasions, such as Triple Witching Fridays).

Table P.1   New Laws of the Stock Market Jungle...and What They Have
Replaced (continued)

	New Law	Old Law
6	**SEASONALITY AND CYCLES**	
	Many seasonal and cyclical patterns are becoming less predictable.	In the past, many seasonal and cyclical patterns were less widely known and were not affected by today's rapidly changing market forces.
7	**IMBALANCES AND UPHEAVALS**	
	Aggressive approaches and tactics are leading to more unstable short-term imbalances.	In the past, institutions tended to rely on more conservative approaches to investing and more passive methods of buying and selling shares.
8	**FORM AND FANTASY**	
	Substance and reality increasingly give way to form and fantasy.	In the past, data produced and distributed by companies, analysts, government agencies, and others was less subject to error, distortion, and manipulation.
9	**MARKET INDICATORS**	
	Many traditional market indicators are becoming less reliable.	In the past, many market indicators were less widely known and were not affected by today's rapidly changing market forces.
10	**GLOBAL FACTORS**	
	Global factors and foreign investors are exerting a growing influence on share prices.	In the past, American investors and domestic concerns were much more relevant to the direction of U.S. share prices than overseas influences.

the reality is that such panaceas do not really exist. Along with myriad individual and institutional players in the equity arena, you cannot always get it right—nor should you expect to. However, it is my hope that with a solid understanding of what goes on in the underbelly of the market, and with the benefit of my 20 years of institutional trading and investing experience, those of you with a thoughtfully constructed and consistent long-term plan will end up as "kings" of the stock market jungle. Under those circumstances, the roar of success is likely to be deafening.

PART 1

EVOLUTION

The Modern Jungle

---

*Developments that have influenced
today's stock market.*

From the beginning, the language of the American stock market has included references to a colorful menagerie of creatures and critters, conjuring up vivid imagery that breathes life into a world of cold numbers and hard facts. Bulls and bears, dogs and dinosaurs, spiders and sharks[1]— all have found their way into the lexicon of equity investing, making for good copy and catchy sound bites. Almost designed, it seems, to keep audiences enthralled with the daily comings and goings of various buyers and sellers. Regrettably, these simple descriptions have sometimes fostered the illusion that coming out ahead is relatively easy—merely a matter of choosing between two extremes—or, to put it in Wall Street terms, of picking winners rather than losers. Yet, whether referring to the hard-charging optimism of bulls, trampling excitedly through fields of worry and doubt, or the grizzly pessimism of bears, chomping on high prices with super-sized incisors, investors have sometimes overlooked a key point: Because of the diverse backgrounds and complex—often irrational—interactions of various participants, making money is frequently a challenge for even the most seasoned players.

This did not always seem to be the case, especially during the stock market bubble that developed in the 1990s. Although many investors did not fully appreciate it at the time, an even more simplistic understanding

1

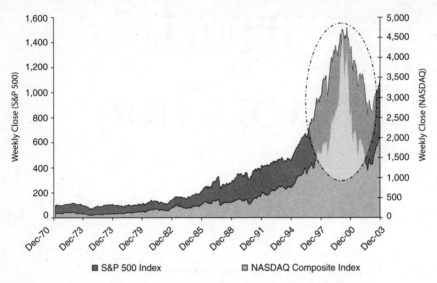

Figure P1.1   Portrait of a Stock Market Bubble (Source: Bloomberg LP).

of how the game was played influenced the collective consciousness during the dot-com[2] days. The battle cry then: Just "buy and hold" until the price—of the stock or mutual fund—goes up. Of course, that view proved to be foolhardy—and expensive—in the wake of the collapse that followed, and nowadays there are signs that at least some of the "irrational exuberance"[3] of the era has been slowly ebbing away. Nonetheless, the echoes of often fleeting successes during that upswing still linger, occasionally serving to hide the fact that the equity market has always been like a dense jungle, teeming with predators and dangerous traps. It is—like many areas of the business world where a potential for sizable returns exists—a place where the strongest, savviest, and most ruthless players tend to dominate the inside ranks. For the most part, they establish the ground rules and influence price action in ways that can seem baffling to a casual observer.

To be sure, this is not just conjecture, as an assortment of qualitative and quantitative data—from tallies of block trades[4] to exchange-sponsored surveys of market activity—generally supports the view that large-scale operators have been—and will probably remain—the driving force behind daily share-trading turnover. Even at the height of the Bubble, for example, when individuals played a starring role in supporting and promoting the fortunes of countless technology, media, and telecommunications companies—or TMTs, as they where called back then—pension funds, mutual funds, investment banks, and other major institutional players generally ruled the investment roost. Of course, size in itself has never been an absolute advantage—in finance or in nature—and there are many examples of investors—and creatures—who, lacking obvious advantages in terms of resources and capabilities, have managed to thrive despite seemingly poor odds.

Indeed, the nimbleness associated with being small can sometimes give an edge to the individual investor, along with the flexibility that comes from being able to trade a broad range of instruments with little need for regulatory approval or committee endorsement. Some professional money managers, for example, cannot buy certain types of securities because of internal restrictions or contractual obligations. They also tend to avoid stocks of companies with capitalizations[5]—a measure of their size—below minimum threshold levels due to worries about liquidity and other concerns. As a consequence, the ability to invest in shares or funds that do not appear on institutional radar screens or to trade in and out of all kinds of markets can offer a useful advantage to smaller players. They can also respond more quickly than in the past to breaking news and rapidly changing developments because of significant improvements in technology and communications networks, as well as the vast information resources now available through the Internet and other channels. Taken together, these factors have made it easier for nonprofessionals to achieve investing success.

Ironically, given the mediocre results posted through the years by a significant proportion of institutional money managers in a long string of quarterly performance surveys, together with positive data on individual investor performance from at least one academic study,[6] it seems that larger share operators do not necessarily have a monopoly on investing ability. This is in spite of their size and many tactical advantages. According to the research, which analyzed the returns of 113,000 accounts at a large discount brokerage firm between January 1990 and November 1996, some 20 percent of the retail investors studied managed to consistently outperform the market throughout the near seven-year time span, while the top 10 percent beat the average by about 38 percent per year. Not a bad showing for so-called amateurs.

Nonetheless, the same forces that appear to have leveled the field for outsiders have had a far greater impact on the mechanisms and methods of the institutional marketplace. Fueled in part by the virtuous circle of investments leading to improvements that stimulate further spending, the structure of the wholesale share-trading environment has undergone a dramatic change during the past two decades. This, in turn, has altered the personal links that were once fundamental to how markets operated. For instance, with the development of electronically connected dealing and back-office systems, it is now possible for an investor to initiate, execute, and settle a trade without actually having to speak to another individual—presumably reducing the risk of human error. Yet without that interaction, today's professionals sometimes miss out on a variety of benefits—such as picking up on unique insights about supply and demand or brainstorming alternative approaches to executing share orders—that have traditionally been available to them.

Other significant changes include the development of powerful processing and data-retrieval capabilities, available in many cases at the touch of a screen or with the click of a mouse. Whether accessed through in-house computers or systems provided by outside vendors, many institutions on the "sell side"—brokers, investment banks, and other intermediaries—and the "buy side"—mutual funds, pension funds, and other institutions that manage money—now have impressive resources at their disposal. They can instantly sift through, sort, and summarize what is going on in the market without having to leave their desks or call on Information Technology professionals for support. They are able to quickly analyze and trade vast portfolios of complex securities in ways which would have been inconceivable even two decades ago. And, in many instances, they now rely almost exclusively on order management systems (OMSs)—rather than paper blotters—to monitor trades on a real-time basis.

Communications methods and networks have also been significantly reshaped and improved in recent years. This has dramatically altered the ties that bind in equity investing. With almost limitless capacity, vastly improved quality, a variety of different avenues featuring numerous bells and whistles, and near universal access, modern communications channels have expanded the number of person-to-person exchanges taking place during—and outside of—trading hours. They have also increased the quantity and speed of interactions between various market participants. At any given time, for example, a sell-side trader might be talking on the telephone, making eye contact with a colleague, speaking on the internal squawk box, reading an email, responding to an instant message, listening to CNBC, and broadcasting informal comments to a preset group of contacts through a Bloomberg terminal—maybe even while sipping some coffee and chomping on a donut. Efficient, but no doubt a recipe for indigestion.

This explosive growth in communications traffic and the overall degree of "connectedness" has been matched by a parallel rise in the volume and quality of real-time, readily accessible data, news, analysis, and other information streams coming from numerous internal and external sources. Whether through informal channels, such as overhead public address (PA) systems, in-house "chat" programs, or mobile telephones; traditional financial media outlets or scrolling newswires; or email, proprietary information vendors, or the Internet, institutional operators are showered with absolute gushers of market intelligence. Or, on occasion, the exact opposite, depending on the nature of the source. Whatever the case, most view the data blitz as a necessary evil for staying on top of the investing game.

On another front, the rise of new technologies at both ends of the trade processing pipeline has accelerated the trend towards lower transaction fees—and related rises in turnover—that began in earnest with the elimination of fixed commissions on share trading in 1975.[7] Spurred on by extensive productivity improvements, increased competition from discount operators and wholesale agents providing execution-only services, and the far-reaching impact of a long-running bull market, banks and brokers developed systems and practices designed to provide better service and handle more trades at a lower cost. Together with the structural changes and substantially increased capacity put into place by the various U.S. exchanges in the wake of the October 1987 stock market crash, commission rates have, at both the wholesale and retail levels, fallen sharply. This has created powerful incentives for investors to boost their overall activity levels.

The rise of the Internet—along with a wide range of proprietary computer networks and user-friendly systems established by a host of modern discount brokers and other intermediaries—has also stimulated increased turnover. The reason? It has simplified and reduced the number of steps needed to buy and sell shares, mutual funds, and other financial products. Instead of following the well-worn path of telephoning a designated representative or call center, placing an order, having it processed through numerous links as it made its way to and from the relevant exchange or administrative center, and waiting—sometimes endlessly—for confirmation that the transaction was—or was not—executed, retail investors now have the option of going online. There, with a few simple clicks or keystrokes, they can usually get their business done fairly quickly and efficiently.

For institutional players, there are even more options. Driven in part by pressure from mutual funds and other large institutional money managers for more electronic "connectivity" and rapid trade reporting—in the name of increased productivity and better risk management—buy and sell orders can now be routed through third-party dealing systems; from internal client OMS programs directly to sell-side computer terminals; through alternative trading venues such as Electronic Communications Networks (ECNs) and Crossing Networks (CNs);[8] or by email, instant message, and of course, the telephone. What is more, the relatively seamless integration of desktop dealing systems with back office operations and settlement functions—which have become, in some cases, nearly "paperless"—has substantially eliminated many of the related processing bottlenecks that were common during the 1980s.

Taken together, sharply falling commission rates and more efficient trading technologies, as well as a turnover-friendly move to decimal pricing,[9] have dramatically increased share volumes and transaction totals in recent years. In many respects, the pattern has mirrored the way traffic expands to quickly jam newly widened highways before the last bit of blacktop is even laid down. The added combination of a fairly supportive macroeconomic environment—for a great deal of the last two decades, at least—intensive marketing and "educational" efforts by the financial services industry, and perhaps, the psychological appeal of hands-on control provided by new and easy-to-use interactive technologies has also helped. Considerable numbers of small and large players alike have been inspired to move away from the long-followed buy-and-hold model towards more active approaches and lower-margin, higher-volume trading methods. While index investing and other passive strategies remain a formidable presence in modern equity markets, the urge to act—and to act more frequently—has been growing.

Along with this far-reaching shift has been the phenomenal expansion in the market for derivatives—instruments, such as options and futures, which essentially "derive" their values from other securities or commodities. Options give owners the right, but not the obligation, to buy or sell an underlying asset at a preset price during an established time frame. In exchange for an initial purchase amount, or "premium," the seller of the option, or "writer," agrees to fulfill the commitment if called upon to do so. Futures, on the other hand, are contracts between buyers and sellers whereby they agree to execute a transaction at an agreed price on or before some specified date, with the seller typically having the right to trigger settlement during the period when "delivery" is allowed. In both cases, either party can usually close out its side of the deal by executing an offsetting trade with someone else prior to the final expiration, or "exercise," of the agreement.

While they have existed in one form or another for centuries,[10] financial derivatives—or "synthetic" securities, as they are often called—really began to take off following innovative moves at two Midwest-based trading venues. The first was the launch of standardized equity options trading on the Chicago Board Options Exchange (CBOE) in 1973; the second was the 1982 introduction of Standard & Poor's 500 Index futures—with a relatively novel settlement feature that allowed the two parties to the contract to close out their interests with cash rather than an exchange of securities—on the Chicago Mercantile Exchange (CME). Combining the power of leverage with increased pricing visibility and a centralized marketplace, these high-octane instruments attracted a wide assortment of private investors and speculators looking for a better-than-average bang for their buck.

Institutional interest eventually came on strongly as well, aided by several important developments. Among them was the formulation of a landmark theory on options pricing by academicians Fischer Black, Myron Scholes, and Robert Merton—referred to as the Black-Scholes model—which allowed for a more rigorous and scientific assessment of valuation and risk. In addition, substantial improvements in computer processing power enabled investors and traders to quickly analyze and manipulate increasingly complex securities and portfolios of unrelated instruments. Academic studies and industry promotional efforts touting the "insurance" benefits that derivatives could provide to managers of large and sometimes unwieldy portfolios, as well as the combination of intellectual firepower and financial market intelligence stimulated by the rise of large-scale Wall Street operators, added to the growing attractiveness of the instruments.

Like waving a lit match near gasoline, however, it took the euphoria of a breathtaking bull market, sharply falling interest rates, and a decisive change in compensation preferences away from cash towards "paper"[11] to really get the derivatives market going during the Bubble years—and beyond. Inevitably, a range of products popped up to satisfy the rapidly rising demand. Aided by a parallel acceptance of leverage and risk among an ever-widening circle of investors, derivatives have become an important fixture of the U.S. equity markets—but not without controversy. The

1998 U.S. Federal Reserve-led bailout of Long Term Capital Management, a highly-leveraged derivatives player that nearly got wiped out by unusual conditions in global fixed-income markets, as well as negative comments from knowledgeable hands such as famed investor Warren Buffet, who described these synthetic instruments as "weapons of mass financial destruction," were not taken lightly.

Nevertheless, this speculative shift echoed another major development taking place in the marketplace. Many investors—as well as the managements of publicly listed companies—were becoming increasingly short-term oriented. For whatever reasons—the speedier pace of the Information Age, the increased volatility associated with aggressive portfolio strategies and unfamiliar macroeconomic conditions, or even a more superficial approach to life—small and large players alike began to focus on quarterly, monthly, and even daily returns and performance benchmarks. Other none-too-disinterested parties also did their part to reinforce the swing away from a long-term investing perspective. The brokerage community, for example, always eager to satisfy a budding demand for more commission-paying action, redirected its efforts accordingly. The financial mass media, increasingly striving for the business equivalent of "leads that bleed," juiced up reports and added experienced market operators to their lineups.

Compensation arrangements, altered to reflect the modern perspective, also reinforced it. Corporations, institutional money managers, and investment banks structured deals that almost seemed tailored to capitalize on quick fixes and stepped-up speculation, while offering relatively little in the way of downside risk if circumstances did not work out as planned. Moreover, stimulated to a great extent by investors' and managers' unfortunate reluctance to look beyond surface facts and figures, as well as a corresponding gullibility with respect to modern performance measurement data—or "metrics," as the trendier breed of analysts coming onto the scene called them—many beneficiaries of the generous new provisions had a strong incentive to focus on near-term results and fleeting accomplishments. In the new era, the long run was quickly becoming a has-been.

Along those same lines, another phenomenon began to take hold, especially during the roller coaster ride of the past decade: the growing importance of trading. Epitomized by the widely reported exploits of independent "day traders" during the go-go days, the professional dealer's role has actually undergone a substantial metamorphosis in recent years, especially on the money management side of the business.

Once viewed as overhead and regarded as little more than order clerks at all but the largest institutions, buy-side traders' primary responsibility in earlier times was to execute investment strategies on behalf of portfolio managers, the "real" decision-makers. They doled out trades to counterparties on the sell side and ensured that transactions settled properly. However, with the growing complexity and variety of financial instruments that began appearing in the marketplace, and the threats posed by increasingly sophisticated competitors employing multiple investing styles, professional money managers began to rethink the situation. They recognized the advantages that could be gained—and the disasters that could be avoided—by relying on in-house traders to closely monitor news and short-term supply-and-demand imbalances.

Together with this newfound importance came the recognition that these execution specialists, by virtue of having their ears constantly to the ground, might be good at detecting anomalies that could prove valuable at the earliest stages of the investing process. They could also help uncover interesting opportunities and round out a potentially one-sided analysis with valuable color on market psychology and complicated technical issues. Reflecting a change in status and influence that was stoked in no small way by the media-driven promotion of active traders as swashbuckling buccaneers during the Bubble years, centralized dealing desks began taking on more of a "partnership" role at many traditional fund management firms. They gained a larger say in setting policy, making investment decisions, and allocating commissions. Eventually, this paved the way for a significant cross-pollination of methods and mindsets.

This combination of circumstances—an increasing emphasis on the short-term, the rise of trading, and a rapidly growing derivatives market—also laid the groundwork for another revolution. Suddenly there was a significant expansion in the number of modern operators in the marketplace, primarily hedge funds, offering alternative approaches to familiar "long-only" investing styles. Dating back to 1949, when Alfred W. Jones created the first such approach to capitalize on inefficiencies by buying undervalued stocks and selling overpriced shares "short," hedge funds were once viewed primarily as a "rich man's game" because of U.S. regulatory restrictions. In fact, the sector was relatively unknown before the 1990s; what little public awareness that existed was driven largely by the media-reported exploits and long-term successes of global big picture—or "macro"—players such as George Soros. Following the post-2000 collapse, however—when the realization took hold that paper gains could

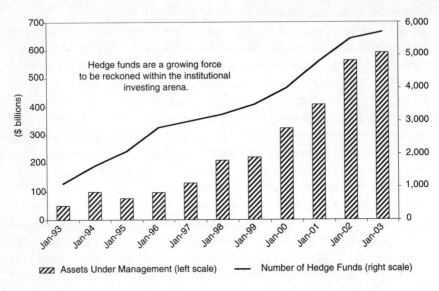

Figure P1.2   Hedge Funds—Assets Under Management and Number of Funds
(Source: Hennessee Group LLC).

quickly evaporate into painful losses—a more widespread interest in the
"alternative investment sector" developed, as Figure P1.2 makes clear.

   At the same time, the increasingly unsettled economic outlook, relatively cheap credit,[12] and the widespread fallout from the bear market—
which pressured financial services firms, in particular, to cut costs in the
face of declining revenues—led to another shift. Considerable numbers of
traditional money managers, analysts, traders, and others, lured by the rising demand for talent and a performance-based compensation structure,
decided to stake their claim in the growing hedge fund sector. Relying on
a variety of sometimes exotic strategies, they were welcomed into an
industry that prized flexible approaches to making money. Many also had
a perspective that was clearly in tune with the revolution taking place
throughout the investment world. Leverage, active trading, short-selling,
derivatives—all were seen as potentially lucrative sources of advantage in
the new stock market jungle.

   Indeed, the rapid expansion of the sector mirrored and magnified the
broader trend towards a more speculative, shoot-from-the-hip style of
investing that was gaining ground in the share-trading arena. With operations that were opportunistic, secretive, and lightly regulated, hedge fund
players could evaluate and execute investment strategies that might not

pass muster with traditional money managers. They were also not held to the consensus-oriented approach favored by conservative players, and they created flat organizational structures designed to speed up the process of converting ideas into action. The result is an industry made up of aggressive operators overseeing more than $700 billion in assets. While not all of the funds are linked to equity markets, the numbers are substantial any way you look at it. The ripples from their expanding influence began poking holes in such long-held institutional safety nets as broad diversification requirements, minimum liquidity preferences, well-defined risk parameters, and portfolio turnover restrictions.

Accelerating demand for the modern approaches, along with the numerous professionals and support teams required to make them tick, had interesting consequences—though not necessarily what conventional wisdom might have indicated. For example, many of the newer arrivals to the hedge fund sector, despite their sometimes considerable talents, seemed to lack the maturity, experience, and temperament needed to comfortably operate in free-wheeling and unfamiliar working surroundings. This was especially true given the unsettled market conditions of the past few years. Moreover, because scores of them were formerly specialists of one sort or another, a significant proportion did not appear to have the hybrid skills necessary to analyze and implement often complex strategies in a real-time trading environment. Some also brought with them lots of unwelcome biases and emotional baggage. The learning curve for these relative novices—as well as the subsequent impact their missteps and mistakes have had on the markets—has been steep—and often expensive.[13]

In contrast, those who did come from the small and close-knit core of long-established operators, while not exactly clones of one another, frequently relied on familiar investing strategies and proven tactics borrowed from their former employers to generate outsized returns. This has contributed to repeated instances of "overcrowding" that have often had a disruptive impact on share prices. Many also continued to depend upon regular daily contact with—and the ongoing support of—a fairly closed network of colleagues-turned-competitors to ensure their long-term success as they moved on to other firms or set up shop on their own. The result has been the emergence of "virtual" communities within the investing world, rife with catty gossip and rumors, arrogance and narrow-mindedness, and the secretive paranoia associated with a small-town mentality.

Interestingly, given the recent widespread academic and professional fascination with Behavioral Finance, which explores the irrational factors that can influence investor actions and approaches, there does not seem to have been much interest in analyzing the psychological and emotional elements churned up by the rapid expansion of the hedge fund segment—which, by some estimates, now accounts for up to 50 percent of daily share-trading activity.[14] These sophisticated operators are not necessarily the voice of reason, either. According to one recent study, rather than exerting a correcting force on stock prices during the Bubble, many of them actually went along for the ride.[15] Aside from that, little attention appears to have been paid to the host of relatively alien attitudes about money and investing that have been brought to the surface in the post-Bubble share-trading environment, especially given the rapidly evolving dynamics of the market. For instance, fear, rather than greed, seems to be the dominant emotion currently influencing individual attitudes. That has helped to boost the daily quota of jerky moves and panicky reactions, which few had been accustomed to during the seemingly never-ending bull run.

Similarly, the pressure-cooker environment stirred up by intense information overload,[16] the need to make rapid-fire decisions under occasionally extreme duress, and aggressive competition from sharp and well-funded rivals has had a negative effect on the state of mind of countless investors—especially those with little experience operating in such hostile surroundings. Many of the hedge fund newcomers—as well as the broader range of individuals and institutions swept up by the tide of a more active investing approach—have sometimes found themselves unwittingly seduced by dark forces. Some have been overwhelmed by the emotional sway of the speculative crowd, while others have been drawn in by the siren song of overtrading that has sunk many dealers in years gone by. Likewise, intoxicated by feelings of empowerment, the allure of instant gratification, and the childish pleasure that comes from being able to act on nearly every whim, more than a few had to learn the hard way that the market is very efficient at doling out punishment to the self-absorbed, the foolish, and the unwary.

Certainly the challenge of performing even routine tasks in an atmosphere of chaos and confusion can be overwhelming. In an energetic trading environment, where mistakes and bad decisions can have particularly nasty bottom-line consequences, the stakes are high and the pressures are that much greater. Various studies have shown, too, that there is a downside risk—in terms of physical well-being and mental sharpness—to operating in a continuously stressful working environment. In sum, not everyone is inherently capable of successfully employing intensive multitasking skills under severe time constraints or facing the unique strains of wheeling and dealing for a living. Unfortunately, it seems that few of those who jumped on board the quick-response, high-turnover train looked to see whether they had what it takes to complete the journey.

Numerous investors have been caught out by the asymmetric price action and vicious "spikes" that are fairly common during choppy or down markets. Many have been affected as well by the unsettling lopsidedness of leverage, which seems to work wonders on the way up, but which strikes fear into the hearts of even the most battle-hardened speculators on the way down—especially when there are derivatives or other complex securities involved. Some money managers, particularly those who had achieved success at traditional firms—where performance is usually measured in "relative" rather than "absolute" terms—have been intimidated by the ever-present need to generate continuous positive returns under widely varying circumstances. No doubt, a few have even discovered a fear of large numbers—as when a seemingly minor 50 basis point, or half-percent, short-term swing in a $1 billion portfolio equates to a nerve-wracking $5 million. That is an effect that may not have even been on their radar screens during earlier—but smaller—investing triumphs.

While the emotional dynamics of the marketplace were being altered by evolving conditions, structures, and perspectives, other more concrete developments were also having an influence. In particular, new investment strategies cropped up that took advantage of improved technologies, revolutionary products and methods, and the infusion of considerable academic and analytical resources. They provided diversification benefits and the prospect of above-average returns that many old-line managers—and a growing minority of individual investors[17]—were looking for now that the easy-money days had passed. Some were designed to exploit discrepancies in prices or relative values. They relied on sophisticated models, specialized skills, or distinctive information-gathering networks for their success. Others incorporated big picture—or "top-down"—approaches that scrutinized sector and thematic trends, economic influences, technical conditions, or asset allocation preferences. A growing assortment depended on "black box" mathematical models, arbitrage methods, and computer-driven buying and selling to capture small but consistent gains from market inefficiencies. All were aimed at grabbing a share of the alternative investment pie.

At the same time, inspired in part by sell-side efforts to develop new sources of revenue in the wake of the deflating Bubble, as well as the hedge fund industry's quest to cut costs and achieve a scale necessary to boost returns from high-volume, low-margin strategies, numerous intermediaries stepped in. They began offering a relatively modern form of bundled service called prime brokerage. Combining back office support, securities lending arrangements that made short-selling easier, and perhaps most importantly, lines of credit that enabled aggressive players to gear up their assets with borrowed funds and potentially magnify their winnings, these operations played a key role in increasing the already growing clout of the sector. They also opened the doors for a multitude of start-ups, providing turnkey facilities and formal introductions to potential investors looking to place bets with rising stars on the alternative investing scene.

Sensing a major moneymaking opportunity in their flagging brokerage arms, many of the multiproduct Wall Street operators brought together firm-wide resources to tap into the activities of this rapidly expanding segment of the institutional investment industry. They put dedicated hedge fund teams in place to generate specially targeted research and short-term trading ideas, brought together experienced and aggressive relationship managers, salespeople, and sales-traders[18] to service the often demanding accounts, and offered streamlined execution capabilities and plenty of market-making[19] capital to encourage the steady flow of commission-paying business. Overall, these efforts were designed to capture a substantial measure of the hefty fees these 800-pound gorillas were throwing off on a regular basis.

Undoubtedly, this new breed has driven many of the changes that have taken place in the equity market during the past few years. It is worth bearing in mind, however, that a wide range of individual and institutional investors, industry intermediaries, and others have long taken steps to avoid being stuck at the bottom of the financial food chain, even during the most euphoric moments of the last decade, when almost everyone appeared to be making money. Before the 2000 peak, for example, one especially aggressive segment of the long-only investing crowd embraced strategies that singled out companies with accelerating earnings or share price "momentum." Once the shares were identified, the operators would leap on to the rapidly advancing uptrends and hang on for the ride. Although successful for a while, these "greater fool"[20] approaches proved to be a disaster when the Bubble burst and formerly high-flying stocks and sectors came crashing down to earth.

In the post-Bubble era of increased competition, unsettled markets, and outsized returns being registered by various segments of the alternative investment universe, it was inevitable that many traditional managers would try to follow in the footsteps of the newer operators. In numerous instances, they significantly stepped up the pace of their buying and selling activities. Occasionally, they granted centralized dealing desks the discretion to trade in and out of portfolio holdings on a short-term basis, or even to manage separate "pads." A variety of mutual funds began offering products featuring short-selling or leverage strategies.[21] Some launched—or contemplated setting up—internal or affiliated hedge fund operations designed to compete with their modern rivals—and, ironically, even their own in-house teams. Faced with pressures from within their own ranks, many established operators also appeared to put in place a conscious policy of reducing cash cushions and increasing holdings of investments at the farthest reaches of their allowable comfort zones, potentially boosting relative performance. In general, the institutional universe seemed to be moving up the risk curve.

Similarly, many Wall Street firms, already well-versed in trading a vast array of securities in a variety of markets—with sophisticated risk management tools and structures at their disposal—went along with the shift towards a more speculative approach to making money. For instance, they granted market-makers and proprietary dealing desks increased authority to buy and sell issues unrelated to servicing clients' immediate needs. The hope was that those activities could generate sufficient revenues to offset the overall drop in fee income that had taken place in the post-Bubble period. Small investors, meanwhile, stung by the double whammy of plunging portfolio values and a sharp decline in dividend and interest income, were under considerable pressure of their own. They, too, moved into more aggressive investment vehicles and adopted riskier trading strategies than many had been conditioned to do during the long-running upswing.

Even foreigners, who throughout the past century have played a significant role in the fortunes of the American markets, have gotten caught up in many of the same influences affecting domestic operators in recent years. Heavily invested in U.S. securities for an assortment of reasons—the nation's standing as a global superpower, efficient trading structures and shareholder-friendly policies, relative economic vitality, and vast holdings of offshore dollars—overseas players have long viewed the American marketplace as a natural second home for long-term investment. They have also found it to be a powerful magnet for speculative "hot money" flows when things are really hopping. Because of their strong support during the past decade, domestic consumers and investors managed to reap substantial rewards in terms of cheap imports, low interest rates, and stock and bond values that were firmer than they might otherwise have been.

In recent years, though, the staggering increase in the size of overseas holdings of U.S. assets, combined with global financial strains and politically charged trade and exchange rate policies—which have become the focus of overseas attention amid a worldwide economic slowdown—have introduced an element of instability to our markets. Many domestic investors, it seems, are not even aware of the scale of foreign dependency that exists. Using the classic example from Chaos Theory[22] of a butterfly flapping its wings in Brazil influencing the weather in Texas, there are clear signs that even relatively minor events outside our borders will likely have a substantial impact on domestic equity prices and broader macroeconomic conditions in the years ahead. A Latin American politician barnstorming about the perils of Western values, a terrorist attack on an Asian tourist attraction, a magnitude 7.9 earthquake in Eastern Europe—these and countless other developments have the potential to echo, abruptly and loudly, throughout the land.

Meanwhile, the influx of foreign players with unique cultural biases has added to the ongoing "democratization" process that has taken place in the U.S. market during the past two decades. Aided in part by the rise of English as a universal business language, as well as enormous improvements in global telecommunications networks and a growing interest in international affairs, outsiders have joined the millions of small and large domestic investors who have become more actively involved in buying and selling shares. This broadening process has made the landscape somewhat less homogeneous than it used to be, and because the range of activities, attitudes, and perspectives has expanded significantly, it seems more difficult to get an accurate read on what the "average" investor is doing, saying, or thinking these days. Moreover, it appears that widely varying levels of sophistication, knowledge, and ability frequently lead to odd market moves in reaction to ordinary events. In fact, it often seems unclear exactly how participants will react after unexpected developments. In general, modern analysis now requires intense second-guessing and an increased reliance on pretzel-like twists of logic.

Finally, changes in the regulatory environment since the Bubble burst have altered the landscape as well, though the implications are not yet as apparent. As with many reactionary efforts by politicians in response to headline-grabbing crises, they frequently end up "fighting the last war" or they create unintended consequences that can sometimes cause more harm than good. For example, the implementation of rules such as Regulation FD[23]—Reg FD, for short—which is designed to prevent individuals such as brokerage analysts from gaining an advantage over others by obtaining important company information "first," should theoretically make markets fairer. While that may or may not be true, what occasionally happens now is that unwanted volatility soars as market-moving news is abruptly, rather than slowly, assimilated into stock prices. Similarly, statutes such as Sarbanes-Oxley,[24] which was created to protect shareholders in the wake of Enron and other scandals by subjecting companies to added oversight, is probably causing managers to refrain from providing important—though potentially questionable—guidance about future prospects. Under such circumstances, investors may be denied critical intelligence they need for effective decision-making.

Whatever the case, all of these developments—changes in technology, economic circumstances, regulatory policies, investing perspectives, infrastructure, the range and variety of players, strategies, and products in the marketplace, the fallout from the boom and bust, and so on—have created a new investing climate. One that is fraught with perils for the naïve and the uniformed, but offers profitable opportunities for the knowledgeable and fleet of foot. It goes without saying, of course, that while the equity markets have been transformed in recent years, human nature has not, and successful money management will continue to depend on having the appropriate skills, emotional makeup, self-discipline, and consistent approach to capitalize on any opportunities that may arise, as well as weather the inevitable storms. Nonetheless, for most investors, understanding the forces at work in today's investing environment—*The New Laws of the Stock Market Jungle*—will make it easier to achieve long-term success.

PART 2

THE NEW LAWS

CHAPTER 1

Intraday Volatility

Intraday share price volatility is on the rise.

Volatility is a word that usually strikes fear into the hearts of investors. Many who hear or read about it almost instantly imagine cliff-like drops in share prices or scenes of battered traders being dragged off the exchange floor—casualties of an especially nasty bout of market turbulence. Like rainy days and Mondays, volatility often seems to get people down, and positive associations are usually hard to come by. However, choppy, wide-ranging moves are not, in themselves, inherently negative, nor should they automatically be interpreted as a sign that participants should pull back and sit on their hands. They can, in fact, trigger profitable opportunities for patient and well-disciplined investors looking to take advantage of favorable entry points when acquiring new positions or to lock in extraordinary gains on existing holdings. Nonetheless, increasingly unstable market conditions can pose a threat to investing success—one that must be understood to be challenged and outmaneuvered to be overcome.

The first difficulty, of course, is that volatility is one of those concepts, like "beauty" or "quality," that everybody believes they have a handle on, but which few can really explain in any great detail. A dictionary provides some guidance with descriptions such as "changeableness" or "fickleness," but these meanings seem somewhat vague in the context of

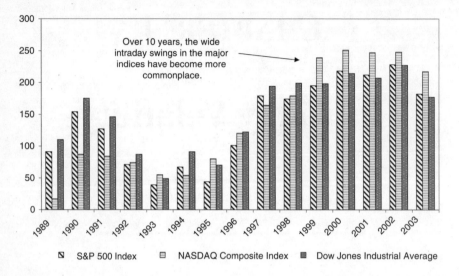

Figure 1.1 Number of Days per Year When the Range Between the High and
Low Exceeds 1 Percent (Source: Bloomberg LP).

modern financial markets. For academics and investment professionals,
the term does have a more precise technical meaning, though it is something of a mouthful. Essentially, it refers to a measure of the annualized
standard deviation—or statistical variation from the average—of the daily
percentage price changes of a security or commodity. In other words, it is
a degree of uncertainty based on historical moves over some set period.
While critical for fully understanding derivatives and a variety of related
strategies, this definition is not necessarily what matters to most investors.

In general, when traders and money managers discuss share price
volatility, they tend to look at it in terms of the impact it is having—or
will have—on their own bottom-line performance, rather than in any academic or technical sense of the word. Consequently, it is the relevant time
frame and nature—or character—of the unpredictability, as well as the
underlying directional bias of the shares or index they are making reference to, that seems to give it real meaning. Although it is correct to say
that equity markets have been more volatile in recent years because the
annual totals of daily swings of more than one percent have gone up compared to earlier periods—as noted in Figure 1.1—it does not seem to
completely capture the essence of the term as it applies to everyday buying and selling.

In the case of those with a very short-term perspective—day traders, for example—fluctuations in the "ticks"—the smallest changes in price that a security can make—are almost always the primary focus of attention. For these players, the moves that unfold over the course of a minute—tracing out, perhaps, a series of uneven peaks and valleys on an intraday graph—are the main triggers for increased stress and worries about profits and losses. That is the case even if things settle down only moments later. For traditional investors—those whose outlook stretches beyond the reaches of today's closing bell—it is usually the range between the daily or weekly high and low, as well as the most recent price compared to the level during some earlier reference period, that determines the indigestion point.

The emotional "flavor" is important, too. Those who follow markets closely—usually on a real-time basis—can often detect subtle distinctions rarely picked up on by casual observers. As with lightening or love affairs, the intensity of the volatility can vary a great deal: Occasionally it is slow and smooth, and at other times it discharges with a kick that is frantic and draining. It may suddenly let rip, like the bullfrog's long tongue snapping out to capture its unsuspecting prey, and then recoil, returning prices to the steadiness of a few moments earlier. At other times, the intraday price action might resemble the motion of a downed electricity cable, sparking wildly as it whips and thrashes throughout the course of a stressful and seemingly neverending trading session.

Volatility can also follow a series of progressions. Now and again, the build-up resembles the one-two-three burst of a triple-jumper, quickly escalating to peak form. It may increase gradually, in a well-ordered stairstep move to higher and wider levels of choppiness. Occasionally, the variability is, strange as it sounds, completely unpredictable. In those instances, the market might be merrily rolling along in one direction, when it will suddenly turn on a dime, sputtering off on some new bearing before slipping back, perhaps slowly but often quickly; then, it will veer off again in a jerky new series of stumbles and bumps. Interestingly enough, depending on their perspectives, some equity players might notice and react to every gyration, however small, while others might see nothing at all.

Action Point

Certain kinds of volatile price action can provide useful information about underlying market conditions. For example, when a stock abruptly breaks out of a clearly defined trading range on relatively heavy volume, creating visual "gaps" on a daily bar chart, this is often a sign that a dramatic change in the outlook has taken place. Although such moves sometimes turn out to be false starts or overreactions to unexpected developments, investors should nonetheless pay heed to this sort of technical message, especially when there is follow-through momentum in the days ahead. What this sort of pattern often signals is that the bulls—on an upside breakout—or the bears—on a move to the downside—have gained the upper hand and are not keen to let it go. More information on relevant screening tools can be found at Web sites such as *www.marketscreen.com* and *www.incrediblecharts.com.*

Market direction can have a lot to do with what people see. On the whole, it seems that perceptions about volatility, as well as investors' responses to it, are often lopsided, depending on which way the investment wind is blowing. If the overall trend is up, erratic twists and turns, while tiring, do not seem to have much impact on spirits or sentiment. Although the reasons are unclear—perhaps it is because of the warm and fuzzy optimism that bull moves bring out or the fact that most investors tend to be long—filters in the brain appear to dull the senses and make people believe prices are steadier than they are. When a company releases better-than-expected results, for example, causing its stock to open sharply higher and zoom to new highs in the days that follow, there seems to be little fear—or even recognition—that prices are more unstable than they were previously. In a roaring bull market, dramatic intraday moves are often seen as "noise" that only serves to liven up nightly financial reports.

When the economic outlook is questionable, the trading environment is unsettled, and many portfolios are underwater, topsy-turvy price action seems to be anything but irrelevant to investors. As with the anxiety stirred up when night falls in the scariest parts of the city, feelings of fear and uncertainty are often magnified by random outbursts and strange goings-on in the stock market when people are prone to see things that way, especially in light of the difficult conditions and dramatic events of recent years. Nowadays, many participants have almost been trained to expect the worst and are often very sensitive to bad news. Volatility under such circumstances is not only viewed as a negative for stocks, it is sometimes seen as a measure of how terrible things are across the board. Although the long-term betting has generally favored better times and higher prices, a noticeable decline seems to promote and gain momentum from greater instability.

There are various reasons why prices seem to swing more often and more widely in a general downturn—apart from the nervous energy stirred up by negative emotions. On the whole, market instability reflects doubts about underlying conditions, growth prospects, and a variety of other factors that influence investor perceptions. When people are unsure about what a stock is worth, what the economic future will look like, whether they will have a job in six months, and even about their own abilities to make informed judgments, they tend to be insecure and somewhat passive in their investing approach. In trading terms, they are likely to be price "takers" rather than price "makers." In other words, they will more readily allow random influences or the actions of other operators to define at least a momentary sense of what the "right" level of a security should be.

In contrast, when participants are confident and self-assured, know where they are and where they want to be, and have been conditioned by positive circumstances or long-term success to rely on their own judgment, they are usually more than willing to vouch for a price they believe is the correct one. They will also be prepared to adopt a view that goes against the grain of short-term supply-and-demand influences and back it up with cold, hard cash. Generally speaking, it takes extra energy and resources to move values away from equilibrium levels that have been established by a solid consensus with a strong conviction. During a garden-variety bull market, commonly held views, supported by widespread faith and enthusiasm, are difficult to shake, and volatility often—though not always—remains somewhat dampened as a result.

Available "trading liquidity" can have a strong influence on volatility. During an upswing, money seeps into the market in various ways, serving as a sort of shock absorber that cushions share prices from the ripples of short-term activity. Investors of all shapes and sizes may leave multiple buy and sell orders in place, market-makers and specialists[1] stand ready to honor sometimes sizable customer demands to smooth the flow of business, and investment banks, reassured by the belief that rising markets will bail them out if they make a bad call, allocate a significant proportion of their resources to speculative activities such as overnight position-taking and block trading. Whether through confidence or complacency, stock traders are generally less worried about being exposed to near-term uncertainty when overall circumstances seem favorable, and will often get involved even if they do not have a strong view. Consequently, the pool of liquidity in the good times is notable for its consistency, depth, and reach.

Since share prices peaked in 2000, however, various cracks have appeared in this backstop. Faced with unsettled economic conditions, falling commission revenues, and diminishing client interest, sell-side institutions have taken a fresh look at some of their activities. They have become more selective in terms of how they use their capital. Large and small investors, meanwhile, hit by large losses and a host of other threats, have become less willing and able to provide consistent support for the market, either on a day-to-day basis or with respect to overall equity allocations. There are also fewer players in the game now than there were during the late 1990s, as the post-Bubble decline chased out some shaky operators who lent a measure of support to a wide range of issues. The result is that there are more temporary air pockets appearing throughout the day that can be popped by short-term supply-and-demand pressures.

Action Point

When volatility begins to intensify after share prices have fallen for an extended period of time, it often indicates that a downtrend is nearing an end, at least in the short run. In other words, if the daily range between the highs and lows of a stock or index expands significantly beyond recent bands and volume picks up following a decline of 10 percent or more, it is likely that emotional decision-making has started to take over and many investors are throwing in the towel. As during the U.S. stock market selloffs in September of 2001 and 2002, such a phenomenon frequently reflects negative sentiment extremes that can spell a major buying opportunity. While somewhat less reliable, a similar sort of signal is sometimes given after extended upswings. To look for such opportunities, check out the screening tools at Web sites such as *www.marketscreen.com, www.incrediblecharts.com,* and *http://moneycentral.msn.com.*

Falling values have also had an effect on volatility for fundamental, as well as mechanical, reasons. Historically, institutions on either side of the Street have avoided investing in or researching companies with low share prices, even if they were brand-name businesses or former high fly-ers, because of the limited impact such investments could have on the per-formance of large portfolios. Typically, the capitalizations of these firms made it impractical to accumulate large enough holdings to make their efforts worthwhile. There is also the view that these sorts of securities—sometimes referred to as "penny stocks"—are inherently dangerous and unsuitable for long-term investors. Moreover, as is common knowledge in the field of marketing, there are strong biases associated with price: A low figure suggests little value and vice versa, regardless of how irrational that might seem at first glance. All of these factors have led to a decrease of support for a broad range of issues, making them more vulnerable to being knocked around by sporadic buying and selling.

The relatively wide bid-offer spread and minimum price change increment of lower-priced securities also creates the impression that they are more unstable than their double or triple-digit counterparts. The rea-son? A one cent move—about the minimum these days—in a two-dollar stock equals one-half of a percent. That is significant, considering the same adjustment on a $40 share price works out to about two and a half basis points, or one-twentieth as much. Moreover, with some broad-based indicators, such as the NASDAQ Composite Index, now made up of many more lower-priced issues than they were at the height of the Bubble, the overall variability of the these popular market measures has seen at least some slight increase because of the larger percentage moves that now take place in a greater number of their underlying shares.

Interestingly, the move to decimal pricing that began in August 2000 seems to have made shares more volatile, too. Under the old system, where the smallest ticks were generally denominated in eighths,[2] it was only natural that greater energy and conviction were needed to shift val-ues away from existing levels. This was because of the built-in transaction costs associated with the gap between the buying and selling terms. For example, if a stock was quoted on the exchange at $40-1/8 bid, $40-1/4 offered, an investor who sent an order down to acquire 100 shares "at the market" would need the indicated price level to move up by one-quarter of a dollar—around 62 basis points—to make a profit—excluding any commission costs—on the $40-1/4 purchase price. Otherwise, that indi-vidual would have to offer out the security at $40-3/8 and hope someone else stepped in and purchased the shares. Although this might not matter much to long-term investors, the math tended to limit participation by various speculative operators. That, in turn, curbed some measure of short-term supply and demand.

After "decimalization," the prospective cost of buying and selling shares fell sharply. It became possible for a trader to make money even if the displayed market moved in the desired direction by only two cents, or roughly five basis points—again, excluding any commissions—if the quote was $40.10 bid, $40.11 offered, for example. Furthermore, the greater number of increments from one "big figure" to the next—say, from $40 to $41—softened up any sense of price "stickiness" that seemed to exist when there were only eight steps between the round dollar values that many share traders focused on. Psychologically, at least, the existence of more than twelve times as many potential stopping points seemed to reduce the "anchoring" effect that was in place when prices had to travel through a smaller number of gaps. In addition, the fact that liquidity was spread out, instead of being concentrated, also had the effect of encouraging institutions to break up large orders and deal more actively, as Figure 1.2 seems to suggest.

Declining commission costs have played a role in stirring up instability by helping to cut expenses for short- and long-term operators. As was the case with decimalization, this development reduced another barrier to increased turnover. For most investors, the break-even hurdle on every trade was now set at far lower levels than before. In the early 1990s, there were $100 per order minimum commissions and variable charges—

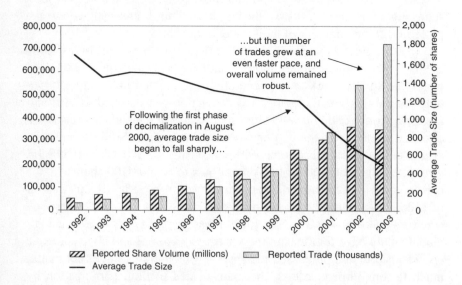

Figure 1.2 New York Stock Exchange Annual Reported Share Volume, Reported Trades, and Average Trade Size (Source: New York Stock Exchange).

depending on whether the client was an individual or an institution—of six cents a share and up. Now, flat-rate or ultralow-cost fee schedules are common—and readily negotiable. It is not unknown for hedge funds to pay one or two cents a share for domestic equity trades done through a full service broker, or even half as much—or less—to execute transactions by way of electronic trading systems. It is even possible to receive a rebate or credit for some orders routed through ECNs because those venues are trying to lure business away from traditional exchanges.

This has had several effects. First, it has encouraged a pick-up in short-term speculation, because some of the dangers associated with trying to capture minor moves in the market have been reduced. If a trade goes wrong, it no longer has to cost a fortune in terms of round-trip commissions and wide bid-offer spreads to unwind it. This has also helped to accelerate the trend by institutional and individual operators across the investment spectrum towards increasing activity levels. Consequently, there has been a general uptick in intraday buying and selling which has added to temporary price pressures. Along the same lines, falling commissions have removed at least some of the obstacles that stood in the way of careless and sloppy investing behavior such as overtrading. It has become easier for operators to boost their involvement when it might not necessarily make sense for them to do so.

As noted, lower fees have also encouraged many traditional money managers to adopt more flexible strategies for acquiring new investments and getting out of existing holdings. They could use tactics that were more opportunistic than in the past, and orders could be worked with an eye focused almost exclusively on current supply-and-demand considerations. Already motivated to some degree by competition and a broader shift towards more active participation in the market, buy-side institutions have steered the emphasis away from upfront costs in favor of minimizing the negative impact of moving in and out of large positions. Ironically, while this has often benefited managers' performance, it has likely added to overall instability. With operators now handing out orders that are more unpredictable with respect to size and timing, it has become increasingly difficult for sell-side counterparties to anticipate their needs and position themselves accordingly.

Action Point

With the depth of available liquidity decreasing, average quote sizes getting smaller, and institutional activities becoming less visible, it can make sense for individual investors to rethink execution strategies and trade smaller amounts than they used to when buying or selling stocks. While it is more labor intensive than the alternative, breaking a 5,000 share order—or one for a tenth as much—into five or more pieces can help to minimize slippage and reduce the incentive for short-term "scalpers" and others to step in front of potentially market-moving trades. Arguably, such adjustments will probably mean very little in the case of the most active shares or at the beginning and end of the session. However, with air pockets increasingly cropping up in various issues over the course of the day, the strategy may help to minimize the long-run costs of consistently giving up a larger-than-necessary edge.

Although increased uncertainty, reduced liquidity, heightened speculation, and declining share values have likely been the main culprits behind rising intraday volatility, it seems a good bet that other influences have also served as catalysts or magnifiers. In all markets, of course, there is a certain amount of truly random noise, triggered when buyers and sellers act for reasons that have little to do with valuations, news, or recent price swings. Shares get sold to finance weddings or bought as birthday presents, people experience lifestyle changes, judges make legal rulings, and sometimes simple mistakes get made. These are all factors that can exert at least a short-term influence on equity prices in the absence of "real" fundamentals. Even some sudden and supposedly relevant event can occasionally cause a reaction that is little more than a blip when the realization takes hold that the item was inconsequential or otherwise misunderstood when it was first released.

Nonetheless, much of the activity that occurs during market hours seems to have at least some link, however tenuous, to where values are and what they are expected to be, and all of it can significantly affect prices. This includes program trading in particular, and electronic trading in general, which contrary to what some would argue, appear to make stocks more unstable than they used to be. There are several reasons for this. In the old days, players depended on what is now seen as a relatively inefficient telephone calling chain to execute one or more trades, and the idea of sending out simultaneous orders in a large number of stocks was viewed as somewhat impractical. Now, with sophisticated computers and trade routing systems, it is easy to transmit virtually any request to nearly every exchange and electronic network with little effort or worry.

Some mechanisms, in fact, require very low levels of active involvement or do not depend on real-time interaction with a human being at all. There are systems in place—some based on off-the-shelf products, others using customized software—that can be programmed with simple "limit minders"[3] or complex formulas to trigger pop-up messages on a computer screen or send orders directly to a trading venue when interesting opportunities develop. Once executed, the details are usually sent back electronically to be input, either manually or automatically, into order management systems. Arguably, such methods help to eliminate potential emotional and psychological biases, and they can ensure that successful investment strategies—presumably based on extensive analysis—are properly implemented. The problem, as with all mechanical approaches to investing, is that the realities of the marketplace can sometimes differ from theory or the expectations resulting from back-tested success.

Indeed, despite the apparent benefits modern methods offer, the "ancient" voice-based approaches actually had an advantage: intelligent safeguards built right into them. Specifically, clients, brokers, clerks, traders, and others would naturally query orders that seemed out of line with previous transactions or were viewed as impractical under current conditions. In other words, a human element was routinely available that allowed for one-off changes and alternative strategies when the situation warranted. However, in cases where orders are sent out electronically, there is usually not much analysis performed except for simple checks that certain limits are not being breached. Consequently, requests made by mouse click that would not get past the first gate in an investor-to-broker telephone call can easily slip through. Mismatches then crop up between what players want to do and what the marketplace can handle, and prices can be knocked askew.

Here is an example. When a dealer decides to execute a "program" in the shares of an index such as the S&P 500 and transmits an instruction to buy or sell the underlying securities[4] as one "basket trade," some orders in thinly traded issues can stir up brief imbalances when they hit the market. Under those circumstances, the crowd often ducks, like bathers at the ocean, to avoid being blindsided by the sudden swell, and prices shift to absorb the volume. While there are some simple measures in place that are designed to prevent transactions from being executed on completely ridiculous terms, the general idea is that orders in thinly traded securities are not given any special handling. The market will likely be out of kilter in those stocks, at least for a while, and prices may vary considerably from where they were only seconds earlier. While not a problem, of course, for a potential buyer in the moments after a sell program arrives, it can put other vendors at a temporary but distinct disadvantage.

Sometimes when a large cluster of orders hits the trading floor, the overall effect, like the concentrated beam of light generated by a laser, triggers a burst of energy that has a widespread effect on players and conditions, especially if traders are somewhat sensitive to unusual flows and events—as they often seem to be nowadays. A sudden surge can cause people to react abruptly and erratically. When there is a flurry of activity, they may withdraw bids and offers or reduce the size of outstanding orders, weakening support for current values. This sets prices up to slide easily out of equilibrium. Even though many operators are tuned in to the factors that can set off program or other arbitrage trades, wariness remains—large flows into or out of the market might mean something else. As recent history has shown, they could represent the fallout from an unexpected and unwelcome geopolitical event.

Electronic execution techniques, even in single securities, have contributed to the problem in other ways. They allow participants to transmit buy and sell orders with much less effort—and consequently, less thought and analysis—than was previously required. Rightly or wrongly, there is often little reason needed to click a mouse or type a few keystrokes to kick off a trade. Moreover, once a request is made, there is limited room for reversing course. With the old-fashioned approach, which involved direct contact between two or more individuals, there was usually some underlying emotional connection that served as a restraining influence. Generally speaking, when people communicate with others, elements of judgment and approval come into play, and conversations that are meant to lead to action usually stir up some question of whether a request is logical or appropriate. Not so with automated methods—all orders, good or bad, get carried out in the same way. Regrettably, the most ill-conceived requests invariably slip through as well.

These include garden variety mishaps and those based on serious errors in judgment. As is the case with most email systems, geared as they are towards speed and efficiency, there is no "retract"[5] button to recall efforts that, after even a moment's pause for reflection, should not have been made. Once a message escapes into the network ether, the electronic genie usually cannot be put back into the bottle. How many times have people erroneously forwarded tasteless remarks or sent confidential information about salaries or business plans to a long list of colleagues by choosing the "Reply to All" function on software applications such as Lotus Notes? Sometimes individuals attempt damage control, but that frequently make matters worse, as when the follow-up message not only fails to resolve the situation, but ends up highlighting the original error for those who missed it the first time around.

In terms of losses made and opportunities missed, the impact can be substantial when it comes to automated execution methods. Many institutional systems feature shortcuts for transaction type, stock symbols, price increments, share amounts, etc.—all packed tightly together in small menus on a computer monitor. They can be easily—and wrongly— selected in the heat of the trading moment. Although most systems have query boxes that pop up on screen and force requests to be confirmed before they are transmitted, or other built-in safeguards to prevent break-the-bank type orders from getting through, they are still part of a process streamlined for speed. And, as when individuals arrive home after a long highway commute wondering how they got there, much of the design, despite the precautions, ensures that participants, including those who are not paying nearly enough attention to what they are doing, can function with as little thought and effort as possible.

Once an order is entered—often by completing a minimum number of data fields and having the rest filled in automatically as system defaults—and then transmitted, that is it. There usually is no way of stopping the process—not even in those cases where a mistake is almost immediately picked up on and followed by a swiftly sent "cancel" instruction or a frantic telephone call to market-makers, trading counter-parties, or contacts on the exchange floor. Generally speaking, it is extremely difficult to "undo" a slip-up before at least some damage is done. And given that Murphy's Law always has a way of cropping up at the worst of times, the likelihood is that the biggest blunders will be the ones that Mr. Market takes the greatest advantage of—as quickly as possible.

Whether through inadvertent error or, as has occasionally been rumored, intentional effort, clumsily transmitted orders of a sufficient size can trigger shockwaves that can have a far-reaching impact on near-term volatility. For example, on July 3rd, 2003, during a shortened and relatively quiet preholiday session, a trader reportedly entered an electronic market order to sell 10,000 contracts—an amount 100 times larger than was apparently intended—of e-mini futures on the Dow Jones Industrial Average (usually referred to as the Dow Jones, or Dow).[6] This set in motion a chain reaction that caused not only the derivative and related

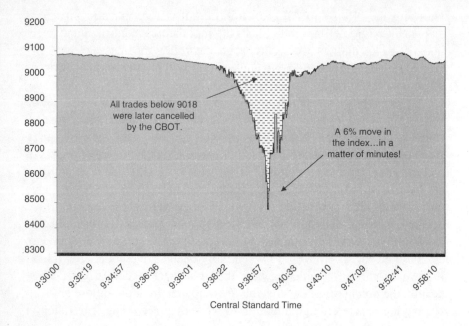

All trades below 9018 were later cancelled by the CBOT.

A 6% move in the index...in a matter of minutes!

Central Standard Time

Figure 1.3 July 3, 2003. Plunge in the E-mini Dow Jones Industrials Futures: An error...or an "intentional" effort to unsettle the equity markets? (Source: Chicago Board of Trade).

index to gyrate wildly—as seen in Figure 1.3—but other well-known market measures as well, including the S&P 500 and the NASDAQ Composite—not to mention the underlying shares that comprised those indices. Partly as a result of arbitrage activities and partly because of fear among traders that the sudden surge reflected an unexpected news development, the investing crowd ended up intensifying the original disturbance. It eventually took a half hour or so for conditions to finally settle down, but the damage was essentially done.

Action Point

Technology has made many aspects of life much simpler and more efficient, but the ease with which a range of complicated tasks can now be tackled can also lead to carelessness and dangerous complacency. When using mechanical methods and computer programs for evaluating markets, assessing risks, or executing orders, take the time to purposefully focus on, read

over—out loud, if possible—and write down observed results
and intended actions. These steps can force the conscious mind
to pay heed to what is going on, and will go some way towards
minimizing   costly   trading   errors   and   lost   investment
opportunities.

Panicky contagions have always been a feature of financial markets.
Triggered by "fight-or-flight" instincts associated with the oldest parts of
the human brain, and reinforced by the same group dynamics that come
into play when someone shouts "fire" in a crowded theater, automatic
physical and emotional responses usually kick in to weaken individual
resolve as fear and uncertainty spike. When that happens, raw emotions
and basic instincts take priority over thoughtful consideration. In addition, the speed and volume of information that is circulating throughout
the marketplace, and the instantly available buying and selling power that
most institutional players have at their disposal, almost ensures that an
efficient mechanism is in place to get everyone heading for the exits at the
same time—especially nowadays, when many find themselves rushed
into trades that suddenly get very overcrowded. This likely facilitates and
promotes wavelike responses to significant events and trading flows.

Interestingly enough, the size of any prospective groupthink "infec-
tion" has grown as well, despite the fact that an ever-increasing number of
players are located away from the trading floor. Why? Because modern
communications systems have created rich and multilayered real-time
links between traders, brokers, speculators, and others. All of them are
now plugged into a vast electronic network that seems to convey not only
words and data, but some measure of the energy and emotional intensity
normally engendered when individuals are physically close to one
another. Boosted by the highly charged current associated with an uncertain outlook and unsettled market conditions, the momentary buzz of
trader hysteria regularly lights up share prices in a variety of ways.

That is not all. Because they are becoming increasingly skittish about
the new geopolitical state of affairs—a world of random acts of violence
and once unimaginable terrorist threats—market operators of all shapes
and sizes have steeled themselves to respond quickly to even a hint that
something big is going down. Sometimes they back away instantly from
perceived supply-and-demand pressures; alternatively, they might jump
on board and try to capture some part of the momentum for themselves in
the form of a quick "scalp," or short-term trade. While the two sets of

actions—prompted either by choice or through instinct—are at opposite ends of the trading spectrum, the combination tends to reinforce near-term instability instead of counteracting it.

The increased use of leverage, especially among aggressive, often large-scale players, such as hedge funds, together with the widespread shift towards a more speculative approach, has also contributed to market instability. In addition, some participants now seem to be taking on additional risk exposure by operating with thinner capital cushions than in the past to protect themselves if trades go wrong, or by choosing heavily geared securities tied to short-term moves. The expansion in the quantity and availability of various derivative products has also aided these efforts. At the same time, because of restrictions imposed by prime brokers or others, and a reduced tolerance for large losses among some backers and investors, many operators are adopting tactics that professional traders have long relied on to control risk or reduce the chances of disaster. These include the use of automatic stop-losses[7] and the practice of reducing overnight positions on a regular basis.

As it happens, these mechanical measures, while designed to protect the primary users, can often have a negative impact on the activities of other participants in the marketplace. Typically, such strategies leave little room for finesse or negotiation, and they generally do not take account of conditions at the moment of impact. In fact, they often serve as a form of rocket fuel, fanning the flames of near-term chaos. They can set off a chain reaction that mirrors the impact of the bull in the china shop, smashing tables and pottery as it jerks and wobbles its way towards escape through a narrow front door. Although they clearly offer some sort of prudent safeguard against disaster, these automatic approaches occasionally fail to work out as planned for either traders or investors—or innocent market bystanders.

One reason why is that many operators tend to set trigger points for stop-loss orders at widely watched technical levels or familiar round numbers, creating a potentially large build-up of concentrated firepower that the market cannot absorb quickly enough should circumstances warrant. Similarly, when numerous operators put investment strategies into place at around the same time, either because they rely on common methods or widely followed analyst recommendations, or because they are part of the informal hedge fund idea-swapping network, the mass of get-me-out orders often seems to bunch up at familiar percentage loss levels—10 percent, for example—relative to where many trades were initiated. Sometimes the prices themselves have no specific importance, but more players in general might be putting a greater number of protective measures in place because of an overall rise in macroeconomic and geopolitical uncertainty.

All this seemingly beneficial behavior can produce side effects that are dramatically unwelcome. It is almost a given, for instance, that many of the bunched stop-loss orders will be "elected." History has shown, time and again, that the market tends to zero in on hot spots, inflicting the maximum pain, as trading lore has it, on the largest number of participants. Sometimes the process is spurred on by aggressive speculators, such as floor traders who are only too happy to give prices a bit of a push to get them going in the "wrong" direction. Then they can cash in with a quick in-and-out transaction that involves relatively little risk. The result is often a whir of self-reinforcing orders that worsens an already unfavorable technical situation. Soon, supply and demand imbalances appear that can last anywhere from a few seconds to several minutes or longer. Once in motion, prices may also grow legs as others amplify the swing with additional purchases and sales.

Sometimes this leads to even more breathtaking moves, especially when the action triggers a series of cascading stop-losses. Placed at what were thought to be relatively safe levels outside widely anticipated short-term trading ranges, these automatic orders can sometimes cause havoc if they actually see the light of day. What happens is that prices, jolted by an unusual charge of market electricity, break through "normal" levels and move to rarefied air, with little in the way of opposing influences to hold them back. At that point, they can often travel for at least short distances on momentum alone. Then, especially in situations involving illiquid securities or issues traded on electronic exchanges lacking price-limit safeguards, the later executions end up creating a sort of "piling on" effect. As in the Dow Jones e-mini futures debacle cited earlier, the fallout can wreak temporary havoc until some semblance of order returns—and cooler heads prevail.

Action Point

Some investors automatically assume that dramatic moves in share prices happen for the "right" reasons. While this is usually the case, such a narrow view can prove to be naïve in markets that are affected by patchy liquidity, increasing sloppiness, and traders with itchy trigger fingers. It is important, of course, to try and get some sense of whether unsettled conditions reflect changing fundamentals or a significant shift in supply and demand, but for investors who have done their homework and who are comfortable with their investment assumptions, a sudden though favorable jolt in prices often represents an ideal time to enter the fray. Whether you set formal or informal limits beforehand, be prepared to act purposefully when others seem to be reacting blindly.

The rise of a host of aggressive and well-funded operators with flexible approaches and opportunistic perspectives has most likely increased instability as well. Their trading activities often seem to account for at least a few of the odd moves that take place during some sessions. Although it is not actively commented on by the media, or even discussed in some circles, the footprint of manipulation seems especially evident when there is little else going on in terms of news or traditional investment flows. In many respects, the situation can be similar to what regularly occurs in the commodity pits. There, many have witnessed, and occasionally experienced firsthand, the odd swings and one-off spikes triggered by locals—independent floor traders—"gunning for the stops." Driven by nothing more than the urge to activate temporary buying and selling orders that automatically kick in at key trigger points, such activity is a game where players capitalize on momentary gaps in liquidity by abruptly setting minitrends in motion. After prices start moving, they let the autopilot orders take them out.

In addition, while there has generally been less money flowing through the share-trading arena in recent years to dampen choppy price action, some larger players, in actual fact, seem to have almost limitless resources at their disposal. This allows for the possibility of sizeable bursts of buying and selling that can further unsettle markets. Indeed, there has often been talk from the trading pits and exchange floors that certain operators have been the driving force behind early session swings that later evolved into much larger moves. It is difficult, of course, to prove intent, and manipulation is clearly illegal under U.S. laws. Nonetheless, market history is filled with stories about traders "cornering" markets in attempts to drive them higher or launching "bear raids" to force prices down. During the Bubble years, there was even an informal network known as the ShortBusters Club, founded in 1990 and organized by maverick stock promoter Ray Dirks, that publicly orchestrated efforts to force short-sellers in some speculative and thinly traded issues to buy back positions at sharply higher prices.

Ironically, while manipulative tactics are generally frowned upon in traditional investment circles, governments around the globe have relied on such measures for centuries to "stabilize" economies and markets. From overt cheerleading to covert buying and selling of securities using taxpayer funds, politicians and central bankers regularly attempt to influence prices in the name of public policy. Similarly, they often act to smooth the bumps of normal cyclical activity or, on occasion, to achieve outcomes driven by less-than-honorable ends. Although it has sometimes been rumored that U.S. authorities have had a hand in steadying domestic share prices—in the same way that they regularly buy and sell currencies and fixed income securities—the allegation remains unproven. It seems likely, though, that certain official actions, such as currency intervention by some other nations, have had at least an indirect influence on short-term movements in equities, if only for psychological reasons.

One phenomenon that has also contributed to near-term volatility is the practice of short-selling. While it is covered in more detail later on, suffice it to say that the technique can trigger a range of emotional and technical responses that can often stir up markets. For many investors, it is a relatively unfamiliar animal, and once unleashed, it is difficult to keep under control. Also, it goes against the grain of a traditional investing—and even a human—perspective. Moreover, selling securities one does not own and speculating on falling share prices are two activities that require considerable expertise and a nose for danger. While it is easy to say that the process is a mirror image of going long, battle-hardened experience suggests otherwise. In the hands of novice operators, misuse of the tactic can be like walking in a minefield. Even for experienced professionals, the pain when things go wrong can be exceptionally difficult to swallow.

Information overload and the pressures of multitasking under extreme stress can also cause wide swings in share prices for various reasons. With more data to look at, a greater number of factors to analyze, and numerous actions to consider, modern operators are frequently pushed to the brink of what they can handle. Under normal circumstances, this range of activities is usually manageable, especially for seasoned professionals. However, when it all becomes too much, participants sometimes opt for the wrong choices—or they make no decisions at all. Occasionally, people seize up, as if caught in the glare of the market headlight, and withdraw—mentally or even physically—from the center of the action. This can be a serious problem if they have open orders or positions that need to be unwound, and the fallout from cleaning up the mess can be substantial. Alternatively, they may decide to begin across-the-board actions or adjust their positions all at once, with little regard for trading conditions. Regardless, when players are out of phase with supply and demand, prices invariably bump and grind.

Investors and traders sometimes find themselves inadvertently operating on autopilot, reacting instinctively to every blip and blob that floats by. Headlines, instant messages, PA announcements—they all keep on coming, sometimes in a jumble. It can be difficult to sift through the whole lot when the flurry is intense and seemingly neverending. Even long-time veterans can find themselves reacting, zombie-like, to each and every development in a relatively disinterested manner. When conditions are right and one's state of mind resembles the "zone" that professional athletes enter when they are at the top of their game, profitable things do seem to happen. Bids appear when investors want to sell, and offers come into the market when it is time to buy. However, if it all goes wrong, the groove can soon become a rut, where air pockets continually get popped, triggering losses and unsettling prices.

Finally, a few other factors also contribute to market instability. For example, some hedge fund players, especially those without established track records or a solid base of patient investors, occasionally look to lock in monthly gains—or limit losses—if desired performance parameters are met relatively early on in a measurement period. While helping to paint a positive picture for the aggressive manager's short-term return profile, this sort of activity can create seemingly random disturbances in securities where there are no other developments around that might have otherwise knocked prices out of whack. And, because of the sizable positions a variety of modern operators can take on board, as well as the ham-fisted approach many use when they eventually decide to head for the exits, the short-term effect can sometimes be dramatic.

Regular and seasonal money flows into mutual funds and other pooled investment vehicles have always played an obvious and well-known role in pushing shares around. In the past, the pressures tended to be most acute at times when many automatic investment programs, such as employee deferred compensation plans, kicked in. Although they have occasionally had a dramatic overall effect on the market, especially around calendar turning points, the inflows and outflows in previous years generally seemed to be spread throughout the course of one or more trading sessions. This effectively minimized the appearance of disruptive flare-ups and large intraday gyrations. Recently, however, for reasons that are not entirely clear, fund managers seem to be concentrating buying and selling activity associated with these streams at certain times of the day, usually in the first or last hour of the trading session. Perhaps they are trying to avoid creating gaps between executed prices and closing valuations, or maybe they are attempting to influence existing portfolio values. For whatever reasons, volatility and the clock now seem to be more linked than in the past.

Action Plan

Timing, of course, is usually a critical component of investing success. In fact, the returns from a solid investment idea can easily turn sour if the entry and exit strategies are poorly handled—which can happen if no allowance is made for conditions at the moment of execution. Though it may seem obvious, one of the best ways to minimize the risk of being blindsided by choppy price action is to regularly stand back and try to assess what is actually going on in the market. If trading has been volatile, what are the possible reasons? Is activity being driven by fundamental developments, or does it seem to reflect the fallout from a widespread mood swing? If unexpected data or surprise geopolitical events are responsible for increased instability, does it make sense to wait for the dust to settle before getting involved? Generally speaking, markets tend to quiet down significantly in the hours and days following event-driven disturbances.

Putting circumstances in context can also provide valuable insights. Some questions to ask when the investing landscape becomes unsettled are: Where were share prices headed beforehand? Has the overall market or the securities you have been monitoring been in clearly defined trends, or just treading water? Is it just one security or sector that is volatile, or have many different markets become destabilized at the same time? Intense price swings in a variety of arenas often indicate that the overall economic environment—or, at the very least, investor expectations about it—is changing. If the instability is confined to asset classes other than equities, could it reflect circumstances that may ultimately affect stock prices? Dramatic selloffs in the bond market, for example, may indicate that investors perceive the economy is poised to recover or inflation is set to rise—or both.

It is also possible that unsettling developments in any of the commodity or financial markets could be largely technical in nature, but which may nonetheless have implications for share prices down the road. In the modern investing environment, severe losses in one market can sometimes force heavily leveraged players to raise cash by selling other holdings. This can create a cascading effect that can put pressure on a wide assortment of traded instruments, many of which may have little in common with each other. Under these conditions, lateral thinking can often provide additional insights. Weakness in fixed income securities, for example, may signal rough sledding ahead for banks and insurers, given the substantial size of their interest-sensitive portfolio holdings.

History suggests that understanding your adversaries is the first step to victory—the same usually holds true when it comes to volatility. To make a full and accurate assessment, however, it is usually necessary to look at a cross-section of fundamental and technical data. For example, if a company's stock trades in the low single-digits or its market capitalization is below $500 million, the odds are good that its average volatility will be higher than the market as a whole, as there will often be little broker research to alleviate uncertainty or institutional support to provide a backstop of liquidity. Alternatively, when average daily volumes and intraday ranges decline noticeably from historical averages, it can often indicate that short-term buying and selling activity is likely to be dominated by floor traders and market-makers, who can move prices sharply in response to minimal stimulus.

Sometimes events on the calendar or action in related markets can provide useful insights about the nature of potential instability. If the current date is within a week or so of the day when quarterly results are set to be released, there will likely be little in the way of direct comment from the company during the period. Consequently, speculators and other short-term operators may step in and begin to hold excessive sway over the near-term price action. In addition, the information vacuum may boost the significance of updates and news from rivals, customers, and suppliers, or even those events that have little to do with the company's immediate prospects. Generally speaking, it is a good idea to stay tuned to the potentially market-impacting news and developments highlighted at Web sites such as *www.wsj.com*, *www.investor.com*, *www.bloomberg.com*, *www.reuters.com*, *http://moneycentral.msn.com*, *www.thestreet.com*, *http://finance.yahoo.com*, and *http://cbs.marketwatch.com*.

Once again, the point to remember is that while choppy prices may not matter over the course of a long-term holding period, the instability can dramatically affect performance if it crops up at an inopportune time—say, when a position has to be liquidated to meet obligations or to adjust asset allocations. Consequently, it usually makes sense to have effective execution strategies in place from the outset that can be called on when circumstances warrant. Many institutional operators, for example, prefer to use limits, rather than market orders, when dealing conditions are particularly unsettled. The reason is because, during those occasions, the trading crowd tends to back away from even routine supply and demand flows, and they will generally treat every order as a threat rather than an opportunity.

Adjusting limits to match market swings can also be a worthwhile strategy. In other words, the wider the intraday price range, the more aggressive your limit-setting approach should be. If, under average conditions, you would normally target your buying levels at a discount of one to three percent from the previous close, a recent 50 percent increase in the daily price range would suggest that a discount of two to four percent might be more appropriate. If your level is ultimately hit, you will have a bit more margin built into the price if things go wrong. If not, you end up missing out on a trade. If that is the case and it is a new position, so be it. For most successful players, one of the golden rules of making money is to walk away from investments that cannot be acquired on favorable terms.

Of course, it may be necessary to execute an order to realize a gain or to minimize the loss on an existing position. One approach that many institutional players will often use in this case is a split strategy. They will set limits on a portion of the trade, and use market orders for the balance. While that still leaves the position open to the effects of short-term instability, at least some of the exposure will be reduced. Other operators may use a piecemeal method. Essentially, they divide the order up into relatively small chunks or gradually spread it out over some period of time. This can produce an average price that may help to cancel out some of the choppiness. Whatever the case, the goal is to have volatility as your ally, not as your enemy.

CHAPTER 2

Trading Like Commodities

Stocks are increasingly being bought and sold like commodities.

The financial markets are a mirror image of what goes on in the outside world. Every day the pace quickens, the level of complexity grows, and the challenges people face just to survive become ever more daunting. Some cope by becoming better organized or by trying to improve their level of skill and understanding through training and education. Others adopt more flexible approaches, choosing to "go with the flow" and adjusting strategies as best as they can. Various individuals call on specialists or bring in systems that can take on at least some of the dirty work, so they can focus on what they do well. Many, however, make the choice to rejig their decision-making and direct their efforts towards circumstances most likely to affect them in the near term. In the stock market, as Figure 2.1 seems to indicate, countless operators appear to have moved in that direction, and in doing so, they are changing the nature of the share-trading game. Like it or not, to succeed in today's world, investors must take account of this new, more speculative reality.

Although there are many reasons why the shift towards a more active approach seems to be taking place, unsettled conditions since the Bubble burst have likely had a major influence. Despite the mantras preached by the financial services industry that "stocks go up in the long run" and

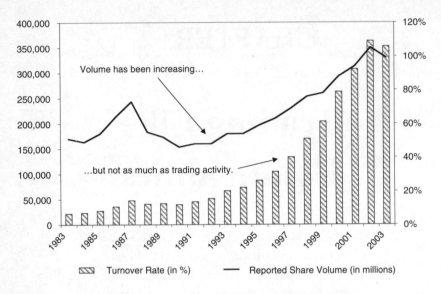

Figure 2.1   New York Stock Exchange Turnover and Volume (Source: New York Stock Exchange).

"buy-and-hold" investing is the key to success in good times and bad, significant numbers of investors learned the hard way that personal timetables do not always jibe with those of the equity market. Compounding gains were a potent drug while prices were moving higher—the reverse, however, tended to be pure poison. The severity and speed of the post-2000 collapse wiped away substantial paper profits for a broad cross-section of investors. Market participants became increasingly cautious about how quickly the downside risks could turn into reality and were reluctant to wait around for the next upswing.

In fact, many now seem to believe that those who relied on an active approach fared somewhat better than the buy-and-holders. While there were a few dramatic stories circulating in recent years about aggressive traders who ended up giving everything back after riding the huge speculative wave skywards, it appears that numerous professionals did indeed cash out in one form or another before prices took a turn for the worst. Admittedly, some drew their rewards from advisory fees and the revenues associated with higher turnover. They took on little of the principal risk that investors naturally assume when they buy and sell securities. Nonetheless, justified or not, the view has become increasingly widespread that those who acted sooner, rather than later, during the Bubble years did the right thing. Perhaps it is a case of rewriting history, but more than a few individuals now believe it makes sense to "lock something in" before circumstances go awry. This sort of mindset favors the bird in the hand over two "special situations" in the bush. As a consequence, the traditional investing culture is being slowly transformed, and a trading mentality is gaining ground.

The approach of a speculator is different than that of a traditional investor. Generally speaking, traders are, by nature, less concerned with textbook fundamentals than with the technical state of the market. They tend to assess the directional outlook in terms of near-term prospects— long-term factors usually provide just an overview or a loose framework. Most rely on some combination of "gut feel" and indicators that attempt to measure current supply-and-demand forces, rather than valuations, in deciding on a course of action. It is probably fair to say, in fact, that nearly all short-term players utilize some form of price-based analysis in their decision-making. While most are, to some degree, aware of influences such as monetary and fiscal policy[1] or the various financial measures "fundamentalists" rely on, dealers usually pay heed to those issues only to the extent that they can make things happen. On the whole, they focus mainly on catalysts that can trigger potential trading opportunities.

Hardcore speculators, at least the successful ones, also tend to be much less concerned with the "whys" and "wherefores" of market moves than traditional operators. The majority do not care whether prices go up or down, as long as they are on the right side of the move. Moreover, most have opinions that are as fleeting as the wind: They are bullish when the markets are heading up and bearish when they are going down. It does not seem to bother many in this group if they start the day with the wrong view—as long as they are able to reverse course and get back in synch with what eventually does take place. After that, early mistakes are forgotten in a matter of minutes. The point is that unlike many conventional investors, especially those with an intellectual bent, most traders are unconcerned about whether a rally makes sense or if the market is "wrong" in interpreting some piece of news or data. If they make money, they are right. Nothing else matters.

For some short-term operators, this perspective also supports the idea of locking in gains whenever possible. Although there is an old adage that says the key to success is "cutting losers and riding winners," many experienced traders have modified the approach somewhat: They are disciplined, but they also like to see the bank balance growing with some degree of consistency over time. This is especially true of those who make a living buying and selling. For some, this means taking profits on purchases and short-sales at regular intervals, often at the conclusion of a trading session. In fact, there is usually a tremendous flurry of activity in many modern-day markets at the beginning and end of the day, as speculators—and others—jump in and out of the game. In recent years, many formerly long-term operators, looking to imitate the approaches of their nimbler counterparts, seem to have moved in this direction.

Action Point

Short-term speculation is a treacherous game that is not for everybody. It requires steely nerves, relatively deep pockets, a unique set of trading skills, and ready access to top-notch information and dealing technology. Most investors, however, can learn something from the wheeling-and-dealing crowd. For example, one trait that successful operators have in common is a lack of emotional attachment to the investments they make. Falling in love with the shares of a company because of the positive fundamentals it once had or staying wedded to a position because of the gains achieved in the past can be a significant and costly mistake. When evaluating what is out there, always remember to take a fresh look at existing shareholdings as well.

There are also deeper societal influences at work that put the accent on the here and now. In a culture where the average length of words, sentences, and paragraphs has declined dramatically since the days of Charles Dickens, where pop videos and nonstop action flicks have become the preferred form of entertainment, and where an alarming number of individuals are being diagnosed with Attention Deficit Disorder, the new realities are already obvious. The emphasis is on the near-term, the superficial, and the exciting. Many people now seem to care only about what is in front of them or what is likely to happen next—with "next" having a much shorter ring to it than it used to. For the most part, there is less interest in probing and challenging, or in taxing what little remaining patience people have, to look into future mysteries. Whether the emphasis was originally three months or even a year from now, the population at large, like growing numbers of market operators, seems to be suffering from rapidly diminishing attention spans.

With all the strains of modern life in the age of information overload, it appears numerous individuals are choosing to simplify matters, too.

Often this involves breaking information, activities, and interactions down into smaller, simpler-to-manage chunks. In the investing world, there are signs that a similar evolution is going on. In fact, given the speed and complexity of global financial markets, it is not surprising that various investors are fine-tuning their perspectives to focus on matters that are not only more digestible, but easier to control and, potentially, profit from. Many have decided to specialize in one way or another: They concentrate on fewer activities, monitor a smaller number of securities, or direct their attentions to narrower time frames. Whatever the case, the results are the same. Despite the apparent contradiction, there seems to be a shift away from the elaborate entanglements associated with the modern age towards a more uncomplicated approach. With its relatively simple perspective, short-term trading appears to provide a solution for some.

The financial roller-coaster ride in recent years—from the shocks and spurts of the 1990s to the euphoric optimism at the peak of the Bubble to the post-Y2K[2] collapse and subsequent choppiness—exhausted a lot of people. While the intensity has mellowed somewhat, and conditions are no longer as continuously charged as they once were, the share-trading arena still mirrors in many respects the accelerating rush of the technology boom. However, like the population at large, it seems more market participants are looking for opportunities to step back and occasionally catch their breath. With a significant proportion pushing into middle age and beyond, many appear keen to take "time outs" and temporarily get away from the hustle and bustle, even if only mentally. Numerous players seem to be creating artificial break points where they go flat or reduce their positions to a minimum. Others are relying on natural barriers, such as the closing bell, to regroup and reassess their outlook for the following day.

Interestingly, the broader shift towards a more speculative approach, and the simultaneous rise in the power and influence of traders, has stimulated psychological urges that have inspired for some market participants something akin to a return to childhood—a time when they discovered with awe how wonderful it was to manipulate the world around them and to experience the pleasures of instant gratification. When things are going well, pulling the trading trigger offers an enjoyable experience that is fun to repeat over and over again. It combines a feeling of control with the prospect of almost magical gains that are not necessarily dependent on hard work or long hours. In a dangerous world where people sometimes feel detached and helpless, buying and selling securities can provide an exciting interactive relationship that is addictive and empowering.

Indeed, without a clear sense of discipline and restraint, it is easy for even experienced professionals to get caught up in the exhilaration of the process itself, instead of remaining focused on what it is meant to achieve. Whether admitted or not, trading offers many of the same thrills as gambling, though arguably it is easier to come out ahead in a game that is not based solely on chance. Consequently, the urge to speculate can generate a feedback loop that is relentlessly self-reinforcing—and potentially very dangerous for the bottom line. While gamblers and other addicts have any number of resources to help them overcome compulsive and self-destructive urges, there does not seem to be any support network in place for those who trade excessively. Usually, they end up lagging in terms of relative investment performance, or if circumstances are especially bad, they lose their jobs or find their financial security is at risk. Although an organization such as Traders Anonymous might be an invaluable resource for curbing the growing urge to speculate, it does not exist, and every day more players seem to get involved—and probably overindulge—in short-term wheeling-and-dealing.

As with gambling, the other great temptation speculation offers—in contrast to patient, long-term investing—is the immediate and spectacular results it can sometimes produce if things go well—especially if the returns are multiplied through the use of leverage. It is a prospect that seems to have appeal in an age where salaries have not kept pace with rising costs, and where the fleeting gains of a few years ago induced a sense of want and despair that now has people thinking of ways to make it all back. Moreover, the Bubble era itself instigated and promoted a sort of get-rich-quick mentality. Historically, such perspectives often crop up after an extended period of economic growth where many people have not had to struggle all that much to get by. They also appear to be a common feature associated with the waning fortunes of great hegemonies—global superpowers—where populations adopt a broad sense of what they are "entitled" to just as the best days of the empire are behind it.

Like many far-reaching trends, the shift towards a more speculative approach reflects both a long-term development—as is made clear in Figure 2.2—and a sudden increase in contagiousness. In today's market, it is apparent that numerous operators have been infected. Moreover, in a world where people learn rather quickly what is going on and what everybody else is doing, active investing has become a popular topic in some circles. Aggressive gunslingers such as hedge fund managers are all the rage—a view helped in part by enthusiastic media coverage—and "trash talk" has even begun to surface that long-term players should call it a day.

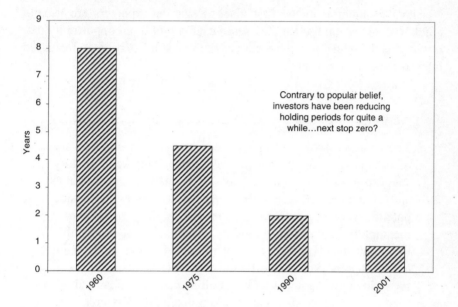

Figure 2.2   Average Holding Period for a NYSE Listed Stock (Source: Bain & Co.).

Living for the next in a series of data points, interacting on a real-time basis with the buzz of the market, exerting a measure of immediate control that is exciting and intoxicating—under these circumstances, it is not difficult to see why risky speculation appeals to many people. Of course, not everybody is or should be "doing it," but even those who stick to their knitting and either ignore it or dismiss the turn of events as dangerous cannot help but be influenced by it.

The fact is that most people, like mice trained to seek out a pellet reward, respond to interesting and potentially useful things going on around them, especially in the financial markets. If they observe operators making money by moving in and out of securities at key technical levels, or if they see it often makes sense to jump on board a sudden trend and quickly exit before the momentum fades, it is hard to sit back and say those methods are not fundamentally sound—that they are merely a form of gambling. One thing about trading or investing is that people are almost always keen to copy strategies that work—or appear to work—if there seems any likelihood that the results can be repeated. Invariably, of course, once a winning tactic becomes too popular, it tends to lose its appeal, as self-correcting forces alleviate some of the conditions that created the situation in the first place. Regardless, players are usually quick to come around when they sense even a hint of an opportunity that might give them an edge. In recent years, the result has been an increased interest in being more active.

Action Point

Though it may sound old-fashioned, it makes sense to be wary of complexity and change in the financial markets. History suggests that the downside risks of newfangled instruments and strategies are generally understated, while the upside potential is often exaggerated. Nonetheless, the world is evolving rapidly, and certain kinds of technology can ensure that important developments are not missed. For example, many online content providers offer customizable Web sites that can filter "in" important news. Others offer access to updates about fundamental data that can be automatically forwarded by email or text message. In both instances, investors can gain access to intelligence that might not appear in the mainstream media until days later—if at all. To get started, check out what is offered at sites such as *http://moneycentral.msn.com, http:// finance.yahoo.com, www.wsj.com,* and *www.thestreet.com.*

As is often the case when people latch on to something new and exciting, there always seems to be someone around who can supply all the action that is needed. In the financial markets, not surprisingly, many vested interests fit the bill. The brokerage industry, for one, has always done its share to keep things humming. Structurally dependent on dealing activity for survival, financial services intermediaries are essentially colossal selling machines. True, they employ lots of smart people, have plenty of good research ideas, and usually have helpful structures in place that can make the process of investing easier—and potentially more successful—than it might otherwise be. Some individuals and firms, in fact, can add real value when it comes to deciding which situations are worth looking at or where shares stand on the value scale. A few even get kudos for helping clients to make money on a relatively consistent basis. Most representatives and their employers, however—especially those focused primarily on equities—could not exist without regular turnover.

There have been a few exceptions. Some retail firms have tried to establish relationships with clients that generate revenue based on the size of investment accounts, rather than the amount of commissions produced. They introduced quarterly or annual charges, usually tallied on a percentage-of-assets basis, which provided a regular income stream for brokers—and which presumably got them thinking about customers' long-term financial well-being. These arrangements were also seen as a way of tying investors to a stable relationship, rather than a short-lived one depending upon the level of commission rates. Rolled out in earnest during the late-1990s, when euphoria was widespread and the prospect of never-ending portfolio gains was becoming accepted wisdom, fee-based accounts remain an important fixture of the industry. Nonetheless, the structure of the overall investing environment, as well as the institutional marketplace, has always been largely transaction-oriented.

During the long upswing, the rush to invest made matters relatively easy, of course. Buying and selling activity naturally picked up as fresh funds came into the market. A sizable interest in Initial Public Offerings (IPOs)[3] developed, as a variety of start-up companies and established firms looked to tap into soaring investor demand for shares. The often spectacular gains that many new issues registered in the minutes and days after they first started trading further stimulated a growing desire to hop on board the equity gravy train. Moreover, an abundance of new products and loads of high-powered research contributed to a sharp rise in strategies that could capitalize on divergences and inconsistencies, many of which were short-term in nature. Numerous operators also appeared who were looking to profit from day-to-day price movements. Significant improvements in technology and communications networks made it easy to grant them their wish.

There was also the mathematics of greed. Some market participants looked at the huge percentage advances that numerous shares were making and began projecting those trends forward. They estimated that continuing gains on an ever-increasing pile of winnings could lead to fantastic wealth in relatively short order. In simple terms, the thinking seemed to go like this: If someone could make 10 percent—say, in a month—and reinvest those proceeds, realizing the same return in a subsequent period and repeating the process over and over again, the individual could retire and live the good life after only a few years. Unrealistic, to be sure, but not a completely alien line of thinking when people get caught up in their own euphoria. A cynic would say that sort of perspective gets people into trouble. True, but it seems that the compounding issue, which reared its head during the Bubble years, has not gone completely away. In some minds, at least, the view remains that increased turnover leads to greater gains.

Active buying and selling produces an environment that is ideally suited for those who stand in the middle, collecting a cut on every deal. Not surprisingly, the number of brokers and scale of their operations expanded significantly during the boom. They not only capitalized on the movement, they reinforced it. Despite the fact that commission rates had been falling steadily for years because of competitive pressures, improvements in technology, and other factors, revenues continued to increase, as new issue fees and overall volume growth outstripped declines in per-share charges. However, as is common in any boom, fixed costs rose relatively sharply. Short-term demand for space and resources far outstripped near-term capacity and availability. Variable expenses also soared, especially those associated with payroll costs, as vast numbers of new bodies were brought on board to serve the needs of the rapidly expanding customer base. It seemed like things could only get better, and many firms threw caution to the wind as they positioned themselves to take advantage of a widely expected multiyear run.

Then in the spring of 2000, the Bubble burst, and the fallout ever since has been relatively severe. Declining share prices slowed volume increases, as numerous speculators fell by the wayside and others reined in some of their more exuberant activities. IPO activity shrank to a shadow of its former self. The gusher of money that had poured into the market throughout the last few years of the twentieth century slowed down significantly, and although many regular monthly investment programs remained in place, overall interest in equities faded from the near-euphoric levels that existed only a short while earlier. Stuck with bull market overheads and bear market revenues, brokers who catered largely to the equity crowd came under considerable pressure to close the gap. The implications were clear: Costs had to be cut and revenues boosted.

The former was relatively easy: They laid off lots of employees, subcontracted back office functions out and sublet office facilities. Luckily for many brokerage houses, a few things were going on at the time that also aided the latter. While it was not a cakewalk, these factors—along with the money being generated by other product areas, such as fixed income—helped to ease some of the pressure. Trading, for instance, was becoming an increasingly important focus across the investing spectrum. This meant that aggressive clients' turnover would likely continue to rise, and the firms themselves could potentially make up some of the slack by engaging in more buying and selling on their own account. Meanwhile, vast numbers of modern operators, such as hedge funds, were also arriving on the scene. Comprised of sharp and flexible individuals who were well attuned to a variety of modern developments, this group was not only comfortable with an active approach, they often thrived on it.

Action Point

As has been the case in the fixed-income, foreign exchange, and commodity markets for years, it seems that the sell side of the institutional equity business is moving away from servicing customers towards a principal-driven trading model. Under such circumstances, the natural tension between the interests of intermediaries and those of clients is likely to grow, regardless of intentions. In all likelihood, the fallout from this structural change will eventually spill over and influence dealings on the retail side as well. Hence, it is more important than ever for investors to figure out the basis and cost-effectiveness of their financial relationships, determining what they are paying and what they are getting in return. For example, the first question to ask on low-cost, flat-rate, or "free" deals is: How does the "other side" actually make its money?

There are many reasons why this is so, but perhaps the most important has to do with the way these alternative investment managers are evaluated and compensated. Generally speaking, traditional buy-side firms are assessed on how well they do relative to their peer group or some predetermined benchmark, together with the long-term consistency of their performance. They are not judged on how much money they make—or lose—for their underlying clients. In other words, what usually matters most is whether they have earned more—or lost less—than the standard they are being evaluated against. For example, if traditional manager A drops 10 percent this quarter and all the other institutions which employ the same investment style end up losing 11 percent or more, A has scored an impressive victory—despite the portfolio's sharp decline in value. Of course, if the "winning" manager also manages to make money, it would not be viewed as a negative.

In the alternative investing world, however, the primary determinant of success is absolute return. While factors such as an operator's long-term track record and comparative ranking versus rivals are usually taken somewhat into account, the key question is: Did the fund manage to achieve not only a minimum required level of performance—sometimes equal to the risk-free[4] rate—but a net positive return after that? Regardless of whether the market goes up or down, these players are expected to make money for their backers by the end of the year. Sometimes it gets a bit more complicated than that—when, for example, a manager fails to come up to snuff or even loses money during one period. In those cases, there is typically a "high-water" mark, which must be exceeded in the following term—assuming the investor sticks with the manager—before there can be any prospect of a payment for performance.

This brings to mind the other significant difference between old-line and alternative investment managers. Most traditional firms are compensated with a percentage fee based on the total assets under management, rather than on how successful their particular strategies have been. The primary means for rewarding or punishing these institutions is to keep investments in the hands of those who are relative winners and take them away from those who are not. In the hedge fund sector, however, there is almost always some sort of incentive-based fee structure, sometimes combined with an additional kicker in the form of a percentage charge on the overall portfolio. Typically, the bonus element works out to a straight or graduated share of the profits above preset levels, with more successful operators sometimes arranging to receive a larger slice of the pie. Under these circumstances, when the investor does well, so does the manager.

In the case of some relatively young funds, especially those just starting out, the performance-based reward is occasionally all they get—at least until a longer-term pattern of success is established—which creates some interesting incentives. For a start, it almost encourages a riskier approach to investing—one that depends on the manager putting money to work under all sorts of market conditions, even those which might be considered hostile to that operator's particular investment style. It also creates, especially in the case of relatively flexible equity-based hedge funds, an urge to do something—perhaps *anything*—to make money, because certain minimum percentage gains must be achieved in order to have any fees coming in the door. Finally, because the rates of return they are expected to earn are typically higher than those sought from their more traditional counterparts, modern operators often feel the need to adopt a speculative posture. In a few cases, it almost comes down to the view that "to trade is to eat."

The pressure to be more active has as much to do with the mindsets of hedge fund managers and their underlying investors as it does with the reward system. For the most part, the sector grew out of a unique approach to making money that broke the mold, so to speak, of traditional equity investing, and one of its key long-term appeals has been the flexibility most operators have been afforded in their approach to markets. While a relatively recent influx of institutional interest from pension funds and others has forced some measure of the fast-and-loose approach to disappear—especially at larger, more established hedge funds, many of which have started to look and act like their long-established rivals—this new breed is still allowed considerable leeway in terms of aggressiveness and turnover. Moreover, alternative investment managers tend to pay less attention to the potentially negative tax consequences of active trading than traditional firms, for various reasons.

The result is that, as a group, most equity-based players, at least those that are not restricted to pure arbitrage strategies or otherwise prevented from aggressive buying and selling, are usually expected to be intimately involved with what is going on in the marketplace—and they are. And, as is the case with many who take that stance, the focus often quickly turns to potential short-term catalysts, such as earnings reports, economic statistics, and news events. The list of possible market-moving events has grown in recent years, helped by the creative input of vested interests and the research done by players looking for unique insights on underlying conditions. This has pressured time frames. On the one hand, everyone now has at their disposal a set of pending data points almost guaranteed to trigger market responses; on the other, no one wants to be exposed to factors that can knock existing positions out of kilter. Taken together, the two forces promote an in-out-flat sequence that reinforces the shifting perspective.

Action Point

One of the many things that set humans apart from their counterparts in the animal kingdom is their ability to easily learn from others and absorb second-hand insights that can have as much value as those which are acquired through first-hand experience. For example, an endless stream of data points might seem, at first glance, to offer little direct benefit to a long-term investor. Yet, the reaction of other players to the information, as well as the issue of whether or not prices exhibit follow-through momentum, can often provide critical intelligence on expectations and short-term supply-and-

demand facts. Generally speaking, if news leads to an unantic-
ipated reaction, it is usually a good reason to reassess the facts.
When it comes to getting a handle on where expectations are,
the Preview section of *Barron's* provides an excellent starting
point.

Measurement benchmarks also play a role. While it has been apparent for some time that the emphasis in the corporate and investment communities had shifted from annual to quarterly assessment periods, the
growth of the hedge fund market has given rise to an even more dramatic
reduction in the evaluation window. The sharp expansion in the number of
new operators, combined with their fairly secretive ways and the potential
volatility associated with riskier strategies, has caused some backers to
zero in on monthly returns. Not surprisingly, this development has influenced the investment horizons of the managers themselves, especially the
newer entrants. Often, start-up hedge fund operators will strive to measure up at the end of each month during the first year in order to keep nervous underlying investors in tow. Sometimes this means they close out
positions for no other reason than the date on the calendar. At other times,
managers may decide to cover shorts or liquidate longs at mid-month
because things have gone about as well as expected and they do not want
to tempt fate.

There are even greater extremes. For example, independent operators
such as floor traders, as well as some proprietary Wall Street dealers, are
often evaluated within a much narrower timeframe. Their positions are
"marked-to-market"[5] daily for regulatory or accounting reasons, for margin
purposes, or as part of a process of managing risk. The goal in most
instances is to make certain that sufficient funds are on hand to clear the
day's transactions and to ensure that nobody ends up breaking the bank.
Profit-and-loss data—P&Ls—are also recorded and added up at the end of
each period, and everyone pretty much knows where they stand before the
start of the next session. With more players going this route, it adds to the
overall sense of time compression. For these short-term speculators, there is
often a clear motivation—not necessarily driven by internal rules or management edicts—to regularly close out positions at the first opportunity.

Also worth mentioning, though it might seem obvious, are the reasons why brokers are quick to respond to the needs of aggressive operators. For the most part, it has to do with the way the institutional market
tends to work. Along with the flexibility many modern players have in

terms of when and how they choose to operate, traders and hedge funds can usually do business with any counterparty they like, as long as they themselves can pass muster with sell-side credit committees and compliance departments. For most established firms, this is usually not a problem. Consequently, if they desire, they can dole out trades to a broker the first time they discuss an idea, even if there was no prior contact or relationship between the two. In addition, because the majority of alternative investment managers have flat organizational structures, the chances are good that a solid investment pitch will lead directly to a commission-paying order.

That is a substantial incentive for sales-oriented individuals, and it generally means that representatives will go out of their way to give these operators what they want. Dealings with traditional institutions, however, are not always so easy. To begin with, there is often a divide between the discussion and implementation of an investment strategy because, in many cases, a proposal must be vetted first by others. In addition, most long-only firms, especially those overseeing multibillion dollar portfolios, separate the analytical and execution functions, dividing the relevant tasks between portfolio management staff and centralized dealing desks. For risk-control purposes and other reasons, managers typically do not give orders directly to their sell-side contacts. While this helps to ensure that trades are handled by specialists who are plugged in to what is going on and that legally mandated "best execution" practices are followed, it nonetheless creates a disconnect that can sometimes dampen motivation.

Perhaps more importantly, many old-line firms have adopted commission payout schedules that favor brokers who provide consistent long-term service. Usually, they award points for research and trading recommendations, as well as other services, such as arranging visits with company managements. Then on some sort of regular basis—often quarterly, though sometimes annually—they evaluate the universe of authorized counterparties in terms of their overall performance. They may also give them a "report card," although the actual level of disclosure can vary considerably. Sometimes the results are not revealed at all, but are only used to produce internal guidelines. Whatever the case, this process establishes a framework that governs how resources are allocated, usually in the period ahead. Although many well-known investing institutions can pay out substantial sums, it generally takes considerable effort over many years for intermediaries to share in the wealth or move up to more prominent spots on broker lists. As might be expected, the emphasis tends to be on long-term investment ideas.

Consequently, no small number of intermediaries find the active investing community to be a much more tempting target, especially in the wake of the overall damage the post-2000 collapse did to share prices. Available commission dollars from traditional managers naturally fell as portfolios shrank in value. While the sell side has obviously not ignored this segment, numerous representatives find it easier to promote ideas to those who have plenty of money and the ability to deal on the spot. This provides not only financial incentives, but psychological ones as well. Modern buy-side players also welcome short-term trading recommendations, which certainly does not hurt. Adding further fuel to the fire, sales-traders' roles have also changed. Once mainly advisors and facilitators to centralized dealing desks, many have now become active marketers, pitching ideas to aggressive trading accounts. Moreover, by focusing on what they know best—short-term supply-and-demand conditions and real-time developments—they end up leaving plenty of fundamental details out of their daily chatter—the kind of details that long-term investors rely on.

In the wholesale and retail markets, the combination of a creative infusion of intellectual resources and an explosion of new products, especially in the derivatives arena, has had far-reaching consequences, particularly in the aftermath of the boom and bust. For one, it has given brokers a fresh opportunity to teach old-dog clients a host of new tricks—the kind of tricks that can generate lots of commissions. It has also caused a variety of interesting and complex strategies to bubble to the surface. Some allow minute price discrepancies, for example, to be captured by a wide range of operators, aided by improving industry economics. In addition, there has been increased issuance of all sorts of exotic and hybrid securities, such as convertible bonds,[6] which has triggered active buying and selling of shares for hedging and arbitrage purposes. On the whole, much of what has arrived on the equity scene in recent years seems designed to boost turnover and short-term speculation.

Action Point

One of the common assumptions that market participants on both the wholesale and retail sides of the equity business make when they learn of new investment ideas and potentially market-moving developments is that they are hearing it first. This is usually a mistake. In reality, there are very few investors who get such exclusive access—unless, of course, they are among the top commission-payers on Wall Street or are equally valuable as sources of unique insights in exchange. In an era of broadcast messaging and the rapid spread of information, it does not take long before a sizable cross-section of operators is aware of even the most valuable facts and figures. Consequently, rather than reacting as though the news is hot off the presses, look beyond the data and try to focus on what others in the crowd may be missing.

Another factor that has changed perspectives has been the dramatic increase in the number and availability of equity-linked derivatives that can, as will be explored later, have a major impact on the related "cash" or physical markets. Unlike shares, these instruments almost always have a fixed maturity date, with the most actively traded issues generally having the shortest lives.[7] This has important repercussions in that it has introduced an artificial but powerful new rhythm to stock price movements. Short-term swings in the market are now more closely tied to the life cycle of synthetic securities than they were in the past. For example, when options mature, there is often activity in the related equities that can temporarily unsettle the forces of supply and demand. Similarly, the expiration of a futures contract can push the underlying index in a variety of directions within a matter of minutes.

The intense interaction between the cash, options, and futures markets, as well as the increased preference for simplification by many players, has had another interesting effect. In essence, stock markets have become more "commoditized." For numerous reasons—available liquidity, easy access, and the perception, rightly or wrongly, that share prices can be easily manipulated by insiders or others—growing numbers of operators prefer to speculate on the direction of indices or sectors, such as those comprised of banks, pharmaceuticals, or semiconductor makers, rather than individual equities. Simplistic as it sounds, many seem to find it easier to choose some widely followed measure as a "punting" vehicle, rather than trying to wade through the complex details that make every company's stock inherently unique. Consequently, the action in listed derivatives or, especially in the past few years, Exchange-Traded Funds (ETFs),[8] has seen a marked increase, and a significant proportion of recent volume seems tied to the buying and selling of index-related securities.

In a sense, much of the activity fosters a sort of "homogenization" process, blending cream with milk to create a churn that is frequently unrelated to underlying fundamentals. Sometimes, for example, a stock will rally on relatively bad news, not because the information is already discounted and bargain-hunters are stepping in, but because there is widespread index-related buying pushing the overall market higher. True, the real dogs might underperform on a comparative basis, rising less in percentage terms than the broader averages, but the direction of the moves themselves can still defy logic. For the most part, it seems equities are taking on more of the "look and feel" of physical commodities. As has been the case with oil, gold, pork bellies, and other products, it is now quite easy to wade in and out of stocks as though they were just another simple asset class. What is more, little knowledge of valuations, earnings, management qualities, or other factors is required to do so.

Once viewed as a three-dimensional puzzle requiring years of study and practical experience to master, the stock market now appears to be nothing more than a collection of trading baskets to numerous players, with a few paying almost no attention to what the underlying securities actually have going for them. Not surprisingly, this bundle-oriented approach has not only minimized the differentiation of companies within sectors, it has even led some participants to question what individual equities have to do with the stock market. This is a bit of an exaggeration, of course, but the broad measures do seem to be the main draw for an increasing number of operators. Consequently, price movements and trading patterns now appear to have more in common with what goes on in the commodity pits than they do with the way shares used to act. Short-term speculation is widespread, with a significant emphasis on technical factors. In both arenas, players are keenly focused on the action that lies immediately ahead.

Since the Bubble burst, financial services firms have, as suggested earlier, encouraged this shift in perspective to keep business coming in the door—and, perhaps, to sustain the relevance the stock market has had with respect to the overall economy, as Figure 2.3 certainly demonstrates. They feed customers aggressive investment ideas and boost the number and pace of research calls, especially those tied to upcoming releases and events. They supply reams of information about technical factors and arbitrage situations. On dealing and sales-trading desks, representatives send out time-sensitive data about flows and supply-and-demand needs through a combination of telephone calls, emails, Bloomberg messages, and Indications of Interest (IOIs).[9] Sometimes they slash commission rates on individual orders and program trades to generate business with

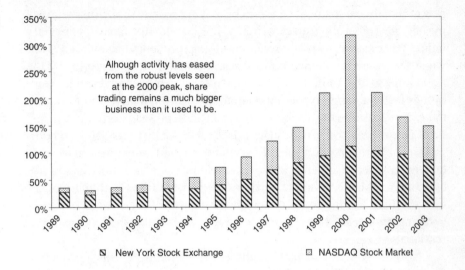

Alhough activity has eased from the robust levels seen at the 2000 peak, share trading remains a much bigger business than it used to be.

☒ New York Stock Exchange   ⊠ NASDAQ Stock Market

Figure 2.3   U.S. Stock Market Traded Value as a Percentage of Gross Domestic Product (Source: Securities Industry Association, U.S. Bureau of Economic Analysis).

other clients or provide "swap" opportunities for in-house dealers. They may even break apart and recast statistics in a new light—or create their own measures—to draw in speculators looking for a unique angle on what is happening. Not surprisingly, other interests, such as the media, are happy to play along as well.

Driven in part by developments on the artistic side of the fence, many general and business news organizations have, for some time, been moving towards providing information that is easy to digest, requiring little effort on the part of readers, listeners, and viewers. Weighed down by the costs of far-flung operations and competition from a variety of modern day providers, many have also striven hard to raise awareness and stand out from a competitive crowd. They offer exciting nuggets and tasty morsels on a near-continuous basis and shove breaking developments out the door as quickly as possible—sometimes allowing quality control to slip a notch. Overall, it seems a great deal of the formerly serious output has taken on more of a showbiz flavor in recent years—the sort some highbrow organizations once scorned. In many respects, it almost seems that many modern news providers are bent on giving pop video producers a run for their money.

As it happens, the Bubble years were extremely rewarding for "hard-content" generators, especially those that cranked out business-related

news. The almost magical euphoria of making money in the markets per-
meated nearly every aspect of daily life, while the financial services
industry boosted advertising spending to unprecedented levels. However,
when the go-go days ended, most media-oriented firms were hit by the
same squeeze that rattled the brokers. Costs were high, and revenues were
falling fast—a dangerous combination. While competitive forces during
the boom had already triggered frequent teasers and more "juiced up"
news reports, the collapse in share prices really kicked marketing and promotional efforts into high gear. Everything was suddenly directed towards
creating a sense of urgency and excitement that people simply had to pay
attention to. Airwaves and television screens were filled with more bulletins, scrolling headlines and tickers, breaking news flashes, and constantly
updating on-screen "bugs" to catch the eyes and ears of amateurs and professionals alike.

Now there is a constant emphasis on upcoming events—economic
data, live interviews, domestic and international bulletins, and even garden-variety hype. Services like Bloomberg and Reuters offer not only
proprietary news and data, but all sorts of other information put out by
third-party services and research boutiques, injecting lots of high-impact
color into an already frenetic trading day. Weekly and daily calendars
have become commonplace, as are reports discussing potential short-term
influences in the period ahead. Market participants even have access to
material that is aimed primarily at editors and beat reporters, such as day-
books and electronic press releases. A host of free and members-only
Web sites have also popped up, offering insights on technical levels, price
trends, supply-and-demand conditions, money flows, floor trading activity, and even the latest "whisper" numbers.[10] Without a doubt, content
providers are doing their part to feed the need for action and speed.

Finally, corporate America has helped to keep the speculative ball
rolling as well, which appears to suit their interests. Many firms continually pump out management interviews, financial data, and news releases,
supposedly to keep investors informed, though much of it seems to have
more in common with public relations puffery than anything else. Part of
the reason, of course, is that increasing numbers of executives are being
rewarded on the basis of short-term financial performance and share price
movements. The view seems to be that if they can create enough positive
data points to keep investors buying, the process might just create self-
sustaining momentum. While regulatory changes such as Reg FD and
Sarbanes-Oxley have made it more difficult to paint an unrealistic picture
for the masses—or to offer a realistic look to a favored few—companies

appear to have done what they can to "manage" expectations so that market responses lean towards the upside. Like numerous vested interests, a variety of public corporations seem determined to give participants what they want, which, for many, is the possibility of short-term action—and the chance to buy and sell stocks with a vengeance.

Action Plan

Such an environment can frustrate long-term investors. They may find that the chaotic conditions and frenzied activity that accompany, for example, an "unexpected" earnings release make it difficult to separate out what only seems important from what actually matters. For speculators, irrelevant news and fanciful rumors usually carry the same weight as "real" fundamentals, so long as they move prices in ways that offer opportunities for short-term gain. In addition, it can be difficult to avoid getting caught up in the constant whirl of activity. Much like the glittering serenade of a large Las Vegas casino, with its flashing lights, beeping slots, and crackling chips, there is a hypnotic allure to short-term trading. Unfortunately, unless you have the right emotional makeup and skill set—the ability to cut losses quickly, for example, or the knack for reversing direction in a heartbeat—rapid-fire trading is a very difficult and risky way to make money.

Nonetheless, keeping an eye on what speculative players are up to can offer interesting insights. It can also help to fill in some of the critical pieces of the supply-and-demand puzzle. Generally speaking, in a market dominated by traders, it is likely that their perspectives will matter most with respect to near-term action. How to tell? Look for the types of publicized chatter that signals this group is currently holding sway. For example, if daily market reports make many references to "technicals" and "charts," that is a usually a sign that traditional fundamentals—and investors—are temporarily out of the picture. Alternatively, if news stories remain fixated on the degree of "bullishness" or "bearishness" that exists on Wall Street, it can also serve notice that short-term operators are in charge. Finally, if bulletins and discussions are centered on rumors and catalysts, it suggests long-term operators are probably on the sidelines, watching and waiting. Without the support of big money players, it is a good bet that prices will tend to remain choppy and range-bound.

Of course, it is worth paying attention to activity levels, too. Regardless of whether you believe in technical analysis or not, the pace of turnover is one of the clearest signs around that something "real" is going on. There are, of course, a host of activities nowadays that can artificially inflate volume statistics, but the key is to look at the up-to-date numbers and weigh them against historical patterns. If prices appear to be treading water, yet volume seems to be picking up significantly, that often indicates something interesting is brewing—but has yet to be publicly revealed. To get a good sense of perspective, compare current and five-day average volume data to longer-term trends. Web sites such as *http://moneycentral.msn.com* and others can provide this information. A pickup in recent activity, along with a move to new price levels, can be a sign that institutional players are on the scene. Alternatively, if the pattern is reversed, the possibility looms large that the shares, or the market as a whole, may be set for a period of meaningless meandering.

While it may not necessarily be a good idea to act like a short-term trader, it can be helpful to know what some of these players are focusing on. Many rely on a host of technical signals, for example, to determine exit and entry points, and to set levels for stop-loss orders. Consequently, it can sometimes give you added insight to take even a brief look at a three- or six-month bar chart to gauge where the potential flashpoints may lie. Although it is easy enough to record the levels of visually important peaks and troughs, there are a number of resources around, such as *www.stockcharts.com*, that can give you a more detailed picture of what trigger points the speculative types may be keeping an eye on. It is worth noting that, historically at least, certain indicators have often served to identify levels that function as catalysts for speculative interest. These include measures such as the 50- and 200-day moving averages. Finally, pay attention to widely-watched "round numbers"—even fundamental traders sometimes cannot resist the attraction of prices that end with "00."

One advantage that many long-term players have over speculative operators comes from the fact that a significant proportion of the activity the latter group engages in can be somewhat involuntary in nature. Because of capital constraints, risk-control measures, or basic personality profiles, many short-term speculators frequently close out positions at the end of a day, a week, or even a month—regardless of market conditions. Often there seems to be an abundance of operators who are similarly positioned—who apparently begin contemplating their closeout moves in the early afternoon. Pay attention to price action that takes place on either side of the midday hour: If a sharp early morning decline reverses course into the latter part of the session, this is often a sign that late trading is likely to be dominated by fast money players cutting short positions and vice versa.

Short-term operators are always on the prowl for catalysts, and even though it may not make sense for you to view them from the same perspective, awareness can be a useful accessory when formulating execution strategies. In modern markets, it seems that once a theme or product becomes the center of attention—whether it is a particular commodity market, a geopolitical phenomenon, or even pronouncements coming from the mouths of certain individuals—it tends to remain so for at least some number of months. Consequently, staying in tune with what the latest linkages are by reading daily market updates in the *Wall Street Journal, Investor's Business Daily, New York Times, Washington Post*, and other newspapers can help you to avoid getting run over by potentially foreseeable events. If developments in the Mideast and sharp moves in the price of crude oil, for example, have become particularly important influences in the stock market, it is not a bad idea to stay on top of when the next OPEC meeting is likely to take place.

Because of the excitement it creates and the commission revenues it can bring in, short-term trading sometimes brings out the worst in a host of vested interests. Many are only too happy to clutter the landscape with an assortment of meaningless catalysts and lots of irrelevant noise, just to get the speculative juices flowing. At the worst extremes, the logic they offer seems to follow along the lines that the best reason to actively buy or sell is because everyone else is doing it or because there is nothing better to do. If you find yourself getting caught up in this unhelpful sales pitch—impatient and anxious to deal—or putting on boredom trades that regularly end up costing a lot of money, then it is time to take a break and get back to the basics.

CHAPTER 3

Approaches and Attitudes

Investing and reason frequently give way to speculation and emotion.

Although attitudes have begun to change in recent years, there is still widespread reluctance to admit that market players are often irrational. This is despite the fact that most people, even those who have never traded a share in their lives, intuitively understand the cliché that fear and greed are the primary drivers of investor behavior. Some textbooks and personal finance tomes make reference to the emotional elements that influence buying and selling, but many commentators still appear to believe otherwise. They argue—or tacitly support the view—that thoughtful analysis and levelheaded decision-making invariably dictate future stock price movements. That is somewhat ironic, of course, in light of the equity bubble that developed during the 1990s, the collapse that followed, and the recent resurgence of interest—as Figure 3.1 seems to suggest—in the most speculative shares. Nonetheless, for today's investor, it is more important than ever to understand the emotional elements that have come to the fore in the share-trading arena. Otherwise, they risk being swept up in a tide that can lead to underperformance and substantial losses.

One of the things that some observers fail to see—especially those who have not had real money at stake in volatile conditions—is that, contrary to desire, people cannot always help themselves. Rather than seek-

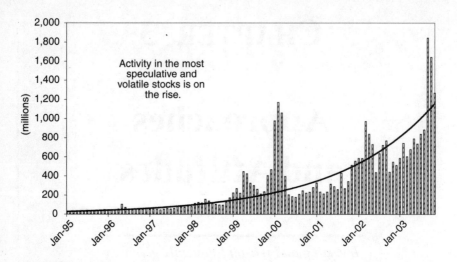

Activity in the most speculative and volatile stocks is on the rise.

Figure 3.1 OTC Bulletin Board Average Daily Share Volume (Source: The NASDAQ Stock Market, Inc.).

ing to maximize returns and coolly looking out for their own interests, individuals occasionally stray from a preferred course of action because of fear, anxiety, impatience, or other distractions. However harmful it might be to their bottom lines, they can get "spooked" into doing things they really should avoid. Or, they give in to a moment of temporary madness, which they later regret—even if they have considerable experience or a long-term record of success. Regardless of whether they rely on others for stock selection and timing or come up with investment strategies on their own, market participants are vulnerable to a variety of negative influences that lurk in the trading arena—and in themselves. Arrogance, stubbornness, and complacency, for example, can be real drags on performance when they cause players to misstep or otherwise take their eyes off the ball.

Investors can also be affected by concerns about forces that are supposedly capable of pushing prices up, down, and around at will. To a certain extent—more so, it seems, when conditions have been especially unsettled—share traders almost always have an air of paranoia and suspicion about them. Sometimes they fear there is a wild marauder out there with the inside scoop just waiting to pounce and take advantage of their naiveté or misfortune. Although logic and history suggest otherwise, some participants worry, in fact, that an abundance of such creatures exist, and are secretly on the lookout for any sign of them. Strange as it sounds, more than a few occasionally accept as true that these "insiders" are all-seeing, especially when it comes to an awareness of supply and demand. "They" know, for example, when most players are wagering on a short-term rally, and "they" immediately take advantage of this by driving prices down to trigger stop-loss selling. That is a bit ridiculous, of course, but the view is not totally out of line in a world where people are quick to blame others when things go wrong.

Ironically, the belief that there are those in modern times who have the ability and resources to impose their will on the marketplace is not as far-fetched as it sounds. As the old saw has it, just because you are paranoid does not mean they are not out to get you. Conventional wisdom says that no one is bigger than the market. While true in a general sense, there are increasing occasions—throughout the year and during the trading day—when air pockets form in the prices of shares and related securities because of the overall decline in trading liquidity that has occurred since the Bubble burst. When this happens, it allows operators with ample resources, an opportunistic approach to making money, and the ability to act quickly, to seize the moment and shake things up. By spending a relatively small amount to kick-start short-term momentum, an aggressive player can often trigger a forceful response from other traders looking to pounce on whatever action crops up. Ultimately, the instigator hopes to unload the recently acquired position at profitable levels.

There is no shortage of such operators, either on or off the exchanges. What makes life difficult for the speculative crowd, of course, is not knowing who is ultimately behind any of the buying and selling that does take place. For example, while a floor broker[1] on the New York Stock Exchange may represent various institutions—some small and others large—for reasons of client confidentiality, other participants can never really be sure who the agent is acting for on any given occasion. Mind you, educated guessing is a frequent pastime. The same applies to the various electronic dealing networks, which generally promote anonymity as a selling point, especially for institutional fund managers who are worried about the impact of their potentially market-moving interests. As a consequence, when orders do come in, there is usually some momentary combination of wariness and expectation that arises in players' minds that the flow may be part of a much larger picture.

Not surprisingly, many sharp operators try to capitalize on these sentiments, aided by electronic capabilities that allow individual and program orders to be quickly routed to an appropriate venue. They hope that by sending a well-timed burst of business, they can set off a charge that can boost their own performance. Nonetheless, sometimes the interest is for real, and the buying or selling that initially knocks the market off balance is the beginning of a significantly larger order. The reasons for this type of approach are numerous, but much of it has to do with style, perspective, and the resources at the disposal of many modern operators. A significant proportion of hedge fund managers, for example, are assertive by nature, and many are willing to stir up potentially self-defeating momentum at the outset of a trade to quickly get a large chunk of the position on board. Psychologically, at least, it can be quite beneficial to have a purchase or short-sale "in the black" almost from the get-go. For executions that do not work out, the activity sometimes gives a useful read on sentiment and supply-and-demand conditions. It can also provide interesting feedback on stock selection methods—and, perhaps, an opportunity to go the other way.

Action Point

Although the immediate financial and psychological consequences can be upsetting, poor investment decisions often provide uniquely valuable information. On the one hand, they can open up an opportunity to explore personal shortcomings that need to be addressed; on the other hand, they may reveal useful data about underlying technical factors that can help investors to fine tune their overall approach. The key point is not to treat such events as skeletons in the closet but as valuable lessons in the art of investing. When incorrect choices are made, try writing the facts down and focusing, dispassionately, on what went wrong. Apart from anything else, this will help desensitize the ego to any sense of vulnerability associated with admitting mistakes. That alone can often make the difference between mediocre returns and star-quality performance.

Traders and alternative investment managers are less hemmed in by turnover restrictions than many traditional buy-side operators. For a start, most old-line firms generally prefer to work quietly and limit the collateral damage caused by their buying and selling activities. This is mainly because positions are usually acquired with a longer-term perspective in mind, often following a lengthy review process. The underlying premise is that these fund managers are taking advantage of opportunities on behalf of their clients; they are not trying to rattle the market. Similarly, it is difficult for these investors to rapidly cut positions that fare poorly or to trade out of a string of short-term winners without raising more than a few eyebrows. Although many long established players have, in recent years, joined others and adopted a more active approach to investing, the shift has not been so dramatic as to turn them into poster children for institutional speculation. They also have reservations about being seen to be pouring fuel on the volatility fire.

Most hedge funds also do not have the same restrictions in place that their long-only rivals have with respect to position limits and portfolio concentration. Although the majority are subject to some sort of risk-control procedures and exposure is monitored by prime brokers and principals—and, to a lesser extent, large institutional backers—they often have considerable leeway in how they structure the makeup of their investments, at least in the short-term. Aggressive operators, especially those with a well-established track record, frequently have very flexible parameters under which they can operate. In addition, because they tend to be lightly regulated and fairly secretive by nature, it is usually difficult for anyone but the employees of their clearing firms to know exactly where they stand. This can provide an easy opening for managers to adopt potentially risky weightings.

Resources are usually not a problem either. While not all alternative investment funds employ leverage or trade derivative instruments, many do, and this can substantially boost their firepower when they need it. Combined with the willingness and ability of hedge fund managers and large speculators to take sizable positions on a moment's notice, it gives them the potential to throw their weight around and unsettle short-term equilibrium. While manipulation *per se* is prohibited under current laws, aggressive trading tactics are not. This opens up the possibility that those who choose to do so can cause some real damage in the marketplace—especially if they are reasonably plugged into what is going on, as most sizable operators are. Consequently, there is some justification for fears that players may come in and wreak havoc in the equity market, and traders' antennae are sensitive to that possibility. If there is even a hint that such activity is on the way, the crowd is usually quick to respond.

It is not only flesh-and-blood operators who can upset the applecart, but "virtual" players, too. Not the kind found on some kid-friendly Web sites, but those that seem to form from the mass of concentrated energy that frequently builds up as a result of various modern developments. Technological advances, for instance, have provided a wealth of benefits to people inside and outside the investment world, but they have also had another effect. They allow many market activities that were formerly staggered because of structural or other limitations, or that required some measure of human intervention, to proceed unchecked and at breakneck speed. With a few keystrokes or the click of a mouse, it is relatively easy for an individual to send one or more trades to any number of venues without thinking twice. Although there are restrictions on the size of orders that can be funneled through some electronic gateways because of exchange rules[2] or built-in safeguards, rapid-fire wheeling-and-dealing can be a potent weapon.

When several operators start heading in the same direction at the same time, it can create a short-term tidal wave of buying or selling pressure that can temporarily disrupt markets, causing prices to swing sharply. Partly because of the way breaking news is widely and quickly disseminated, and partly because there are many more active players in the game looking to pounce on anything that moves, the pulse from even a few tiny orders can sometimes set off a feeding frenzy that fosters the illusion, at least, that a major trend is underway, or that a large-scale operator is aggressively trying to get a position on board. Regardless of whether it is true or not, the simultaneous actions often set off a self-reinforcing response from others in the crowd. Some traders quickly join in, looking to scalp a small profit from the short-term momentum. Others move out of the way, hoping not to get badly caught on the wrong side of things. Those that remain soon learn the hard way that it usually does not make sense to stand in front of a speeding train—even an imaginary one.

Sometimes the action is not just a coincidence. Because of significant improvements in the quality and reach of numerous communications networks, passing information along to others is a cinch nowadays. Emails can be forwarded to group contact lists at the press of a button, recommendations can be sent out by broadcast fax or telephone messaging programs, comments can be shouted through squawk boxes or overhead PA systems—all offering ways to let many people know fairly quickly what is going on. In addition, most market participants have multiple points of contact with each other, as well as with information sources such as Bloomberg and Reuters. Hence, when something big—or potentially big—is going down, global voice and data pathways quickly fill up with intense two-way traffic, mirroring the flash of activity that appears on a brainwave scan when complex thoughts set multiple nerve endings alight. This real-time storm can generate significant power that usually finds its way to the trading floor.

Arguably, while much of the synchronized reaction is not necessarily the result of collusion, it can often seem that way. At times, in fact, there is a common bond between some market participants that can produce an amplifying effect. As has always been the case in financial markets, there are influential analysts, newsletter writers, investors, and traders that many people pay attention to. Some are smart and savvy operators who are usually on top of things and have a keen sense of timing. Others may have had their reputations strengthened by some degree of investing success, even if it was only recent in nature. A few survive on past glories or the halo effect of an active public relations effort, with little in the way of current results to show for it. Whatever the case, these individuals can sometimes trigger at least a temporary stampede either by recommending an idea or by executing a trade for themselves and letting others know about it afterwards.[3] In some instances, they do not need to say anything at all, as eagle-eyed competitors absorb what is going on and play follow-the-leader.

Action Point

As in most aspects of life, there are generally a few leaders and many followers, and it is usually in investors' interests to know who the movers and shakers in the share-trading arena are. When it comes to analysts, for example, there are services available, such as *www.starmine.com* and *www.zacks.com*, that methodically separate the wheat from the chaff by determining whose opinions matter most in assessing various companies' prospects. On the money management front, consistent long-term performance is usually the best guide, though it is worth remembering that no one always gets it right. As an aside, it often seems that those in the trend-setting group are not necessarily the individuals who get the most air time on radio and television.

Ironically, given the secretive and suspicious mindset that many players—especially traders—have with respect to others cottoning on to what they are up to, it seems that some are only too happy to talk about what they have done once they have established a position. The reason is that while this chatter sometimes provides an ego boost or serves as a method of rationalizing away doubts about a questionable course of action, it also has a valuable marketing purpose. Whether admitted or not, the basic idea is to get other people interested in putting on the same trade. Theoretically, at least, this will then spur additional buying or selling support that can add to the overall momentum, boosting the returns of the earliest players in the game. It is sort of an offshoot, perhaps, of the greater fool theory.

Although such efforts have long been a feature of financial markets, many outsiders, especially smaller investors and some relative novices, have occasionally taken these promotional efforts at face value, not looking at what was being said in the context of why it was suddenly being brought to light. Numerous analysts and firms, of course, also overstepped the line in a major way during the 1990s. They allowed misplaced incentives and various conflicts of interest, triggered in large part by the fat fees flooding into brokers' coffers during the IPO boom, to unduly influence their recommendations and public pronouncements. In some instances, as the press, the SEC and various Attorneys General discovered[4] in the aftermath of the post-Bubble collapse, there were blatantly fraudulent attempts to foist bad ideas onto the public to gain favor with prospective issuers. Nowadays, there are rules[5] in place that bar analysts from being compensated on the basis of specific investment banking transactions. Moreover, researchers generally must disclose anything that might be relevant to what they are advocating. Although it is not a cure-all, it does limit some of the more outrageous puffery.

Still, nothing can prevent some operators from relentlessly tooting their own horns to get a full-fledged concert going. However, for most speculators, motivation does not really matter. In their minds, anything that can serve as a spur to get prices moving has value, especially in an age where many players are aggressively boosting their turnover. Fact or fiction, marketing fluff or overheard tidbit—if it has the potential to trigger notable share buying or selling, many short-term operators will do what they can to try make the most of it. Sometimes that includes passing along rumors or hearsay from the trading floor or other markets that would be given short shrift if analyzed in the cool light of day. At other times, facts can end up twisted or exaggerated, though still plausible, when minced through abrupt conversations and the sloppiness of modern communications. With numerous participants increasingly focused on headlines, tickers, bullets, and sound bites, there is rarely enough digging to see where the roots lie.

As odd as it sounds, many modern players do not even pay all that much attention to "fundamental" information, truthful or otherwise. For

them, it is the trading volume and intrinsic behavior of the prices themselves—range between the high and low, rate of change over time, previous areas of congestion, levels relative to other shares and the overall
market—that really matter. Sure, if an earnings report sets off a wave of
sell orders that drives a stock beneath a previous low—which happens to
be a widely watched technical level—many traders will concede that it
was poor fundamentals that did the trick. But more than a few technical
types will argue that "the charts" indicated a decline was due to happen
regardless, and the news was merely one of any number of possible catalysts that could have caused it to occur. Whether that makes sense or not,
the reality is that numerous operators are avid followers of methods that
focus almost exclusively on divining supply-and-demand characteristics.

In fact, given the expanding interest in short-term trading and active
investing, awareness of key technical levels has become an important priority for many participants—even those who are traditional long-only
investors or who otherwise tend to rely on textbook fundamentals. One
reason why is that the data sometimes creates at least a psychological
draw to certain prices that can be almost self-fulfilling. Like a huge magnet waved over a pile of iron filings, a widely watched chart point can
cause all the action in the market to magically rise up and clump to it—in
spite of anything else that may be going on at the same time. It can also
serve as a sort of energizing force that draws out a range of operators
looking to aggressively tap into the pent-up energy. Consequently, this
can trigger a frenzied round of buying and selling when certain targets are
breached.

For example, if over the course of two weeks a stock has twice sold
off after rallying to $60, and once again approaches that point, several
things may happen. Some short-term players may take the view that
"resistance"[6] will remain intact, and they will look to liquidate longs or
set shorts at or near those levels. They will, however, be quick to reverse
course if the trades do not immediately work out. Others may decide in
advance to buy any "breakout" above that price, speculating that temporary momentum will likely drive the security much higher still. Some who
are already betting against a rise will get set to cover their positions if the
shares rally any further. To cut their losses, they will transmit market,
limit, or "buy-stop" orders, with the latter often placed just above the last
notable high. A few holders may leave offers in the market, but will look
to cancel them at a moment's notice. Others will sit tight, hoping that this
time the shares will finally be off to the races.

Then, especially in the case of a widely followed issue where there has been a large build-up of speculative interest with numerous stops in place, an aggressive operator may try to get something going by force-fully buying shares in an attempt to drive prices above the $60 level. Once that starts—if the initial read of the market is correct—it will likely set off a chain reaction from short-term traders and tape-watchers[7] that will aggravate a temporary supply-and-demand imbalance. Consequently, prices will shoot higher, creating a self-feeding surge that drags the crowd along like a torrent of water rushing through the crumbling wall of a bro-ken dam. Although such efforts do not always work out as planned, the widespread interest in technical analysis[8] has, ironically enough, given many speculators a sort of roadmap, guiding them to stress points where action will most likely be found. Not surprisingly, such moves can create a short-term blast that burns those who are not fast on their feet.

Action Point

Stop-losses offer a useful means of dealing with the uncertain-ties and risks associated with virtually all investment deci-sions. Yet, as with many longstanding share-trading tactics, they have limitations that have become especially pronounced in recent years. For one thing, they should be viewed as a potential form of protection, not as an absolute method of avoiding losses. For another, setting the appropriate levels is an art, not a science. Indeed, there is a real risk that investors may occasionally get "stopped out" at the very point at which a market is poised to reverse in their favor, especially given the approaches employed by today's aggressive operators. Never-theless, one important rule to follow is: once a stop is in place, avoid the natural temptation to cancel it if the price of the secu-rity nears the chosen level. Unless a truly valid reason can be found to justify the action, it can often turn a small loss into a financial black hole.

Gaps in available liquidity and unsettled conditions since the Bubble burst have induced more than a few participants to latch on to mechanical methods and relatively simple, almost instinctual, approaches to playing the market. Even many traditional long-term investors have found it hard to rely on a densely constructed fundamental outlook, because increased volatility, unusual macroeconomic circumstances, and a rise in random geopolitical disruptions are difficult to factor into forecasts. It is also tougher to develop concrete views based on a variety of shaky expectations. In fact, this pall of uncertainty forms part of a broader sense of worry and doubt that has seeped into the investing landscape since the spring of 2000. Not surprisingly, it has created an environment where investors are frequently on edge, and where there is considerably more anxiety influencing behavior than there was during the go-go days. One result of all of this is that participants are often quite jumpy and quick to react to even the threat of danger by relying on reflexes and practiced routines.

In the modern environment, market operators seem to be insecure about many things. For a start, they are not only nervous about the big picture going forward, but about personal financial circumstances as well. Even when participants were rattled by the failure of Long Term Capital Management in 1998, the 1997–1998 Asian Economic Crisis, and the 1994–1995 Mexican Crisis, the collective spirit, while unsettled and downbeat, seemed to be somewhat reassured by the fact that the global economic engine still had a bit of "oomph" to it and that authorities gave the appearance, at least, of being on top of things. In recent years, though, the backstop of hopefulness has diminished to some extent. Despite huge amounts of fiscal and monetary stimuli, conditions have yet to fully return to the lofty levels seen when equities were flying high. Indeed, the mood occasionally seems like that experienced by a lottery winner who somehow loses the ticket—once euphoric, now somber and easily rattled.

A continuing sluggish international economy and increased competition at every level have also stirred anxiety in countless employees, both inside and outside of the investing arena. Many are worried that other countries or companies will continue to siphon away jobs, or force their own firms to economize by firing staff or even by shutting down completely. Aside from that, in the financial markets in particular, there is an incessant fear that only certain operators really know what is going on and will ruthlessly exploit that knowledge. Even those who are intelligent and street-smart in their own right, who focus on specialized areas where they seem to have an edge, feel threatened when prospective rivals even glance their way. What is more, market-moving events that occur outside of their own immediate areas of interest sometimes stir worries that there are forces at work that might suddenly ruin their bread-and-butter investing strategies.

Indeed, it is safe to say that no small number of institutional operators worry about underperformance and failure—and not just from the point of view of their backers or underlying investors either. The financial services industry has been wracked by thousands of layoffs since the 1990s ended, and even the boom in the alternative investment sector seems to have slowed down somewhat following the hectic pace that occurred in the wake of the post-2000 stock market collapse. Although brokers, traders, and investment managers have always known they are employed in a cyclical industry, traditionally subject to great waves of hiring and firing, it seems that for some remaining employees there is—probably justifiably so—a sense that a sudden job loss at this point in time will likely lead to a forced career change, along with all the personal disruption that entails.

There is another, more depressing side to the prospect of investment losses and lagging returns. Financial services industry professionals share with most other Americans of working age nagging concerns about whether they will have enough money to live on when old age sets in. With short- and long-term interest rates having reached historically low levels in recent years, the macroeconomic and market outlook still largely unsettled, and the underfunded social security system likely to be a drag on growth going forward, the prospect of generating the sort of outsized returns that can build healthy retirement nest eggs seems somewhat remote—despite occasional bouts of market euphoria. True, history suggests that when times seem bleakest, the investment opportunities are often the greatest, but some would argue that the paralyzing fear and widespread revulsion for equities that typically accompanies a long-term bottom—a necessary precursor to a major wealth building rally—has yet to be seen. Whatever the case, the emotional fallout from the dramatic boom-and-bust does not appear to have fully played out yet, and money worries continue to have a strong influence.

All of these factors have instilled in a cross-section of market participants a general sense of insecurity that has had a very peculiar effect. Indeed, the contrasts are striking. On the one hand, many players have not fully abandoned riskier pursuits despite the new uncertainties. They have, in fact, moved towards a more speculative approach and are more willing to employ aggressive tactics such as leverage on a regular basis—as Figure 3.2 seems to indicate. They are also becoming increasingly involved with a host of volatile instruments and complex strategies of the kind that offer more bang for the buck—but more reasons to duck. Others have decided to focus almost exclusively on short-term trading, shedding any pretense that they are in it for the long haul. Admittedly, such strategies

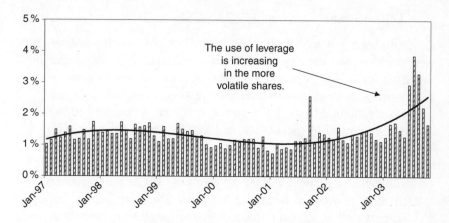

Figure 3.2   NASD Margin Buying as a Percentage of NASDAQ Volume: Ratio of Balances in Clearing Firm Customers' Cash and Margin Accounts to Dollar Traded Volume (Source: The NASDAQ Stock Market, Inc.).

do have an appeal in the sense that there is less exposure to overnight uncertainty and the problems of a world filled with random disruptions. Nonetheless, most require specialized skill sets that many people simply do not have.

On the other hand, countless traders are more concerned than ever with losing money, which is causing them to rely on tactical measures, such as stop-losses and itchy trigger-fingers, that are supposed to take them out of losing positions before too much damage is done. Unfortunately, the problem for individuals who trade—as opposed to invest—is that their emotional state is often a significant factor in their success. Nowadays, that frame of mind is likely to be one of nervousness and confusion. What is more, regardless of what mechanisms are in place, losses are the usual result for those who operate from a position of weakness, with insufficient resources at their disposal to cushion the inevitable setbacks. In the modern era, it seems that many players are like desperate bettors wagering their last few chips at the casino—inevitably left with nothing in their pockets and no way to get home. These two somewhat contrasting perspectives—the urge for fast cash and the fear of losses— have fostered an anxiety-ridden approach based on quick moves in—and even quicker ones out.

Action Point

Although it is usually not the best course of action for most investors and can potentially lead to substantial financial and emotional pain, once individuals have decided to engage in short-term trading, it is crucial that they avoid some of the basic pitfalls. More often than not, a failure to pay heed to the essential rules of speculation will lead to a very unhappy ending. Perhaps the most important are the same warnings given to gamblers on their way to Las Vegas: Do not bet more than you can afford; avoid putting all your eggs in one basket; shoot for the consistent percentages rather than the big score; employ only a limited portion of your capital at any one time; and bet with your head, not your heart. At the very least, these words of wisdom may prevent you from being knocked out of the game before it really even gets started.

As with speculation in general, the downside of this money-making strategy is that not many people have the self-restraint, opportunistic flexibility, self awareness, and hard-knocks experience to weather what can be an extreme roller coaster ride. In addition, even though there seems to be more individuals moving in that direction, modern conditions make high-turnover methods much tougher to work with than they used to be. The pace of the markets has accelerated, and information flows have occasionally become disjointed. Often market participants have little opportunity to really get to the bottom of what is going on and must operate by the seat of their pants instead—clearly not the best way to make significant financial decisions. Under current circumstances, there is rarely enough time to adequately digest new developments because of the lag between when high-impact headlines hit the tape and when the full details are eventually released.

Informal communications are also short and frequently ambiguous in the Information Age. Although most people do not pay by the word to transmit electronic messages, they often act as though they do. In the financial markets, even important details are occasionally sacrificed at the altar of brevity. More often than not, the goal is simply to get something out—orally or in writing—before anyone else. Much like hard-nosed reporters rushing to scoop the competition in order to bolster their reputations, market participants, especially those who interact most closely with active traders and hedge funds, often feel compelled to do the same. They press ahead as if they might live or die by the speed with which they can keep their contacts informed. Sometimes it even seems like a game, as a desk full of salespeople find themselves hunched over keyboards rapidly tapping out the latest updates—often with two fingers—as they look to score points against various rivals.

The other great risk of modern methods is the ease with which errors and omissions can slip by, especially in the heat of a volatile market moment. Mirroring the decline in standards in the population at large, writing skills have been deteriorating for years. Spelling and grammar do not seem to matter much anymore, while the urge to carefully review one's thoughts has largely fallen by the wayside for most routine communications. The financial markets have always favored very short sentences, of course, because prices can whip around in the time it can take to grind out a long request. Indeed, nearly everyone who operates in this environment understands the limited vocabulary of dealing and the invariably negative consequences of sloppy language. To outside observers, trading interactions can sometimes sound like nothing more than a series of grunts and syllables, which might go something like this:

"Coke?"

"20 for 14, 3 at 24."

"Hit it.

"12 Done. Offered at 11."

"8 low."

"Filled."

Generally speaking, this conversation will leave little room for doubt in the minds of most experienced U.S. stock market operators.[9]

The same cannot be said, however, for many other exchanges that are now taking place during trading hours, especially those typed out on a keyboard, because much of the editing and altering that does take place is not standardized. Some operators are choosing to write messages using capital letters, while others prefer lowercase. Periods and commas are frequently omitted, as are transition and linking words that can make rapid scanning easier for the reader. Space constraints also play a part. Reporters, editors, analysts, traders, and others are often hemmed in by the length or width of a scrolling ticker, newswire line, broadcast slot, or electronic message, at least in terms of the most relevant points. Unlike

oral or handwritten communications, it is difficult to squeeze extra characters through a fixed-length window.

The methods for handling the problem can vary significantly. Sometimes writers economize by leaving out words or by substituting others
that do not quite fit in terms of meaning. They may abbreviate terms in a
confusing way or fail to highlight a shortened version with the necessary
punctuation. Occasionally, acronyms that have more than one meaning
are used, and it might not immediately be clear which one is being
referred to until more of the accompanying detail is read and digested.
Once in a while, they leave out quotation marks as well, which can create
major confusion about the actual source of a report. In the case of a few
messaging systems—such as that offered by Bloomberg—the standard
page size used for subscriber-to-subscriber transmissions does not leave a
lot of room for details. What happens then is that participants either cram
as much as they can onto the allotted space, making it difficult to quickly
glance through the text, or they cut out what they believe is unimpor-
tant—and occasionally get it wrong.

While the quality and depth of the information flowing around leaves
something to be desired, the speed and volume of data causes problems in
its own right. When the action heats up in dealing rooms or on the trading
floor, communications networks get hit with large amounts of voice and
data traffic that can be overwhelming. With volatile price action, flashing
quotes and indicators, shouts and squawks, constantly ringing telephones,
and considerable time pressure, things sometimes go wrong. Salespeople
may misunderstand a report, traders may get an instruction wrong, fund
managers may overreact to a news headline, and everyone may feel—
temporarily at least—that they would rather be somewhere else. Nonstop
action can boost energy levels and make the day go by quickly, but too
much of a buzz can be exhausting and unsettling. Throw a few cups of
coffee into the mix, and pretty soon people are bouncing off the walls and
their typing fingers get extremely twitchy.

Action Point

Because the act of buying and selling securities can seem so
straightforward on the surface, especially with all the point-
and-click systems that are available, it is easy to fall into the
trap of thinking that physical and emotional well-being do not
necessarily have any impact on performance. However, experience suggests it is almost always better for investors to walk

away than to step into the mix when distractions such as exhaustion or illness might force them to take their eyes off the investment ball. It also makes sense to be aware of the impact that the modern stock market environment can have on one's state of mind. The pulse of technology and the rhythmic hum as flickering data flashes by can be mesmerizing and almost hypnotic, leading to actions and words that are not necessarily well thought out—and potentially dangerous to the bottom line.

The result is that market participants are often primed to react quickly to anything that comes their way. What makes it worse is that even when individuals are criticized over an erroneous call or are ridiculed because of a poor off-the-cuff interpretation of developing circumstances, they risk either being marginalized in the eyes of clients or colleagues or losing out on profitable investment opportunities if they do not continue to let contacts know what they believe is taking place as soon as new information comes their way. When market-moving developments unfold in the current environment, those who are plugged in and at the center of the action are the ones most likely to benefit—in terms of gains realized or losses avoided. Simply put, many have adopted the battle cry of the Wild West: You are either quick, or you are dead. For most participants, the choice appears to be relatively straightforward. In reality, it tends to pump up the irrational volume.

Unfamiliar geopolitical developments have also played a part in making people anxious and emotional. While a variety of wars, natural calamities, and one-off shocks have affected markets throughout the ages, it often seemed that once the initial reaction wore off, there was invariably some quick rebound towards relative normality. Indeed, despite the frequency of upheavals over time, humanity has usually managed to roll with the punches and bounce back. Events since September 11, 2001, have struck a strange chord in many people, however. The icy randomness of terrorism—in terms of time, place, and the scale of the damage done—as well as the incomprehensible willingness of individuals to sacrifice themselves and others for a cause few in the West understand, has shaken traditional perspectives. In many cases, Americans do not really know where they stand. For some, it is hard to return to normal when no one is quite sure what that term means anymore.

Consequently, there appears to be more of a structural insecurity affecting the U.S. financial markets now, one that echoes with every strange noise, every unusual act, and every odd movement. When traders hear reports of an unidentified explosion in the center of a large metropolitan area, their initial reaction is to try and sell shares. Never mind that it might be an accident, that the incident in question might be confined to one small area or building, or even that it might have nothing at all to do with the securities actually being dumped onto the market. What matters most is that the news might signal the start of something bigger and more ominous. It reflects a generalized fear of a dark and scary unknown, a chaotic force few have reckoned with in their lifetimes. Under those circumstances, it seems that many operators take the view that it is better to act quickly in the hope of saving a lot than to act slowly to avoid losing a little.

The combined power of two modern developments is probably amplifying these worries. To begin with, one of the many benefits improved technology and communications networks have given market participants is a sense of independence and flexibility. Traders and investors no longer need to gather in one location or rely on large-scale intermediaries and single points of contact to get their business done. There are various interactive systems and electronic pathways in place that allow players to be based nearly anywhere and trade nearly everything without needing to have anybody else around. In fact, the current investing framework is well suited to an era where email is gradually replacing "snail mail" and instant messaging programs are gaining ground on the telephone. As anyone who lives or works with the younger generation can attest, it has gotten to the point where individuals will sometimes forego a chat across the room in favor of communicating by IM instead.

The trend towards disintermediation—the gradual whittling away of middlemen—in the financial services industry is also playing a part in minimizing personal contact with others. With the widespread use of electronic trade routing, direct access dealing systems, and ECNs, there are now a smaller number of links between those who have the orders and the locations where the actual trading takes place. True, like an iceberg floating on the high seas, there is often much below the surface that conceals the full extent of the dealing structure that exists. Nonetheless, the reality is that technology makes it easier and seemingly more desirable to cut out much of the human interaction that was a necessary evil of the way things used to work. By eliminating extra steps and minimizing the natural dawdling associated with personal conversations, market

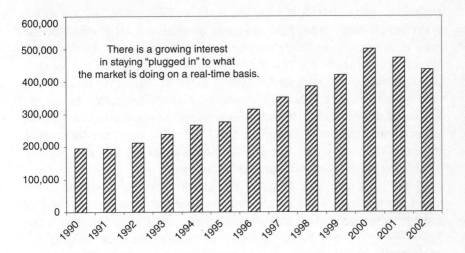

Figure 3.3   New York Stock Exchange Market Data Devices (Source: New York Stock Exchange).

participants can presumably focus more time and effort on making money—bolstering demand, as Figure 3.3 suggests, for an assortment of modern day trading tools.

This efficiency and relative isolation has a downside, though. As in the real world, where many people have migrated away from frequent socializing with others in favor of communicating through electronic methods, the switch from voice to data sometimes causes interactions to be more formal and less open. This appears to reduce the natural bonding associated with oral communication and physical proximity that can often lead to interesting insights and synergies. What is more, human ties, even incidental ones, frequently provide a calming influence and a useful emotional outlet when things are not going well. Sure, typewritten messages can be funny, sad, upbeat, or interesting, but they do not seem to offer enough of the emotional "glue" that enriches human relationships and makes people stronger, especially in the face of uncertainty and turmoil. As a result, while it is now a relative breeze to get on with wheeling-and-dealing, the emotional consequences may be somewhat more negative than people realize.

Industry trends clearly add to the skittishness and insecurity that many professionals face. Various operators have crammed into the marketplace, driving down commission rates, depressing compensation arrangements, and pressuring returns as strategies get overcrowded with too many individuals doing the same thing. Frequently, this creates a shaky supply-and-demand position that can cause a rapid rush for the exits if conditions suddenly change. It can go the other way as well. Sometimes the stampede is not caused by players trying to get out of a position, but by the widespread desire to get in. Whatever the case, in their haste to be a step ahead of the crowd, players sometimes imitate the actions of drag-racers. They rev their engines hard as they anticipate the moment when the run of flashing red and yellow lights will suddenly turn to green. Then, they put the pedal to the floor, hoping that they will be first off the mark—and will not have a false start.

Finally, as with the proverbial chicken crossing the road, one of the reasons players seem quick to trade is because they can. Despite the fact that even a few seconds of thoughtful analysis could provide a more intelligent outlook and a basis for better investment decision-making, the modern day quest for action is difficult to overcome when all it takes is a touch, click, or peck. With the convenience technology has to offer, it appears so easy to sit back and flick a switch or push a button to make things happen. Like playing with the television remote, flicking between channels and never really settling in any one place, jobbing in and out of the markets can seem like an amusing way to while away the time. Unfortunately, this feeling of electronic command and control can sometimes stoke the costly illusion that success can be achieved with relatively little effort. In reality, however, nonstop trading and the urge to act on irrational impulses can be a financially precarious waste of time.

Action Plan

It can be disturbing when people all around you seem to be losing their heads, frantically reacting to developments that seem trivial at best and misleading at worst. Moreover, even a cool and calm perspective can give way to confusion in an environment where emotions are running high and the prospect of economic or geopolitical disruption is dangerously real. Nonetheless, it is usually better to stand back from the turmoil than to be sucked into a frenzy of emotional decision-making. Sometimes those who are caught up in the speculative whirl believe they have matters fully under control. Often, however, what they are experiencing is a fleeting moment of calm at the eye of a passing hurricane. Inevitably, the high winds and chaos reappear, and they are once again stung by the destructive turbulence. While the urge to act quickly can be overwhelming, especially when everyone else is jumping on board, experience suggests it is usually better to keep your wits about you—to ask questions first and keep your powder dry.

Of course, that is sometimes easier said than done. Throughout the ages, markets have almost always had a way of unleashing irrational urges and bringing out the worst in people. Perhaps it comes down to the fact that it is all about money, a subject that has always had an interesting and pronounced affect on psychology and perceptions. Alternatively, it is possible that the wheeling-and-dealing environment gives people some of the pleasures they cannot find in life's daily routine, such as the prospect of scoring "the big one" without having to work too hard for it. Whatever the case, experienced operators sometimes find that a spell has been cast over them, too. Many successful old-timers will tell you, in fact, that the dark forces never really go away, and that it takes a lot of hard work and discipline just to keep them in check. Practically speaking, the best solution is to fully explore why you are in the investing game to begin with, and then to formulate a prearranged plan. In other words, know who you are and where you are going.

Consequently, whenever you think about investing, the questions you should be asking yourself are as follows: Why are you doing it? What are your goals? Are you putting money into the market to prepare for retirement, to have a little fun, or to make up for a shortfall in other income? If you do not know the answers, or choose to get involved for the wrong reasons, there is a good chance that you will suffer substantial losses. The next question you should think about is: What happens if things go wrong? In fact, it might even be better to substitute "when" for "if." One of the biggest problems that unsuccessful investors seem to have is in making the assumption that a particular course of action will be the correct one. Obviously, it is great if that turns out to be the case, but what if it goes the other way? Because of inherent human weaknesses, no one really likes to admit their mistakes, because that is seen as a sign of embarrassing failure. As a result, this tough but necessary question is not really asked often enough.

Sadly, it almost seems, in fact, that many individuals would rather lose all of their money than face up to the prospect of having made a bad call. Ironically, the reality is that there are many long-time operators who manage to achieve investment success in spite of the fact that they get it "wrong" a great deal of the time. That is because they are willing to accept losing trades as a cost of doing business—hence, they are not shaken up when things do actually turn out that way. Once the prospect of making poor choices becomes a tolerable friction, it suddenly gets a whole lot easier to quickly eliminate positions that are not working out. Of course, it does not make sense to focus solely on the negatives. Try asking yourself what will happen if things go right. Do you have a target level in mind? Do you have an order or a reminder in place to ensure that you will take your profits if your selection turns out to be a winner?

There is an old market adage that says if you do not know who you are before you start investing, you will soon find out—the hard way. For many individuals, what can be even more important than formulating an investment plan is figuring out what your needs are, as well as discovering your particular style. For example, are you a bull or a bear? Although it is always best to be open-minded, people invariably have some sort of inherent bias. If you are generally an optimist, take the time to temper your enthusiasm with opposing points of view when looking at prospective buying opportunities. Are you a trader or an investor? Are you risk-averse or comfortable with complex and heavily-leveraged instruments? Do you prefer to focus on long-term investing or short-term trading? If you can answer these few questions at the outset, you will save having to ask many more painful questions later on.

Many of those who have found sustained success in the stock market have done so because they have tended to emphasize what they know and what they are good at. Aside from that, if you cannot sleep at night with the positions you have, find some other investments that will allow you to. The "comfort zone" you operate out of should suit you, not someone else. Some people, for example, are not cut out for the short-term trading game because they find it too hard to detach their intellectual views from the basic forces of supply and demand. Moreover, such an approach usually requires a rare ability to alter one's views without thinking twice about it. Generally speaking, it is best to focus on a limited number of shares or sectors, or to confine your approaches to a select group of strategies. Of course, if performance does really begin to suffer, it clearly makes sense to stand back and reappraise matters, but you should avoid the all too common urge to jump carelessly from one tactic to the next.

Whenever you have exposure to the market, be on the lookout for signs that irrational impulses may be taking over. If you cannot do it yourself, find someone else to help you. For example, if you begin rationalizing or start digging deeply to come up with reasons to stick with a losing investment, that is almost a sure sign that you should be getting out of the position. Moreover, avoid talking about your investments, or even listening to others who would like to tell you about their own interests. The reality is that once a position gets "personalized," it becomes harder to change one's views about it. Watch out for signs of denial, too. If you find yourself leaving account statements unopened, avoiding calls from your broker, or glossing over "paper" losses, it is time to cut and run. Finally, if you start altering your particular style—say, by trading more actively or by choosing unfamiliar instruments or complicated strategies—have a look in the mirror. Are you seeing a new "you"—or the old one, running scared?

CHAPTER 4

Information
and Communications

---

*More information and faster
communications often have unexpected
consequences.*

In the financial markets, knowledge is power. Those who know what is going on invariably have an edge over those who do not. Consequently, savvy operators have always made it a priority to tap into as many sources of information as they can to ensure that they are making fully informed decisions. Ironically, in the modern share-trading environment, it often seems that the complexity, pace, and volume of data flowing through the marketplace—which, if Figure 4.1 is any guide, has expanded significantly in recent years—have not necessarily added to the level of understanding. On the contrary, what should have made people feel more in control has sometimes left them at a loss for words. For today's equity investor, ignorance of the new realities of the Information Age can turn out to be a stumbling block to solid investment performance.

Historically, large institutions have had an advantage over smaller operators in acquiring critical information about the stock market. This is mainly due to the hefty fees they could dole out for intelligence and analytical services, as well as the influence they wielded because of the sizeable assets under their control. When it came to getting their hands on the most interesting data or hearing what the best minds had to say, the major operators usually did not have to look very hard, either. In most cases, the

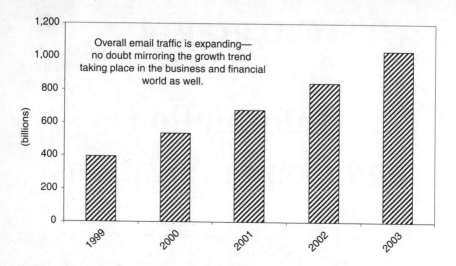

Figure 4.1   Total Email Message Volume in the United States (Source: eMarketer, Inc.).

suppliers found them. For the small investor, however, getting helpful, accurate, and up-to-date insights often proved to be an exercise in futility, and many were forced to rely on the brokerage community or the mass media for word on what was happening in the financial world.

Numerous developments in recent years have, to some extent, altered the balance. Significant improvements in technology and the global telecommunications infrastructure have made it easy for people to send and receive vast quantities of data in a relatively quick and straightforward manner. Communicating with others is much cheaper than it used to be, too. In many instances, the marginal cost of transmission, even over great distances, has fallen to near zero because of flat-rate pricing plans and the glut of capacity created during the Bubble years. This has enabled new content providers to step in and take the place of many established suppliers without forcing audiences to give up a lot in terms of quality or usefulness. Combined with what is available through traditional advertiser-sponsored channels, modern news sources allow individuals to stay in touch with market-moving events at relatively little expense.

Along the same lines, the spectacular growth of the Information Superhighway[1] has played a large part in expanding the overall pool of knowledge, benefiting amateur and professional investors alike. With access prices falling sharply and bandwidth growing by leaps and bounds, nearly anybody can add to or draw from what seems to be an almost limitless resource. Furthermore, they can do it on their own terms, at any time. In fact, this is one of the most significant advantages of many modern communications methods: Information does not automatically decay when intended recipients are temporarily out of touch. This lingering availability allows market players, in particular, to prioritize and adjust their approach, so they can focus on what is immediately relevant. What is more, with the help of tools such as Internet search engines, institutions and individuals can also compare and contrast facts and figures generated at various times by a diverse range of sources. This can occasionally lead to interesting insights and unique opportunities for making money.

It is not only data circulating around the World Wide Web that has a long half-life—the same often holds true for emails, voicemails, faxes, and other forms of electronic communication. Generally speaking, none of these methods actually depends on having a live link present at the time data is sent, and nearly all allow receivers the option of reviewing and responding to messages more or less when they choose. In most cases, information is stored automatically and remains accessible unless or until it is discarded. While some people regularly delete and archive transmissions to reduce clutter, others are hesitant to do so, fearing they may get rid of something they will need in the immediate future. Whatever the case, the fact that securities industry regulations require certain records to be kept for some minimum period of time means that many messages will likely stick around for quite a while.

The ease with which electronic text can be forwarded, stored, printed out or otherwise manipulated often gives time-sensitive and "instant" messages a new lease on life. This brings to mind another reality of the Information Age: Content pushed out into general circulation can sometimes be "reborn." Surprisingly, this phenomenon seems to happen quite often in modern financial markets. For example, a story will appear in a regional newspaper or foreign publication, causing little immediate reaction. However, once it is picked up by influential operators who, for one reason or another, decide to expand upon and promote the development among a wide network of contacts, the interest can snowball dramatically. Inevitably, the mass media catches on and a formerly irrelevant piece of news suddenly triggers a more widespread and pronounced response from the share-trading crowd.

Action Point

The longer shelf life of facts and figures in the Information Age can provide considerable benefits when it comes to making important investment decisions. For the most part, it is relatively easy to access reams of data, news, and insights from online resources such as corporate Web sites, government data banks, and a variety of online information providers. The latter include investment Web sites, such as *http://finance.yahoo.com*, *http://moneycentral.msn.com*, *http://cbs.marketwatch.com*, *www.thestreet.com*, and *www.fool.com*; financial news Web sites, such as *www.bloomberg.com*, *www.wsj.com*, *www.reuters.com*, and *www.investors.com*; and alternative news providers, such as *www.drudgereport.com* and *www.worldnetdaily.com*. With such resources, individuals can often engage in the necessary "due diligence" in a matter of hours or days, rather than weeks or months. Undoubtedly, this eliminates at least one excuse for not doing the requisite amount of homework beforehand.

The fact that digitized information can hang around for a while does have negative consequences, though. For one thing, the continuous build-up adds to the sheer quantity of material that is available, which can leave investors overwhelmed and spoiled for choice. An unrefined Internet search, for example, will often churn up not only recent output, but material from months or even years earlier. While some of it adds interesting color, the investigative process frequently ends up requiring far too much time, effort, and creative analysis to accomplish anything of immediate value. Occasionally, it may be impossible to find the right combination of keywords necessary to generate results that are relevant. And even then, multiple links to other Web sites can sometimes feed a confusing spiral that leaves people exhausted and wondering why they ever got started in the first place. Instead of generating lots of options, huge volumes of data can sometimes produce plenty of confusion.

The other problem with longer shelf lives stems from the fact that much of what is in general circulation in the modern age is unedited and unfiltered. Whether good, bad, or ugly, all kinds of information tend to slip through the cracks and spill into the vast pool of electronic data. While regular cleansing of email, voicemail, and text message inboxes takes some unnecessary fluff out of the mix, and routine archiving at many professionally administered sites keeps them more or less up-to-date, it sometimes takes a complaint to an Internet service provider (ISP) or a service shutdown to get rid of some half-baked ideas or erroneous "facts" floating around the Web. Indeed, despite the benefits that increased staying power brings, it sometimes seems that a great deal of what actually remains available may not even be worth the minimal cost of access.

Whatever the case, the overall quantity of information offered—especially that which pertains to business and finance—has risen substantially. One reason is mushrooming demand, stimulated in part by unsettled market conditions since the Bubble burst. Increasingly unsure about what might happen next, many participants have sought out "intelligence" from any source they can find to help them come to grips with a new and confusing reality. The broad shift towards a more active investing approach has also churned up facts and figures that often evolve into trading catalysts. Indeed, sometimes statistics multiply in ways that can resemble rapid cell division, as formerly one-off reports splinter into a series of separate data points. The increasing complexity of the modern investing landscape and the curious nature of knowledge—the more you know, the more you need to know—add to the pressure.

Multiple layers of connectivity, combined with participants' increased reliance on electronic communications methods, have also had a significant impact on the volume of data flowing around the marketplace. Generally speaking, it is easy to pass digitized information along to others with the technology that is now in place. Most systems have shortcuts built into them that allow text items to be copied or messages to be forwarded to one or more individuals with a few simple mouse clicks or keystrokes. Group contact lists tend to be extensive as well. Many brokers, for example, can target clients, colleagues, and acquaintances more or less at will. When important news breaks, an interesting research idea bubbles to the surface, or unique insights crop up during a trading floor discussion, it is a breeze to make sure that everyone soon knows about it.

This easy-transfer capability has interesting consequences, however. For one thing, it often sets a sort of compounding process in motion that can occasionally unsettle markets. In the old days, for instance, when details about trading flows and potential client interests were passed along by telephone, the procedure was relatively slow and staggered. On the whole, it was very difficult to carry on a conversation with more than one individual at the same time, and the often lengthy nature of the calls tended to limit the number of contacts who could be notified before information became stale or irrelevant. With modern methods, there are no such constraints. Facts and figures can be instantly transmitted through a variety of avenues, including email, instant messaging, fax, and IOIs.

In a typical dealing room scenario, a trader will inform others by shouting, or by broadcasting a message through overhead PA systems or internal squawk boxes, that the firm has a "natural" interest in buying or selling a particular security. This situation may have arisen for any number of reasons. The desk may have had a proprietary position they now wish to unwind, or they may suddenly find themselves exposed because of ongoing market-making activities. Alternatively, a representative may have taken an agency order in a stock and urged colleagues to find the "other side" to get the transaction done. Whatever the case, once the okay is given, sales-traders go out and shop the flow through various channels. Soon, client awareness becomes widespread. At that point, some of the details might seep into other conversations, and that is when things can get interesting.

An institutional investor, for example, might mention to a brokerage contact on a morning call that there is a large buyer around in a particular security. Although standard etiquette dictates that the name of the sell-side firm with the order should not be revealed to rivals, it nonetheless happens. Regardless, the supply-and-demand information now becomes an interesting nugget that can be passed along to others. Soon, the word gets around that there is a significant natural interest building in a stock, and a buzz of excitement winds its way through dealing rooms and trading floors. All of a sudden, as if a switch had been thrown, the original indication changes into something completely different. Whether through misunderstanding or exaggeration, a 50,000 share interest becomes ten times larger—and still grows. This can set off a stampede that temporarily knocks a market out of kilter.

Action Point

In the financial markets, as in life, there is a natural tendency towards exaggeration when information is passed along from one person to the next. Sometimes the distortions are intentional, though it seems most are probably not. Among other reasons, they may reflect people's desire to spruce up information in a quest for recognition or attention, or an in-built urge to distill chunky concepts down to bite-sized pieces that end up losing their relative weights during transmission. Regardless of why, it makes sense for investors to operate with a measure of skepticism when reacting on the basis of oral or informal communications alone. If possible, try to double-check sources or use third parties to verify key details when it comes to making critical investment decisions.

Interestingly enough, sometimes it does not even require a "real" interest to get things going. There is a classic market cartoon that features an illustration of a trading desk with numerous professionals seated around it and ready for action. At the left-hand side is a bubble highlighting the words of one individual as he slyly speaks into a telephone: "By the way, I have got something interesting for you...." Nearby, another colleague, eavesdropping but only half-heartedly paying attention, catches just the first word as "buy" and absent-mindedly utters it aloud. Soon, others along the row start to pick up on what that individual said and they excitedly start dialing and telling their clients about the latest "recommendation." Eventually, the progression moves right to a misunderstood "sell," and at the end of the strip, people are anxiously shouting that word into their handsets. In today's fast-paced and often chaotic dealing rooms, such an evolution is not out of the question.

Even when the facts are accurate, there is frequently some element of puffery that enters into the equation. The brokerage business is a sales-oriented culture, and whether admitted or not, many representatives have much in common with those hawking used cars or vacuum cleaners. Various rules and regulations, of course, prevent anyone from making outrageous claims, such as guaranteeing what will happen in the future or stating in absolute terms how successful an investment opportunity will turn out to be. Nonetheless, those on the sell side are not averse to putting a bit of pizzazz into their pitches to get something going. Not surprisingly, the intense competition that has cropped up in the post-Bubble environment is a powerful motivating factor. When individuals are fighting for scraps that can keep their business alive, it is worth their while to make what they are selling look as appetizing as possible.

Another reason why brokers sometimes resort to "prettying up" the story is because of the age-old hesitancy on the part of clients about making a commitment—especially common under current circumstances. With markets unsettled and subject to volatile swings, traditional buy-side dealers are, as it happens, often cautious about the best way to proceed with an order. This is true even if all of the available evidence clearly favors one course of action over another. Despite their growing influence in recent years, those who handle the trading function are subject to a lop-sided set of organizational risks. On the one hand, when things go well and they execute an order at the best levels of the day, they usually receive little reward or positive feedback from portfolio managers for a job well done. On the other hand, if things go poorly because their judgment turned out to be somewhat off the mark, they often take a lot of heat.

Sometimes the motivations are purely economic. Many institutional investors, especially traditional long-only fund managers, seek to mini-mize the impact their dealings are having on the marketplace to avoid dis-ruptions and costly slippage—the difference between estimated and actual costs of execution. Consequently, buy-side traders may scan IOIs, look at emails, check what is happening on electronic networks, and dis-cretely chat with a few sell-side contacts to try and get a handle on where the natural offset to their buying and selling interest may be found. For many, getting together with matching counterparties is the holy grail of institutional dealing, likely to reduce friction and boost portfolio perfor-mance over time. Most sell-side firms know this, of course, and it often inspires a marketing effort variously described as "fishing" or "spoofing." Essentially, dealers pretend to have client activity in one or more securi-ties, and they use their own capital to complete part of a commission-pay-ing trade in the hope of winning the right to look after the rest of the order.

In some instances, there will be no pretense necessary, because buy-side dealers will have something else in mind. They will be looking to transfer market risk to a sell-side counterparty by executing some or all of the trade on a "principal," rather than "agency," basis. Going this route is like buying insurance. These traders are seeking immediate protection at or close to current prices instead of taking a chance on where things might be headed in the near future. For the brokers, the tradeoff usually seems worth it, despite the capital commitment and additional uncertainty that exposure to the market can bring. In the majority of cases, the transaction will have a commission tacked onto it, which can cushion some of the losses that might result from unwinding the position. Most reasonable cli-ents will also bear it in mind when allocating future business if these sorts of deals start costing counterparties a substantial amount of money.

With many sell-side operators beating the bushes for business, and nearly everyone having access to much of the same news and market data, there is a clear incentive for brokers and other intermediaries to use distinctive communications to stand out from the crowd. Some do this by lacing their messages and conversations with humor, personalized chit-chat, or even a bit of controversy. Others make it a point to be the fastest "relayers" out of the gate when large trades or breaking news hits the tape. Numerous individuals offer their own perspectives on current and future events, or they tap the talents of analysts and specialist-salespeople[2] to provide tailor-made insights on what may happen next. A few depend on a network of contacts to give them gritty color about what is going on in the trenches. Generally speaking, most offer some combination of these approaches, together with regular updates on trading flows, to keep clients interested and informed.

Another way that people try to gain an edge is by quickly passing along gossip and rumors. In fact, all sorts of individuals have always enjoyed this aspect of the market environment, whether they are on the sending or receiving end. Perhaps it stirs up some sort of naughty voyeuristic pleasure, or maybe it allows for some imaginary wandering away from the stressful realities of buying and selling shares under pressure. Whatever the reasons, the whole process seems to trigger an emotional response that, temporarily at least, sets pulses racing and gets people trading. While speculative operators have always made it a point to stay well on top of hearsay and scandal-mongering, these days many more people seem to be sensitive to the things that are going on below the surface, and communications networks are often filled with colorful traffic and the latest buzz from the Street.

Action Point

The newsstands are filled with tabloids and magazines offering gossipy tidbits about celebrities and those in positions of power. The reason is simple: Many people like to hear about such things, and when they do, they often seem more willing to suspend judgment about the truth of such claims than they would about those involving someone they actually knew personally. As an entertainment pastime, telling tales is probably a relatively harmless pursuit; for investors, though, the fascination with such talk can be a distraction that turns out to be a real financial horror story. While it seems that more of the rumors and whispers flowing through the stock market nowadays do turn out to be true than in the past, prudence suggests it is better to err on the side of caution and check facts first before blindly jumping into the fray.

Part of the reason why, of course, is that many participants in playing the market have adopted riskier approaches that depend on the use of leverage, complex strategies, and aggressive trading tactics. When things go even the slightest bit awry, the results can often be quite costly. Consequently, those exposed tend to have their ears pressed firmly to the ground in search of any signs that potential trouble may be brewing. In addition, geopolitical and macroeconomic conditions remain uncertain and unsettled, which naturally keeps participants on edge and on their toes. Under these circumstances, no small number of equity players take the view that it is better to treat nearly everything as true—at least temporarily—than to stand pat as the voice of reason and end up being trampled by the irrational and panicky crowd.

Interestingly enough, many "stories" do turn out to be at least partially accurate; therefore, it sometimes makes sense for players to assume that where there is smoke, there is fire. Part of the reason is that, despite rules such as Regulation FD, which was put in place to stem the selective disclosure of important facts, there still seems to be considerable leakage going on. Typically, this happens when analysts or institutional investors are given some sort of a heads-up by company management before information is released publicly. What often follows then are nods and whispers about what is coming down the pike. While today's corporate executives are more careful about what they say or do in light of the current regulatory environment, some nonetheless find it easy to rationalize bending the rules for influential members of the investing community.

Sometimes all it takes is a "non-denial denial,"[3] where listeners can draw conclusions based on what was actually left unsaid. As in the Sherlock Holmes story "Silver Blaze," where the fictional detective solves a case because a dog did not bark, the clues can occasionally be found in the silence. On other occasions, participants may try to put two and two together to figure out what is really going on by assessing whether corporate executives' words match their actions. In some instances, market players may take the view that certain operators generally seem to be on the inside track when it comes to pending developments, and they pay close attention to what those individuals are saying or doing. Many institutional investors, particularly those in the hedge fund sector, regularly compare notes and swap insights—occasionally using media such as instant messaging—to try and fit the pieces of the puzzle together.

Links between markets have been another source of reliable hearsay. When U.S. corporations contemplate doing deals overseas or weigh issuing securities in markets where the regulatory climate is more relaxed than here, sometimes important details slip out that can affect the price of those companies' shares. One example might be when an American firm is looking to acquire a foreign operation, and because of local reporting requirements or contact with the latter's major shareholders, the information reveals itself before any official U.S. announcement is made. Facts can also come to light prematurely when bankers put together syndicates outside our shores for equity-linked products, such as convertibles. Typically, the process is undertaken on an informal basis, with deal managers quickly calling around to tie up a group of potential underwriters. While conversations are supposed to remain confidential, those who choose not to participate often feel little need to keep quiet about the deal.

Occasionally people draw conclusions that appear doubtful at first glance, but are based on connections that are not widely known or understood. For example, there was a period during the late 1990s when a few individuals started noticing that prior to certain meetings of the Federal Open Market Committee (FOMC),[4] the briefcase that Chairman Alan Greenspan carried with him was "thicker" than usual. It turned out that on many of those occasions, the policy-making group had decided to adjust the level of short-term interest rates, and observers came to the conclusion that the central bank chief had brought along additional evidence to make his case. Some started taking note of this potential signal prior to every gathering and subsequently passed the "news" along to others. Eventually, CNBC made a big deal out of it, but the "indicator" lost credibility over time, as Mr. Greenspan appeared to adjust his habits.

Market professionals also look at a wide assortment of seemingly innocent activities to try and determine what may be going on beneath the surface. In addition, they frequently make sweeping assumptions based on occasionally small changes in routine. For example, if the senior executives of a publicly listed company are set to participate in a broker-organized conference and word gets out that they have suddenly withdrawn, rumors that bad news is coming invariably begin to swirl. Without thinking twice, players start coming up with theories about what may have gone wrong and what impact the "development" is likely to have on share prices. While this may sound a bit over the top—after all, someone may have simply come down with the flu or gotten waylaid by travel problems—history suggests that the decision to scrap a major promotional opportunity is not taken lightly.

Similarly, if word gets out that a previously unscheduled press conference has been hastily arranged, or one which had been expected has not been announced, players immediately begin to handicap the odds of whether the "news" will help or hurt the share price. Where there have been some hints dribbled out beforehand, either through leaks to the press or informal briefings to investors, the process usually produces a consensus view that matches reality. Ironically, though, in those instances where companies have generally been open and upfront and have made a habit of keeping investors informed about developments and operations, sentiment usually leans toward the negative. As matters go, when people have been trained to expect consistency, even a small change in the pattern can lead them to question a wide range of other assumptions.

Action Point

Admittedly, it is easy to go too far when using lateral thinking techniques and scratching beneath the surface for hidden meaning. At worst, such efforts can create a sense of insecurity and paranoia that does little for bottom-line performance. Nonetheless, both approaches should form part of the flexible and inquiring approach that investors need to strive for, one that can help uncover profitable investment ideas and serve as a nurturing ground for creative thinking. Like many aspects of the analytical process, however, it helps to put things down in writing. Use tree diagrams and other similar methods of connecting unrelated thoughts to turn vague ideas into concrete possibilities. And, of course, do not forget to ask: What if…?

The tremendous expansion in the financial services industry during the Bubble years, as well as the growth of the alternative investment sector in the wake of the subsequent collapse, drew in a lot of talent from various markets and industries. Bond traders, corporate researchers, scientists, and numerous individuals with widely varying backgrounds suddenly arrived on the equity scene and brought with them a broad range of unique perspectives. Consequently, they were often able to interpret developments in other specialized realms that purebred equity players might not previously have been aware of. In addition, though share traders now pay a lot more attention to what goes on outside of their immediate purview than they used to—most keep an eye on bond, oil, and gold prices, for example—much of what occurs elsewhere is usually best understood by those who have some firsthand knowledge or expertise in those areas.

One case in point is the action that takes place in a market originally flagged by fixed-income specialists. It involves a derivative product called a credit default swap, which allows lending risk to be transferred from one party to another. Prices tend to move up and down depending on overall views about creditworthiness and the likelihood that a corporate debtor will fail to honor its loan obligations. A significant short-term rise in the cost of this "insurance" often indicates that bankers, rating agencies, and others are getting nervous about a company's finances, and that those with exposure are scrambling for protection. Although every trading arena is subject to erratic moves and false starts, a persistent and pronounced move upwards in this market is frequently a clear sign that something is seriously wrong on the financial front. Not surprisingly, that tends to paint a negative picture for the share price as well. Indeed, it is not unreasonable to assume that a "profit-warning"—an announcement that future results will be below expectations—may soon be on the way. In no time or all, those views start seeping into the trading consciousness and voilà! The "rumored" event turns out to be true.

This does call to mind, however, some of the points raised earlier. From the beginning, information has often gotten distorted as it made its way around the financial markets—as was apparently the case illustrated in Figure 4.2, where rumor has it that the wrong stock symbol was entered into an electronic order system. In fact, there is a classic children's game that summarizes the pattern quite nicely, and it goes something like this: A number of youngsters are arranged in a circle, and the nearest one is handed a written phrase that he or she whispers into the ear of a nearby student. That individual then turns around and quietly relays the information to another child. The next one does the same and so on and so forth, and pretty soon the phrase makes its way around to the end of the chain. At that point the last one to be told what was "originally" said writes down the words on a piece of paper. Then they compare notes—and start giggling. Depending on the number of children involved, there is usually a considerable difference between the two.

When it comes to oral communications—especially those that do not involve ordinary chatter or basic dealing terminology—people rarely seem to get things one hundred percent correct. This is especially true in a

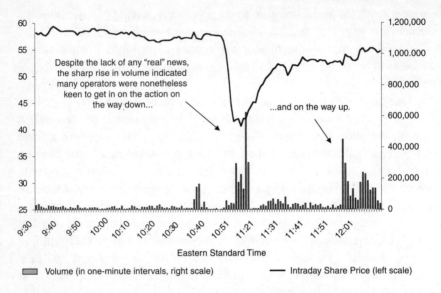

Despite the lack of any "real" news, the sharp rise in volume indicated many operators were nonetheless keen to get in on the action on the way down...

...and on the way up.

Eastern Standard Time

▭ Volume (in one-minute intervals, right scale)   ━━ Intraday Share Price (left scale)

Figure 4.2 December 5, 2003. Selloff in Corinthian Colleges (Symbol: COCO): A case of mistaken identity...or fat fingers? (Source: Bloomberg LP).

frenetic dealing environment, where tensions are often high and time is usually running short. Sometimes slip-ups happen because listeners are not really paying attention—they are doing too many things at once, their minds are somewhere else, or they start shifting gears before conversations actually end. Occasionally, it comes down to expectations: In the market and in life, people tend to automatically make assumptions about most things, which every now and then, accidentally drop in and replace the genuine articles. It can also have a lot to do with how individuals are feeling: On a good day, the glass is half full; on a bad one, it is nearly empty.

In fact, attitudes seem to matter a great deal when it comes to how relevant market information is acquired, interpreted, and forwarded. On balance, it appears that players' perspectives are frequently influenced by two factors in particular. The first is whether they have been relatively successful in generating fees and commissions, making money through astute buying and selling, or providing accurate calls on which way prices were headed. If not, perceptions and judgment will often be somewhat clouded—though, at the other extreme, overconfidence can occasionally cause problems in its own right. The second is whether they have outstanding positions, either directly or "psychologically"—in other words, as a result of recommendations made to clients, colleagues, or others. Subconsciously or not, the existence of some sort of exposure, even if it is only hypothetical, often triggers a directional bias: Those who are "long" will invariably emphasize the good news and vice versa.

Traditional perspectives associated with functional roles play a part as well. Historically, many traders and hedge fund managers have tended to be cynical, looking at markets—and life too, it seems—from a relatively jaded point of view. Although the reasons are not entirely clear, dealers tend to be realists—fantasy does not carry much weight when it comes to buying low and selling high on a regular basis. Moreover, most have been repeatedly exposed to the harsh consequences of getting things wrong. Salespeople and long-only portfolio managers, on the other hand, are generally optimistic by nature. Part of the reason is that—up until the Bubble burst, at least—the established pattern of long-term investing success was clearly associated with rising prices, and the majority of buy-side firms were not permitted to sell short anyway. Their overall mandate, and the approach of those who serviced them, was to focus on securities that had upside potential.

Changing functionality and a cross-pollination of attitudes has tended to muddle the picture, however. With some traders acting like portfolio managers, and many investors operating like speculators, it is not as easy as it once was to figure out where people stand. Many participants' time frames and investment goals, for example, are much more variable than they once were, which can make for a certain amount of confusion when information is passed to others. In the old days, for example, if the principals at an established long-only fund indicated that they were potential buyers on a dip or were looking for long-term investment opportunities, it was usually safe to assume they were referring to double-digit percentages or time horizons measured in months or years. Nowadays, the views can mean just about anything. If operators are currently bullish, they can very easily turn bearish tomorrow, regardless of the number of gray hairs they have on the tops of their heads.

Action Point

In everyday life, people are continually making assumptions about one thing or another, often without thinking twice. For the most part, the process appears to be an instinctual mechanism that allows individuals to cope with an onslaught of data and experiences that would be overwhelming if every little detail had to be analyzed and thought through. Nonetheless, in today's investing environment, it can be shortsighted and dangerous to assume too much, especially with respect to definitions, data, and opinions. When people say they expect the market to move higher, ask how far and in what time frame. If they state that an investment is relatively safe, have them spell out the risks in precise terms. If they recommend a specific course of action, ask them if they plan to do the same.

Sometimes problems crop up because of participants' limited understanding of finance, economics, or day-to-day market dynamics. The vast hiring binge in the financial services industry that occurred during the 1990s drew in people from a wide range of different backgrounds, many of whom had varying levels of education, training, and experience. Not surprisingly, quite a few had almost no prior knowledge of some of the more specialized references and buzzwords that are regularly thrown about in the share-trading arena. Even relatively uncomplicated economic concepts such as Gross Domestic Product or Inflation have been tough for some individuals to get a handle on. More often than not, the terms serve primarily as "hot buttons" for getting clients' attentions or as catalysts for generating short-term trades, rather than as starters leading to more in-depth discussion.

That is not as strange as it sounds, however. When driving an automobile, for example, it is not really necessary to have an intimate knowledge of physics or engineering to get from point A to B, and the same logic often applies when it comes to assessing how markets may react to the latest corporate or economic data. Moreover, in most instances, there are analysts and old hands around who can add some color or interesting insights if necessary. Nonetheless, as when using rusty language skills during an exotic foreign vacation, misunderstandings about what different terms mean, together with local twists of the tongue, can occasionally lead to unpredictable outcomes. Deflation, for example, has been a tough topic for many operators to get their arms around, because historically it has referred not only to falling prices, but a whole set of other notions with respect to debt, investment preferences, lifestyles, and attitudes that most Americans are largely unfamiliar with.

When the potential mishaps of oral communication are combined with the distortions that can result from slicing and dicing digitized information, it is surprising that there are not a lot more half-truths and twisted concepts coursing through the marketplace. For instance, though basic forwarding of messages does not leave much room for error—except, of course, when missives are directed to the wrong people—it nevertheless seems that once electronic data gets mixed in with a little human intervention, a whole host of other problems can crop up. Whether it comes down to a simple mistake—such as choosing the wrong list item with a mouse click or selecting less text than desired for a cut-and-paste operation—or something more complicated, the results can be especially damaging if they are then put into widespread circulation.

Even minimal editing to make data fit the allowed space can cause serious problems. An *alleged* crime, for instance, sometimes translates into actual wrongdoing after sloppy chopping by anxious traders, while words put together by an enthusiastic headline writer can become infamously linked to the supposed source for days—or even years—to come. Moreover, in an age where market participants have become increasingly focused on short-term speculation and rapidly lose interest in the finer details of what is going on, captions and sound bites can occasionally become more important than the stories that brought them to life. This is despite the significant differences in nuance that fleshed-out news reports usually provide. And, like every other bit of information that finds its way into the share-trading arena, most of it will eventually be reflected in prices in one form or another.

Much of the problem, of course, has to do with the widespread desire to be first and fast when it comes to informing others about breaking developments. This perspective is clearly made worse by an emphasis on catalysts rather than fundamentals. It seems, in fact, that even traditionally reliable news providers have sacrificed at least some element of quality in the name of speed. Consequently, there are occasions when erroneous reports can end up moving markets *twice*: once on the initial release and again when the follow-up correction is eventually sent out. As ridiculous as it sounds, sometimes there are wildly divergent headlines describing the same development coming over different newswires. This can set off a burst of activity that can leave even seasoned operators spinning around in circles. Governments have also done their part, of course, by releasing data that is frequently revised, adjusted, or rebased. While volatile statistics provide numerous trading opportunities, the chopping and changing can make it difficult for anyone to know where things really stand.

Another reason why there seems to be considerable misinformation floating around has to do with the constant demand for material to fill space and airtime. Whether it is traders offering knee-jerk responses to queries about a sudden jump in prices, salespeople chattering on about surprise announcements with an air of false confidence, or reporters accepting off-the-cuff interpretations of irrelevant news as the reasoning behind what eventually turns out to be a trading mistakes, many people seem to be plugging holes with little more than fantasy or wishful thinking. Often, all it takes to succeed is a bit of confidence and some degree of plausibility, and suddenly far-fetched opinions can turn into readily accepted "facts." On some days, a little digging reveals that the conventional view of what took place is little more than a pile of sand.

Even when all the news is genuine, the unevenness of daily information flows sometimes distorts reality in ways that can throw participants off the scent of what is really going on. Generally speaking, on "slow" days the minor bits and pieces tend to secure an unwarranted prominence; alternatively, when wires are buzzing with nonstop headlines, important material often ends up falling through the cracks. This latter effect is usually most pronounced during quarterly earnings reporting season, when large numbers of companies announce results in a crush that is typically concentrated into a period of about two weeks. Similarly, at times when dramatic geopolitical or economic developments are hitting the tape, the blitz of continuing updates frequently overshadows everything else. This can mask the impact of events that might have major repercussions down the road.

Action Point

One of the problems associated with the Information Age is the fact that the sheer quantity of available data implies that substantial makeshift editing and filtering regularly takes place. Unfortunately, this means that facts and figures are occasionally compressed into hard-to-understand mush or haphazardly transformed as they pass through a variety of hands. Alternatively, some developments end up being ignored or emphasized to the wrong degree, depending on what else is occurring on any given day. To minimize some of the confusion, take as much control of the process as possible by implementing a regular news-gathering routine that ensures consistency and continuity in terms of which details get through. With modern "push" technologies and a multitude of

information providers allowing customized access to all sorts
of news and analysis, this is as easily done as said.

Many times, in fact, a frenzy of news releases can stir up the confusing data fog that seems an inescapable drawback of modern life. For most
people, an overload of information can be disturbing and disorienting. It
can also trigger cognitive difficulties that cause them to filter out too
much or focus on the wrong stuff. Even when participants believe they are
on top of things, the wide range of constantly updating sources can make
it difficult to get a solid handle on the big picture, especially when markets are really hopping. Moreover, with much of the onslaught taking
place during real time trading hours, it sometimes leads to unhelpful emotional responses. Speculators and hedge fund managers, for example,
occasionally find themselves in a funk as flashing changes in P&Ls, beta-
adjusted[5] positions, and other portfolio measures pulsate in synch with
cascading headlines and constantly changing prices. Under such conditions, it is not surprising that some important material does not get
through.

Nonetheless, it must be said that when there is real money at stake,
financial markets do have a way of separating what matters from what
does not. Often that fact becomes most apparent when observing how
share prices respond to "unexpected" developments—or even those that
everybody supposedly knew were coming. A rally on "bad" news, for
example, has traditionally signaled that the market as a whole has already
discounted the turn of events, or at least a significant number of aggressive operators have. While factors such as derivative trading, lopsided
technical imbalances, or broad macroeconomic and geopolitical influences occasionally muddle the picture, increasingly it appears that the
real story is not the one being widely reported. In those instances, the fundamentals that matter, at least in the short-run, are the influences lurking
below the surface that are moving the stock.

Indeed, it often seems obvious that a great deal of sensitive information is not being publicly revealed before at least some people have had
the chance to act on it, despite rules barring such practices. Part of the reason has to do with the way intelligence has traditionally been transmitted
to and passed around between influential analysts and investors. Typically, operators who have the ability to pay—and the sell-side specialists
who have regular contact with them—get the inside track, usually in the
form of a call, text, or instant message, or at an informal gathering.

Indeed, according to a recent academic study, there is substantial evidence that certain recommendations are "leaked" to institutional operators up to four days in advance.[6] More often than not, it seems, these kinds of early releases end up serving as the basis for rumors and whisper numbers, which have, on many occasions, become more relevant than the published averages when it comes to what people are expecting ahead of important releases.

In the modern equity environment, it is the hedge funds and trading-oriented accounts that are primarily looked after in this respect. They are the ones most likely to respond to potentially profitable insights by stepping up and putting on a commission-paying trade. While it is an unfortunate reality for those who are out of the loop, it does drive home a very important point. One of the key investing tenets that novices and outsiders often fail to grasp is the anticipatory approach most institutional operators employ when trading or investing in the stock market. Their strategy is based on identifying opportunities and taking positions on board ahead of the crowd. Most do not spend time waiting for news and then reacting to it after the fact—they try to figure out beforehand what others may do and position themselves accordingly. Although the success or failure of any one trade may ultimately come down to a bit of luck, the process is invariably an advance bet on how the future will turn out.

This is the essence of what people are referring to when they talk about the market discounting mechanism: Market operators wager on tomorrow by buying or selling today. While risk profiles, expected returns, and time frames can vary—day traders, for example, may try to capitalize on upcoming swings that can be as short as 30 seconds, while traditional investors may look out six months or more—the view is the same: Buy before others climb on board and sell before everyone else heads for the exits. Thus, it is crucial for all investors to continually keep in mind that by the time good news appears in print—or even on the airwaves—it is usually too late to act on it—or at least, to take the information at face value. Ironically, though, it is often the best time to sell—which is what many professionals will undoubtedly be trying to do.

Finally, it is worth noting that there are those who question whether moves in share prices actually do reflect a pending reality or whether they are merely a reflection of how much liquidity is available for investment at any given time. Some even argue, interestingly enough, that the basic premise is actually backwards, and that it is the action in the financial markets that ultimately "creates" the economic world. Their line of thinking goes like this: Confident investors buy stocks and push prices up,

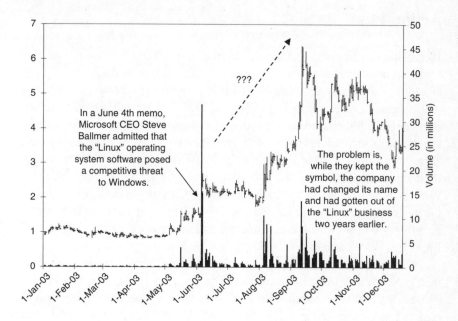

Figure 4.3   VA Software (Symbol: LNUX)—Name-Dropping? (Source: *Barron's*, Bloomberg LP).

causing corporate managements to feel more optimistic about their own company's prospects. This inspires them to go out and spend money on hiring new employees and boosting capacity, which encourages people to feel more upbeat. On the back of that positive sentiment, individuals go out and plow more money into shares—all in a sort of virtuous circle. Could they be right?

Whatever the case, information remains an important driver for understanding what is going on in the market and a necessary ingredient for boosting investment returns. Ironically, though, having more facts and figures at one's disposal does not necessarily convey an advantage, especially if the quantity is overwhelming and the quality does not quite pass muster—or if, as was seemingly evident in Figure 4.3, people are not really paying as much attention as they should be. And even when everything is up to scratch, many players remain hard-pressed to fully understand the implications of what is going on in a rapidly changing global environment. Nevertheless, for today's stock market player, information—good and timely information—remains the lifeblood of investing success.

Action Plan

Increasing complexity, unsettled market conditions, and information overload have caused many investors to scale back their data-gathering in an attempt to clarify thinking and simplify investing approaches. While a worthy goal, this sometimes means that they end up relying too heavily on widely followed and easy-to-digest sources of information to keep in touch with the financial world at large. Unfortunately, as advertiser-sponsored mass-market news providers, in particular, appear to be boosting their emphasis on bite-sized reporting, bringing in more "spin" from a variety of vested interests, and leaning towards one-sided perspectives, listeners, readers, and viewers can be left at risk of not getting as full and accurate a picture of what is going on as is necessary to keep abreast of important developments.

One way to stay on top of your investments is to actively seek contrasts. Nowadays, this is a cinch, as the Internet is chock-a-block with sources promoting a wide range of different perspectives. Although it clearly makes sense to avoid being overwhelmed, multiple viewpoints can often churn up valuable insights, even if you wholeheartedly disagree with what is being reported or how the news is being covered. If you are conservative, explore the liberal media's take on things. If you favor fundamental analysis, check out the views of the technical analysis crowd— sometimes the supply-and-demand picture as reflected in the "charts" is at odds with traditional financial measures. If you have always relied on mainstream news sources to stay informed, become a radical. See what the subversive operators lurking in the information underworld have to say—it might be a real eye-opener.

One of the first rules of success in life is to ask questions, especially when it comes to finance and investing. Unfortunately, many people tend to ignore this philosophy and take too much of what is out there at face value, particularly if the words have been uttered by so-called experts. If certain pundits regularly appear on screen or are quoted in the newspaper, note their perspectives. Do they have a promotional axe to grind? Are they giving you both sides of the story? Are they pitching ideas that make sense for *your* risk and return profile? While it can require a bit of work, it can be useful to keep track of what some of the more visible "talking heads" are saying to see what happens in the days after they have made their opinions known. If their recommendations often appear to precede moves that go the other way, bear that in mind. Despite laws against manipulation and the scandals of recent years, some individuals are not averse to hyping stocks that they or others are looking to sell.

Always have people define as precisely as possible what they mean, and avoid the urge to dive in based on incomplete information. If your broker and your brother-in-law are bullish, for example, what are they really telling you? Do they have a position themselves, or do they otherwise stand to benefit from having a positive outlook? Is there some incentive involved when they favor one investment over another? Remember, too, to question them about when is the right time to sell. If they cannot give you an answer, then they should not be making the recommendation. Always ask—yourself or others—what can go wrong. If the answer is "nothing," than the idea is worth exactly that, because no investment is foolproof. If you rely on your own research, try imagining that whatever investment idea you are thinking about does not turn out as planned— what will you do then?

When it comes to the financial world, everyone is motivated by something, though usually there is no harm in that if the incentives are made clear at the outset. The difficulties come when people refuse to acknowledge their interests or try to hide the real purpose of what they are trying to do. When a strategist recommends a stock idea, a commentator offers a forecast on what might happen next, or an institutional investor advocates a particular approach, try to assess what drives them, and whether they have a hidden agenda that clashes with their apparent intentions. Realistically, the media exists to sell advertising, brokers earn commissions based on turnover, analysts get paid for bringing in clients, and traders look to buy low and sell high. If someone is making a pitch, explore what they have to gain or, if you have the opportunity, ask them directly. If they take offense, take your business elsewhere. Remember, while they may welcome your success, the sad reality is that your performance is often only secondary to their own interests.

Do analysts, brokers, and the media say one thing, while prices say another? If people indicate they are bullish, and they repeat that point of view for days on end, are they trying to inform you or convince themselves? Is the news logical and consistent? Are executives, analysts, and commentators, for instance, promoting the virtues of a company at the same time that various insiders are unloading its shares? Web sites such as *http://finance.yahoo.com* and *http://finance.lycos.com* can offer insights on what they are up to. On a day when a company reports theoretically better-than-expected results, take note of how things end up. Does the stock make a higher high and close at the lows? If so, that is sometimes a signal that much more good news may be needed to drive the stock to new levels. What about the last time? If the pattern is similar, it could be signaling that a major "repricing" is in the cards. More often than not, a failure to react to repeated "surprises" is a sign that the existing trend may be set to reverse—hard.

Always pay heed to how share prices react to unexpected events, but do keep in mind that lurking developments sometimes take a while to become fully discounted by the investing world. The markets are much more complicated than they used to be, and there seems to be a far greater variety of factors that can influence share prices and underlying trends. One way to stay on top of things is to put together an investment notebook and record what is important and what you are thinking about on a regular basis. Apart from giving you a valuable resource to call upon whenever necessary, the act of putting things down on paper, as mentioned earlier, helps to clarify what is relevant. While it may seem that this sort of documenting and recording only adds to the data-compounding woes, you will often find that the process itself tends to filter out a great deal of unnecessary noise.

CHAPTER 5

Derivatives

Derivatives are exerting a growing influence on share prices.

In past centuries, a host of charlatans and colorful characters spent considerable time and effort trying to convince the masses that they could turn lead and other base metals into gold. While these would-be alchemists failed in their quest, attempts to convert simple matter into something more valuable have been a popular pursuit for years. Most such endeavors, of course, have turned out to be nothing more than wishful thinking or elaborate shams. Nonetheless, some would argue that the development of derivatives represents a breakthrough of sorts. In effect, these "synthetic" instruments—created almost out of thin air—appear to allow additional value to be wrung out of a wide variety of securities and commodities. Although there is some debate about whether the phenomenon has, in fact, opened a Pandora's Box, the modern sector's dramatic expansion—as can be seen in Figure 5.1—and its increasingly widespread influence on share prices is a revolution that most equity players ignore at their peril.

Countless individuals find the whole concept of derivatives to be quite mind-boggling. One reason is the complicated terminology traders and specialist operators tend to use. This has largely come about because a significant proportion of the descriptions associated with creating,

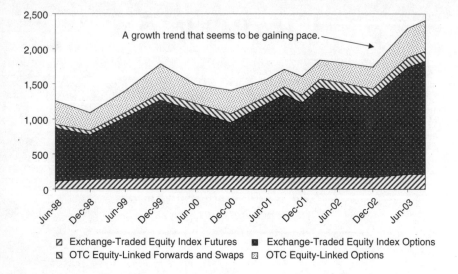

Figure 5.1 Notional Principal Outstanding in Equity-Related Derivatives
(Source: Bank for International Settlements).

trading, and monitoring these instruments, as well as modern methods of analysis, have their roots in the academic world, particularly in the areas of economics, mathematics, and science. Moreover, the use of confusing language is a common problem in the financial services industry. Whether intentional or not, the process of making things difficult to understand seems to be a good way of concealing what is really going on and keeping details about profit margins, for example, under wraps. Complexity also serves as a barrier to entry, helping to prevent too many inexperienced players from moving in and grabbing a share of the spoils.

Regardless, the essence of derivatives is that they are linked to and "derive" their value from other securities or commodities. Generally speaking, there are two reasons they exist. First, these instruments allow some measure of the risks associated with owning, producing, or acquiring financial or physical assets to be shifted to others. This process, often referred to as hedging, can minimize supply-and-demand disruptions and reduce the potential bottom-line costs of uncertainty, which is clearly a benefit. For example, hedging allows farmers to lock in the forward value of their output and bakers to fix the price of the ingredients they will need to purchase at some future date. Both sides can therefore avoid the unsettling vagaries of the marketplace, allowing them to focus on the activities they presumably do best.

On the flip side of the coin, derivatives offer market operators increased opportunities to profit from a variety of risks, potentially enabling them to realize much better returns than they could achieve by simply buying and selling the underlying assets. One way this is achieved is through leverage. In many cases, the amount of money that must be put down—in the form of an options premium or futures margin[1]—to take advantage of moves in a related instrument is a fraction of what would be needed for an outright purchase or short-sale. Consequently, this enables traders and investors to potentially magnify their winnings if they make the right call on where things are headed. While not all derivatives are "geared," this particular feature has certainly been a driving force behind the growth of speculative interest in this sector in recent years.

It is common knowledge, of course, that the derivatives arena occasionally provides a natural entry point for operators who are "in the know," allowing them to profit from advance information about pending changes in the status quo and forthcoming developments that have not yet been publicly announced. Because of the gearing involved, it is possible to realize phenomenal returns on a relatively small outlay, especially in the options market. Although history has shown that many of those who trade these sorts of instruments are nothing more than gamblers, it does seem that, with a curiously consistency, an abrupt change in price and a pick-up in volume in a derivative instrument will often precede a large move in the underlying shares. More often than not, that unusual activity is followed by a "surprise" revelation in the days that follow.

Another reason why derivatives have gained favor in recent years is that they often allow risk to be broken down into its constituent parts. When traditional equity investors, for example, analyze potential investment opportunities, they tend not to focus solely on whether a stock will rise or fall after they acquire it. They also look at how long it may take to reach their target level, how volatile the share price may be during the holding period, and whether the security will actually be trading where they would like it to be when they plan to sell it. By using options, it is possible to bet on or hedge against some or all of these aspects, with the relative impact of each determined by the particular strategy used. Consequently, participants can have a fuzzy view on where things are headed and still make money—or they can get the direction and extent of the move right and yet lose out. Someone who buys a call, for example, following a period when overall premium levels have been boosted by widespread investor uncertainty, might discover that the price does not move up much—or at all—when the shares do.

The derivatives market also makes it possible to create hybrid instruments with an assortment of risk and return profiles from a variety of similar or unrelated underlying securities. In many instances, the end products can be specifically tailored to meet the needs of a wide range of market participants. The process usually happens in one of two ways. In the first case, the various structural attributes associated with one or more assets—any future price appreciation or dividend payouts, for example—are, figuratively speaking, divided up and put back together in new ways to produce synthetic securities with distinct properties. This approach includes the practice of securitization, where numerous home mortgages or car loans, for example, are packaged together in different ways to create fixed-income issues that have different yields, maturities, and credit ratings.

Alternatively, derivatives may be designed to mirror the moves of a group of stocks or other instruments. They may take the form of a claim—or "depositary receipt"—on an actual bundle of securities, or a combination that exists largely in name only. Such products include index futures and options, as well as ETFs. They essentially allow players to bet on the direction of broad-based measures without the inefficiency and expense of having to buy or sell each underlying share separately. They also enable operators to reduce timing risk on related transactions, to lock in the value of large and hard-to-manage portfolios, and to put substantial funds to work with relatively little effort. In addition, they give investors alternative routes for entering or exiting the market, because an active arbitrage community generally keeps the prices of linked securities more-or-less in line.

Action Point

The derivatives arena is the first port-of-call for many speculators and institutional operators when unexpected news or rumors hit the tape, or when word of the latest developments leaks out before details are officially announced. While it can be a fool's game to try and keep pace with the professional "fast money" crowd, it is nevertheless a good idea for investors to pay attention to what is happening in the leveraged hot spots. A seemingly inexplicable move or a noticeable increase in turnover can occasionally provide some early warning about supply-and-demand forces that may ultimately affect the underlying securities or the market overall.

For insights on what may be coming down the pike, keep tabs on the most active options data at Web sites such as *http:// finance.yahoo.com* and *www.cboe.com*, as well as the Money and Investing section of *The Wall Street Journal*.

Not all derivatives, of course, are based on more than one underlying security. Options and warrants on individual shares have long been a feature of the equity landscape, and exchange-listed single stock futures are a relatively recent entry that has drawn some interest. Nonetheless, it is the aggregate instruments that have become the primary focus of attention for many market participants, especially institutions. Prior to the introduction of index-based securities, it was often difficult for sizable players to operate with the appropriate degree of finesse when it came to moving around large chunks of money. In addition, the process was generally very labor intensive, and a surge of inflows or outflows could easily cause self-defeating disturbances when managers attempted to invest those funds in a hurry. Nowadays, however, it is possible to throw $50 million at some broad measures and cause nothing more than a temporary blip.

Increased speculation and the shift towards a more active investing approach have also stoked the growing interest in index-related derivatives, especially on the back of an expansion in the use of electronic order routing and dealing systems. Although the traditional "open-outcry," or auction, methods seen in the commodities pits were originally designed to foster rapid turnaround when it came to wheeling-and-dealing in volatile futures markets, it is the up-to-date automated structures, with easy-to-use front-ends and instant trade reporting, that appeal to today's impatient and technology-savvy operators. Combined with relatively low costs, a wide depth of participation, and readily available price and technical data, the modern model of exchange-listed derivative trading has become the standard to beat for dealings in a variety of securities.

As a consequence, most trading venues now make it very easy to buy and sell index-related products. Invariably, that has whet the appetite of a considerable number of plain vanilla equity investors, too, despite the fact that improvements in technology and communications networks have also made conventional share dealing a more straightforward process than before. In addition, while the action in individual stock options served as the focal point of derivatives-oriented speculation in the late 1970s and early 1980s, the apparent shift towards uncomplicated decision-making seems to have drawn a variety of short-term operators into the basket-trading fold. Spurred by low dealing costs and a desire to wheel-and-deal in the most liquid markets, many players have foregone instruments based on single securities in favor of those based on bundles of shares.

Somewhat ironically, benchmarking[2] and the widespread promotion of passive investing strategies may have also encouraged the growth of the index-related derivatives market. Both during and after the Bubble years, brokers, mutual fund operators, and the media often emphasized the benefits of investing in equities as an asset class, rather than paying much heed to the long-held view that success in the share-trading arena comes from picking the right stocks. In addition, most of the educational and marketing materials the financial services industry has churned out in recent years have made repeated reference to the concept of relative performance versus broader market measures. They have also called attention to the significance and characteristics of sectors and themes. Undoubtedly, all of these influences have had a pronounced effect on contemporary attitudes.

Liquidity has likely been a factor as well. Ironically, while the rush to jump on board the equity train during the 1990s helped to stoke a widespread interest in equity investing overall and inspired a far-reaching obsession with well-known market barometers such as the Dow Jones, the patchiness of trading and investment flows since the peak in early 2000 also seem to have kept participants focused on broad-based measures. This is because the post-Bubble investment streams, like the runoff collecting in the cracks and crevices of an aging roadway, have tended to flow towards those points where the liquidity is deepest. And, as is often the case with most trends of this sort, some of those who have gravitated towards the index-related products have done so because that is what everyone else seems to be doing.

Perceptions also affect preferences, and there is a popular view in the financial community—whether real or imagined—that when it comes to trading "size," the best place to go is the derivative markets. Spurred by negative first-hand experiences and damaging press coverage, many operators have become somewhat dissatisfied with traditional market mechanisms such as the one used at the New York Stock Exchange. Despite the venue's longtime role as the primary source of liquidity for buying and selling publicly listed shares, there seems to be a growing sense that the NYSE's specialist-based system does not work the way it should. Moreover, because of increased volatility in many individual issues, often made worse by the actions of aggressive players and the fallout from rapid-fire trading technologies, the slippage costs of operating in such an environment can seem unacceptably high.

On the other hand, with the vast array of electronic links, alternative dealing venues, and arbitrage efficiencies available to traders in index-related and other derivative products, it seems that there are fewer obstacles to getting sizable business quickly taken care of. Increased competition has helped, as a growing numbers of players look to maintain their share of the action in an increasingly crowded arena. Interestingly enough, there is also the specter of market-making "machismo"—for lack of a better word—lurking in the crowd of those who deal in synthetic securities. This appears to reflect an aggressive spirit carried forward from the earliest days of financial futures trading, when some specialized operators and big-swinging locals exerted a strong influence on short-term market movements. Supported by a feeling of strength in numbers, many players seem relaxed about assuming the other side of potentially risky trades.

In fact, it often appears that professional operators are more inclined to take on a $5 million exposure in S&P 500 Index futures at current market prices than they are to position a portfolio of the underlying securities worth a fraction as much. This is true even if the individual shares can be bought or sold with a small margin factored in, especially if dealers have no way of efficiently hedging the risk. For whatever reasons—widespread familiarity with the products, ease of access, efficient dealing structures, or the number of players involved—derivative securities often seem to offer a better way to trade and invest than the instruments that serve as the basis for their existence. To be sure, it has not only been the demand side of the equation that has boosted the fortunes of synthetic issues—increased supply has played an important role, too.

In recent years, several developments have caused a flood of new derivative products to pour into the marketplace. A large influx of academic firepower, significant improvements in portfolio monitoring and trading technologies, advances in computing power, and a noticeable rise in the sophistication and intensity of sell-side representatives has spurred investment bankers, research firms, and others to come up with all sorts of securities featuring numerous bells and whistles. Part of the reason, of course, is competition, as firms have sought to gain a marketing edge with exclusive new products that also feature outsized profit margins. Generally speaking, the primary side of the equity business, which focuses on the origination and issuance of new securities, tends to be more lucrative than those areas that are concerned with secondary market activities.

Action Point

Much like the instant depreciation that takes place when a car buyer drives a shiny new vehicle off the dealer's lot, freshly minted derivative products offering a range of unique features and fancy extras are often worth significantly less immediately after purchase. Cooked up by creative marketers and drawing upon complicated valuation schemes, these instruments can sometimes have a lot of mark-up fat built into the price that may be hidden by complicated financial wizardry. Experience suggests, in fact, that this is one area where it usually pays for individual investors to keep things as simple as possible. For those who do choose to get involved in synthetic securities, the competitive exchange-traded secondary markets tend to offer the better deal.

One thing that sets derivatives apart from common stocks and other traditional investment products is the fact that their construction, valuation, and risk management characteristics often depend on complex formulas, multifaceted analytical methods, and sophisticated technology. This is especially true in the case of options and similar types of securities with some element of "opportunity" value—or "optionality," as it is called in the trade—built into them, such as convertible bonds. While many speculators operated without the benefit of elaborate pricing models such as Black-Scholes in the early days of the industry, the intricacies of some modern instruments and their complex interactions when hundreds or even thousands of issues are mixed together in large portfolios means that today's operators generally cannot function without the support of such elements.

Interestingly enough, while jargon-laden formulas and high-tech systems seem to convey a sense of mathematical certainty that proponents often allude to when attempting to ease concerns about the dangers of derivatives or similar instruments, the reality is often quite different. Part of the reason is the fact that "implied volatility," one of the key determinants of value in the popular algorithm, is essentially a guess about how much an underlying security is likely to move around in the future. While "historical volatility"—a measure calculated based on prior swings—provides some guidance, and market pricing of the derivative or similar instrument yields a value that serves as a useful starting point, the irony is that the main reason why many people buy or sell these products to begin with is because they think circumstances are about to change. Regardless, though history suggests many smaller options players usually get it wrong, it is not necessarily because the pros have better insights on the future.

There are other factors that help to determine what an equity-based option is worth, though theoretical values can, of course, vary from where securities are actually trading. These include the "strike" or exercise price, the time remaining until expiration, the level of interest rates, and whether or not the underlying shares may pay dividends during the holding period. Generally speaking, in the case of a call option, for example, the lower the exercise price is relative to the market value of the underlying share or index, the more "in the money" and valuable it becomes. In addition, the farther away the maturity date, the more "time value" it will have built into it. Finally, the higher the presumed rate of interest or prospective dividend payout, the lower the premium, because of the potential income that is foregone when funds are used to buy the derivative instead of the shares or an interest-bearing investment.

Although these five variables are the primary inputs used in options valuation models, they are merely the start when it comes to the bewildering array of specialized language that operators employ when evaluating opportunities and assessing risks in the synthetic securities arena. Most rely, for example, on a host of conceptual descriptions identified by various characters of the Greek alphabet—although it seems a good bet that few have actually studied the language. The main reason, as mentioned earlier, has to do with the strong influence the academic world has had in creating a framework for analyzing these instruments. In practical terms, it is not really necessary to have an in-depth grasp of the terminology to understand how derivatives affect the underlying cash markets. It does make sense, however, to be aware of one: delta.

Simply put, delta—or the hedge ratio, as it is sometimes called—equals the expected change in the price of an option given a one-point move in the underlying asset. Without going into all the mathematical reasons why, the general rule is that the more intrinsically valuable the synthetic instrument, the greater its proportional price adjustment will be when the value of the linked security moves up or down. For example, an "at the money," three-month call on the shares of company A, with a strike price of $90, will tend to rise about a half a point if the stock moves up a dollar to $91. In this instance, the delta is 0.50. For calls with a higher exercise price, the comparative shift will usually be less—with a correspondingly lower ratio—and vice versa. The opposite holds true for put options.

What this means is that in order to neutralize, at least temporarily, the market risk on a $1 million long derivative portfolio with an overall delta of 0.30, the equivalent of $300,000 worth of related securities would have to be sold short against it. Moreover, to really make things complicated, the hedge ratio itself is a moving target that tends to vary as the value of the associated asset changes. In the case given above, for example, when the market price of the underlying shares goes up, so does the ratio, meaning that additional shorting would be required in order to maintain a balanced book. Although it is actually somewhat more complex than that, the key point to remember is that "delta-hedging" is at the heart of most risk management strategies involving synthetic issues.

This hedging activity can have a distinctly calming effect on share moves, naturally counterbalancing market forces and, in theory, holding prices steady. Unfortunately, that is not always the case. In particular, matters can get especially tricky when specialist players or market-makers have sizable derivative positions that run counter to the directional bias of the underlying securities. For example, if an operator is net short a portfolio of call options—effectively a bearish bet on the underlying assets—a stock rally will often force the individual to join the fray and do some buying to maintain the calculated exposure at relatively constant levels. Hence, rather than stabilizing supply and demand, this will tend to reinforce short-term imbalances and boost market volatility.

Moreover, in the case of some dramatic market moves—driven, perhaps, by a sudden geopolitical development, such as a terrorist attack—delta-hedging can exaggerate a short-term swing and contribute to a chaotic feeding frenzy. Or, on days where prices gyrate wildly, the strategy can add to overall choppiness, as exposed players sell dips and buy bounces. Contrary to at least some of the arguments put forth by vested interests, it sometimes seems that derivatives-related activity is less of a dampener and more of an amplifier than is generally understood, primarily because of this ongoing rebalancing activity. While it is true that the synthetic securities market is a zero-sum game—for every long, there is a short—the distribution of positions tends to be uneven. Overall, there appears to be a relatively small number of operators who hold and actively manage a significant proportion of the outstanding risk, and their actions can have a noticeable impact on the share-trading environment.

As it happens, the short-term effects of their hedging activities often seem especially pronounced in the week preceding quarterly expirations.

With most exchange-listed derivatives, maturities are standardized: Equity and index options usually expire on the third Saturday of every month, while index futures and related options revolve around a 13-week cycle. Consequently, every March, June, September, and December, there tends to be a cluster of simultaneous expiries that have been popularly referred to as "Triple Witching"[3] Fridays. Although, in past years, all of the instruments used to stop trading at the close of business on that day, when final prices were calculated, expirations are now partially staggered to reduce the unsettling impact of a mass of end-of-session orders.

While it has never really happened, the risk of a large-scale market disruption unfolding on days when substantial amounts of derivative rebalancing activity is taking place theoretically raises the prospect that a self-feeding chain reaction, fanned by aggressive delta-hedging, could be set in motion. Moreover, with a significant proportion of the outstanding exposure in the hands of a fairly limited group of operators, it leaves open the possibility that the financial world could be faced with a systemic crisis. Nonetheless, these sorts of scenarios appear somewhat remote. The key issue seems to be that significant trading and rebalancing of sizable synthetic portfolios creates situations where stocks are pushed around for reasons that have little to do with traditional supply and demand fundamentals.

Action Point

"Forced" buying and selling by index-related players, delta-hedging by market-makers, "volatility trades" by derivative specialists—all of these can create temporary imbalances and short-term swings that can churn up unusual opportunities for nimble investors. Sometimes it is simply a matter of paying attention to the time of day or day of the month when putting together strategies that might be able to capitalize on the moves. One example: Have a look at how trading unfolds in the week before the quarterly options and futures expirations. If share prices are volatile and newspaper and online reports point to significant derivatives-related activity during the early part of the period, it often indicates that major players are unwinding positions prior to maturity. This suggests that Friday is likely to be a yawner. However, if events are quiet early on, it is frequently a sign that intraday volatility may be set to increase during the latter part of the week.

Like many aspects of the derivative market, none of this seems very easy for outsiders—and even some industry professionals—to understand. Arguably, there is a widespread lack of awareness of the full range of risks and potential effects that synthetic securities can have on the underlying indexes or shares. Combined with the fact that the terminology and mechanics are not intuitively easy to grasp, it does not seem all that strange that the industry has been able to ensure that some aspects remain lightly regulated or out of the limelight. Aside from that, when it comes to financial matters, many people are reluctant to admit ignorance or raise questions because they do not want to be seen as unsophisticated or out of touch. Ironically, it does seem that even some specialist operators—who may understand all the mechanical ins and outs—sometimes fail to see the forest for the trees.

Not all derivatives are overly complex, however. In the case of index-related futures and ETFs, for instance, the technicalities are somewhat easier to get a handle on. Equity-related ETFs, which, as Figure 5.2 illustrates, have experienced significant growth, essentially represent ownership of a bundle of shares, and thus tend to closely track the latter's moves and overall returns. Futures, on the other hand, have an element of "time value" built into them, and their intrinsic value may be higher or lower than the underlying assets. Generally speaking, the disparity is due to the difference between the risk-free interest rate and the distributions expected to be paid out to holders of the linked shares over the remaining life of the contract. When short-term interest rates are greater than dividend yields, the "fair value" of these instruments tends to be higher than the cash or "spot" price of the associated index or stock—and vice versa.

As noted earlier, there are two features that set most equity-related synthetic issues apart from traditional cash-based securities and ETFs: limited lifespans and the fact that for every long position there is a corresponding short. Not surprisingly, both aspects seem to have had a significant impact on share-trading in recent years. On occasion, the effect has been pronounced. The regular quarterly lifecycle of exchange-traded derivatives, for instance, appears to influence volatility, investor interest, and turnover levels. Part of the reason probably has to do with the changing cast of characters holding sway in the options market over time. For the most part, activity in instruments with longer lives tends to be domi-

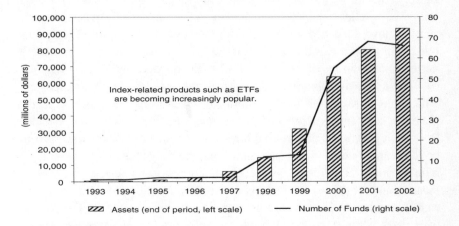

Figure 5.2   Exchange-Traded Domestic Equity Funds—Annual Assets and
Number of Funds (Source: Investment Company Institute).

nated by swing traders and investors; nearer to maturity, arbitragers and
short-term speculators tend to rule the roost.

Whatever the case, the cyclical aspects of the large and growing market in options and futures have not only affected the rhythm of the underlying shares, they also seem to have reinforced an increasing emphasis on
short-term trading. Echoing the on-off chants of cricket chirps on a warm
summer night, the ebb and flow of most equity-related activity seems to
have become tightly linked with the buzz emanating from the world of
derivatives. While seasonal factors have always had an impact on the
stock market, the action in synthetic securities has imposed a pattern that
has little to do with such widely known influences as end-of-year tax selling or quarterly earnings reporting. Moreover, the element of "time
decay"[4] that is peculiar to fixed-life instruments often adds an artificial
sense of urgency, unrelated to traditional fundamental developments, to
share trading.

The fact that much of the trading in the newer instruments is a zero-
sum game has had an interesting impact on the stock market, too. For the
most part, because each derivative position represents a contract between
opposing interests, any adjustment in prices creates some degree of tension between the two sides. Consequently, as the influence of equity
options and futures has expanded in recent years, it has introduced an

intensifying dynamic that has altered the traditional balance between buyers and sellers. Why? Because in the old days, when shares rallied sharply, the move did not necessarily inflict any direct "pain" on anyone—short sellers, in other words. Nowadays, especially when circumstances have seen a dramatic buildup in open interest—total positions outstanding—the emotional pitch is raised because more players have a vested interest in the upswings as well as the downswings.

The leverage available to derivatives players is generally greater than what many pure cash market operators have access to, and this has clearly played a part in boosting interest in these instruments. Under Federal Reserve regulations[5] that govern how much money can be borrowed from brokers and banks to finance new shareholdings, the current margin requirement is 50 percent. This level, which has been in effect since 1974, means that half the value of any new purchase must be put up in cash—or cash equivalents—if loans are used to finance the balance. In the derivatives market, however, the effective cost of taking on equity-related positions is usually much lower than that. Whether it involves paying an option premium equal to a fraction of the "notional," or face, value of the underlying security or putting up margin equivalent to about 7 percent for S&P Index futures, the gearing can be substantial.

Admittedly, the effective difference is no longer as wide as it once was, because "fungible," or interchangeable, credit enables hedge funds, for example, to borrow significant sums from their prime brokers to fund various investments and individual operators to tap a variety of sources—including the equity in their homes—to finance share-trading activities. Nonetheless, the growing level of participation in the futures and options markets, as well as the influence and standard-setting effect these instruments have had on related cash equities, has contributed to a more widespread acceptance of leveraged investing. It has also lessened the impact of traditional margin lending requirements, which have historically served as some sort of a minimal check on excessive stock speculation, thus making it more difficult for regulators to keep tabs on overall risk.

Action Point

Although the potential dangers should not be taken lightly, short-selling—explained more fully later on—can be a useful tool, benefiting investors who need to hedge some or all of their exposure to equities. While the SEC is in the process of re-evaluating the longstanding rules with respect to shorting individual shares, numerous derivative securities already exist that allow downside protection to be acquired in a relatively straightforward and cost-efficient manner. With easy access, generally liquid markets, few restrictions in terms of when trades can be executed, and little or no need to borrow securities in advance, these instruments can provide useful ways of managing portfolio risk. For more information, check out the facts and risk disclosure statements found at Web sites such as *www.cboe.com*, *www.cbot.com*, *www.cme.com*, *www.etf.connect.com*, and *www.indexfunds.com*.

Among other things, derivatives have also opened up the short-selling game to a wide variety of players—occasionally to their peril. They have also allowed participants to legitimately circumvent SEC and exchange-created restrictions[6] designed to inhibit aggressive traders from recklessly driving down share values. Generally known as "tick" rules, these regulations require that in order for individual stocks to be sold short, the trades must be executed at prices equal to or higher than previous levels. Although the specifics vary—policies governing NASDAQ[7] National Market System securities, for example, make reference to quoted bids rather than last sale prices—the idea is to minimize the prospects for self-feeding bear raids. With options, futures and ETFs, there is typically no such requirement under normal market conditions, which allows for the possibility that determined operators could step in and do some significant damage.

That is not to say there are no in-built protections against aggressive tactics in the derivatives arena. The various links that exist between the cash and futures markets, together with the rise in the number of operators and the range of technology-driven strategies being used, has led to continuing increases in program trading[8] and index-related arbitrage, as Figure 5.3 seems to make clear. This means that supply-and-demand pressures can be readily transmitted from synthetic instruments to cash securities and back again. Restrictions put in place by the various exchanges in the wake of the 1987 crash—and subsequently updated throughout the years—limit some forms of this activity when conditions are exceptionally volatile. Collar provisions,[9] for example, require that trades in baskets of shares be "stabilizing" in nature rather than "accentuating." When the Dow Jones, for example, moves up 2 percent or so, traders can only execute program buy orders on "downticks"—and vice versa—until the

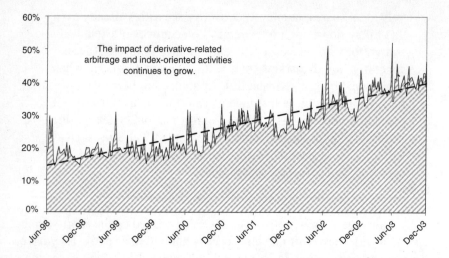

Figure 5.3   Weekly Program Trading as a Percentage of New York Stock
Exchange Volume (Source: New York Stock Exchange).

curbs are lifted. On occasions when markets rise or fall dramatically—10
percent or more—regulators have the authority to halt trading in all
related equity markets for a predetermined period of time. Regardless, the
rules seem to have done little to stem the phenomenal growth of the automated approaches in recent years.

   Despite the emphasis on exchange-traded products, it is worth noting
that there is also an active over-the-counter market in synthetic instruments that caters primarily to institutional investors. Although the bulk of
the activity tends to be centered on fixed-income and foreign exchange
derivatives, the action that takes place in equity-based securities is not
insignificant. Most of the time, though, the business being transacted is of
limited interest outside of professional circles or involves instruments that
have been custom-tailored to meet specific operator needs. Moreover,
over-the-counter trading tends to be lightly regulated and offers little or
no visibility with regard to pricing and turnover. Nonetheless, while buying and selling in this arena pales in comparison to what takes place at the
regulated exchanges, it will inevitably be reflected elsewhere because of
hedging and arbitrage.

   The derivative universe includes a diverse assortment of operators
employing a variety of different strategies. Some engage in straightforward buying and selling of futures, options, and other products to speculate on moves in the underlying securities or the overall market. They

often try and generate outsized returns by taking advantage of the built-in leverage that may be available. Derivative specialists—a loose knit group which includes arbitragers, program-traders, market-makers, and "quants"—focus primarily on exploiting valuation discrepancies and relative price differences between cash and synthetic securities, though many are not averse to placing simple bets on which way things are headed. Indexers and hedgers use the instruments mainly as passive investment vehicles or to control portfolio risk. Some players, such as hedge funds and investment banks, may fit into all three categories.

Apart from outright speculation, which has been a major factor behind the staggering growth of the derivatives market in recent years, one of the biggest reasons why buy- and sell-side institutions employ options, futures, and other such instruments is for hedging and risk management purposes. Sometimes they help to minimize slippage or uncertainties related to timing, especially when operators are moving sizable funds into or out of the market. Alternatively, they are used to reallocate resources between different sectors or individual securities. More often than not, they provide a measure of "insurance" designed to protect portfolio profits or neutralize some portion of market exposure. In the case of some long-only managers, for example, this might only involve the purchase of index put options; for Wall Street firms, it could include buying and selling a dizzying array of complex products.

Various operators also use the instruments as a way of generating extra returns from existing positions. For example, one commonly used strategy is to write "covered"—or hedged—options against an individual security or the overall portfolio. This involves the short sale of equity or index calls—frequently those that are at or out of the money—against newly purchased or existing shareholdings, which can bring in extra income that boosts performance, especially in quiet markets. Others may focus on potential adjustments in the prices of the derivatives themselves, by taking positions that try to capitalize on investors' changing perceptions about future swings, or on their own views about whether markets will break out of or remain stuck in a range. Such tactics, of course, often rely on option valuation models such as Black-Scholes, and therefore might not have any in-built directional bias.

Numerous players employ strategies that feed off some of the temporary mispricings that are occasionally created by basket-driven strategies. With a considerable sum still tied to indexing and other passive investment approaches, and market measures regularly being reweighted or updated to take account of changes in the fortunes of underlying share issues or perceptions about different industries and sectors, sometimes shares *must* be bought or sold by benchmarked players. This turnover usually has little to do with the immediate prospects of the companies involved. It does, however, tend to direct capital from the smallest to the largest companies, which can spur opportunities for arbitragers, value players, and individual investors looking to take advantage of any related discrepancies that might arise.

In fact, there seems to be a multilayered structure associated with index-related investing activities. Generally speaking, the managers who oversee these passive equity pools tend to rely on a variety of approaches in their attempts to keep performance aligned with benchmark averages. Some choose to buy or sell shares being added to or dropped from the indices by using only market-on-close (MOC)[10] orders on days the changes become effective. While this is the safest way to ensure that portfolios properly reflect the broad measures they are based on, the overall impact of many such operators doing the same thing at the same time can be significant short-term imbalances that temporarily knock prices out of kilter. Others may rely on market timing or use derivatives to lock in part or all of their exposure to minimize their involvement in the last-minute frenzy. They may even adopt such tactics with a view to outperforming their "bogey," or target.

Some players try to anticipate the actions of the indexers by positioning themselves ahead of those fund managers as soon as a public announcement is made, or even by trying to anticipate how the makeup of the benchmarks might change over time. In the latter case, if the fundamental fortunes of a company have been somewhat disappointing, for example, causing the share price—and consequently, the market capitalization—to fall to levels that indicate the stock may eventually be dropped from an important market measure, various players will often look to sell it in advance, potentially creating a self-fulfilling prophecy. Others may buy put options or implement spread trades where the security is sold short against a basket of other issues in the sector or the market as a whole. Not surprisingly, with all the actual and pent-up selling pressure, the shares do often lag the market ahead of the actual transition date.

On the day when a previously announced index deletion becomes effective, there is usually a significant pickup in trading activity. Conservative index fund managers who have avoided acting beforehand will be poised to sell at the close of business, as will other operators who may take the view that the shares will continue to underperform once they are dropped from the benchmark. Players who have been shorting the stock in anticipation of the event may look to close out their positions, as will others who perceive the pending end-of-day sell-side imbalance as a temporary fillip and a chance to acquire cheap stock. Some value-oriented types may step in and decide that after waiting for the downward pressure to reach what they believe is an extreme, it is suddenly the right time to make a purchase. All in all, a considerable number of participants will end up getting involved in a situation that is largely a technical phenomenon. Ultimately, their interactions will tend to counteract the preceding move once the trigger point has passed.

Action Point

When setting limits on buy or sell orders, establishing stop-loss levels on existing positions, or assessing the technical state of play in a single security or the overall market, it is important to get a read on any factor that might have a significant influence on prices. This includes the impact of index additions, deletions, and rebalancings that are instigated by providers such as Standard & Poor's, MSCI, Dow Jones & Company, NASDAQ Stock Market, and Frank Russell Company. Although arbitrage and speculative activities can reduce some of the effects, history suggests that stocks that are poised to be added to a widely followed benchmark tend to outperform the index in the period leading up to inclusion, and then underperform in the weeks that follow. The opposite holds true for shares that are set to be deleted.

One of the biggest problems associated with index trading in particular, and the derivative sector in general, is the fact that when money flows into or out of instruments based on broad measures, it tends to break down pricing efficiency. In the modern share-trading environment, both well-managed companies and poorly run firms get rewarded or punished as a group, with little regard for the underlying fundamentals of either. Together with the growing preference for simple trading vehicles and less complicated approaches to making money, this combination tends to undermine the traditional sense that the equity "market," as such, is a collection of unique businesses that run the gamut from good to bad. Practically speaking, this leads to mispricings that can cause capital to be wasted or otherwise misdirected. Of course, it can also mean opportunity for investors who rely on traditional approaches to investing.

Similarly, the fact that the unique characteristics of various securities can be combined, broken down, reconstituted, or otherwise sliced-and-diced creates another set of distortions. For one thing, processes like securitization tend to serve up risks that are detached and spread out, making it difficult for market participants to get a handle on the big picture or even to assess what problems may exist at the source. Aside from the possibility that such instruments could ultimately evolve into financial monstrosities, they also damage the links between investment and performance, leading to curious anomalies. Moreover, in the case of some fairly complex instruments, it is probably fair to say that there may come a time when derivative entanglements will make it difficult to know what the ultimate risks and rewards actually are.

While technology has provided considerable benefits—making it easier and cheaper to buy and sell shares, for example—the downside is that it has made modern market participants very dependent on intricate structures. When the northeastern part of the U.S. suffered a major blackout in August 2003, people learned quickly—and painfully—the cost of such reliance when things go wrong. In a similar vein, there is a risk that the complexities of derivatives may also reveal a woeful vulnerability sometime in the future—especially as some complicated products and large portfolios have become almost impossible to evaluate and manage without a computer nearby. Aside from that, the widespread faith in formulas and technology has also tended to foster a sort of academic detachment from the emotional realities of the marketplace, occasionally leading people into accepting theoretical values as hard facts.

Derivatives can also inspire a false sense of security and an illusion of control. While markets in options and futures seem extremely liquid under ordinary circumstances, that situation is subject to change, as has generally been the case with respect to trading in individual equities since the Bubble burst. Moreover, if conditions go haywire, it is possible that the "insurance" some are counting on will not be available when it is needed most. Part of the reason, as indicated earlier, is that a significant proportion of the existing exposure appears to be clustered in a relatively small number of hands, and a dramatic development could very well trigger a chaotic rush for the exits. As many participants learned during the 1987 crash or the 1998 LTCM debacle, sometimes there is no immediately available counterparty around to take the other side of must-do trade.

Some other modern risks are not so specific to derivatives, but are related to the structural links and arbitrage mechanisms that tie together a variety of different markets. As has been the case in numerous instances involving large-scale "errors" in electronic futures trading, the knock-on effects tend to echo rapidly and loudly through the share-trading environment, aided by the wide range of modern communications methods and ultra-efficient trading technologies. In addition, with many operators taking more of a speculative approach to buying and selling shares, they are quick to react at the first sign something is going on. Combined with the fact that many are using leverage, are operating with thin capital cushions, and are wired up with worry and a persistent fear of losing money, it is not too difficult to see how a short-term stampede can be kicked off at the drop of a hat.

As feedback-response loops have been shortened within the equity landscape, so too have the interactions between a wide range of indirectly linked, or even unrelated, trading arenas. For example, if something unusual happens in the bond market that might have repercussions for other asset classes, it is generally picked up on rather quickly by sharp-eyed operators or large macro players who can readily react to events through exchange-traded derivatives. On occasion, the collateral damage that occurs may have nothing at all to do with economic data or breaking news. It may be the result of margin calls or the negative fallout from unconnected technical imbalances. For some heavily geared operators, stop-loss or forced selling in one area can sometimes trigger a general wave of cash-raising activity that spills over into a host of other instruments and markets.

Indeed, if things do go wrong, derivatives allow operators to inflict a lot of damage because of the substantial leverage that is often available. While the ability to trade huge notional volumes offers considerable appeal to firms controlling billion-dollar investment pools, and gives aggressive large-scale operators the opportunity to potentially maximize returns on capital, it can also put a dangerous weapon in the wrong hands. In some instances, allowing traders access to synthetic securities can be the financial equivalent of giving a soldier a cannon instead of a rifle. Under the wrong circumstances, they can truly become weapons of mass destruction. Moreover, as was the case with rogue employee Nick Leeson, who ended up destroying Baring Brothers with his buying and selling in the futures markets, these instruments make it possible to wreak widespread havoc that can sometimes remain unnoticed until it is far too late.

Finally, although exchange-traded derivatives are regulated and relatively transparent, and the market is governed by rules that tend to keep the game somewhat honest, there is a section of the synthetic securities universe that remains vulnerable to unsavory influences and potentially disruptive practices. With relatively little oversight up until recently, the over-the-counter arena could turn out to be a potential hornet's nest that might negatively impact investors in the years to come. Arguably, with pricing methods that are relatively subjective and not opened up to public scrutiny, it is possible for those who have these modern risks to paint any picture they like when it comes to detailing their ultimate exposure. While the situation is probably on the up and up, it is not hard to imagine instances where such flexibility may lead some individuals or firms to overstep the line.

Action Plan

The phenomenal growth of derivatives trading has had a profound influence on equity investing. For one thing, it has created forces of supply and demand that are not necessarily linked to conventional fundamentals. In fact, sometimes there is little connection between inflows and outflows into various shares and the prospects of the companies those securities represent. Consequently, this can spell opportunity for investors who focus on traditional investing methods, whether they are based on technical or fundamental factors. Perhaps the first question to ask when doing your research is whether a potential investment is linked to options and futures or some widely followed market barometer. If so, are there current or prospective forces at work that are likely to temporarily unsettle supply and demand? Has there been—or is there likely to be—an announcement that a company's shares will soon be added to or dropped from a widely followed index? While there are no easy ways to get answers, heading to the Web sites of the companies involved can be a good way to get started.

Other points to consider are whether the shares you have been monitoring are part of an index that has seen widespread speculative interest or, alternatively, that has significantly lagged behind other bellwether averages? Relative weakness may reflect theme-based trading that has little to do with the business success of the companies whose shares are being affected. In addition, the periods when monthly and quarterly expirations come around, far from being a time to stay away, can represent potentially profitable opportunities to jump in with both feet. If the stocks on your radar have listed options, the appearance of a significant level of open interest at the start of the final week of trading—more, say, than the average daily volume that occurs in the shares—often indicates that technical forces may dominate the price action in the days ahead. For insights and further information, Web sites such as *www.cboe.com* and *http:// finance.yahoo.com* can help.

One of the most ironic aspects of derivatives-related trading is the fact that while synthetic instruments depend on the underlying securities for their existence, they are often an entry point for speculators and other operators who are looking to wager on swings in the shares. When analyzing your equity investments, it makes good sense to keep an eye on all the relevant markets—not just on how the stock itself is trading. If you believe something interesting is going on, what do the options say? Because of the leverage that is available, these instruments are frequently the first to move, sometimes days earlier than the associated equities. Alternatively, if there is unusual volume in the cash issues—two or more times the daily average—and there is little going on in the related derivatives, it may reflect the footprint of traditional institutional accumulation. That can be a bullish signal for long-term investors.

Pay close attention as well to daily market-on-close imbalances for potential late-day timing signals that can often prove useful when getting into or out of positions. Under the present system, preliminary indications of unmatched NYSE trades scheduled to be executed at the end of the session are broadcast at approximately 3:40 p.m. EST, with the final data revealed 10 minutes later. For whatever reasons, there is often a cluster of relatively one-sided orders announced at the earlier time that not only set the tone for the shares in question, but for the market as a whole during the last half-hour of trading. Try to assess whether the buying or selling you may be seeing in the securities you are following is linked to this sort of activity. If so, it may offer an opportunity to step in and beat the arbitrageurs at their own game.

While the presence of an active program trading and arbitrage market apparatus makes it difficult for individuals to take advantage of pricing discrepancies between the cash and futures markets, it is sometimes possible to discover interesting situations that fall below the radar of institutional interest. When looking to take investments on board, do not automatically assume that the best way to go is directly through the share market. Explore the various derivative securities that exist for signs that neglect or temporary imbalances in supply and demand may have created an opportunity to execute trades at better terms than would be achieved by going the traditional plain vanilla route. Of course, if something seems too good to be true, it often is, so make sure you engage in an appropriate level of due diligence beforehand.

Remember, too, that despite the widely used valuation formulas, there is an element of guesswork involved in options pricing, and there are a host of aspects to consider when exploring and participating in the derivatives market. Generally speaking, players are wagering on a variety of factors, and it is naïve to think that an option, for example, is merely a leveraged directional bet. When you buy a call, you are not only speculating on which way the underlying share or index is headed, but on the timing of the move and the potential future volatility as well. As such, it can be a bit like betting on a trifecta—picking the first three horses of a race, in winning order—which is, of course, a whole lot harder to do than choosing just one.

Lastly, pay heed to the greater emotional tension in the modern share-trading environment, and the impact that it may have on your own actions and judgment. Is the tail wagging the dog? In other words, are you buying and selling for its own sake, or are you getting involved because it is the right thing to do? Among other factors, the growth of the derivatives market has helped to foster a casino-like atmosphere in the equity world, and the overall increase in leverage has raised the stakes considerably. With a whole host of vested interests looking to see you trade more often, this can seriously take you off your game.

CHAPTER 6

Seasonality and Cycles

---

*Many seasonal and cyclical patterns are
becoming less predictable.*

The stock market, like many aspects of business and the economy, has
long been subject to a host of cyclical influences. Compensation schedules, tax laws, specialized investment programs, asset allocation preferences, mutual fund practices, and budgeting processes have regularly
affected the flow of funds into and out of the share-trading arena. Even
mood swings and shifts in psychology, stimulated by such recurring factors as the changing seasons, have likely played a part, though the specific
impact of those has been difficult to pin down. While destabilizing
events—earthquakes, assassinations, terrorist attacks—have occasionally
muddied the waters, historically at least, there appears to have been some
measure of consistency to the rhythm of share prices. Indeed, numerous
studies have noted the existence of such patterns,[1] though in reality, few
generate much in the way of tradable profits after transaction costs are
taken into account. Nonetheless, investors have often tried to adjust the
timing of their buying and selling activities to capitalize on the ebb and
flow. In recent years, however, it seems that distortions caused by various
modern developments have made that process much more challenging.

One of the better known market patterns is what the *Stock Trader's
Almanac*[2] refers to as the Best Six Months effect. Together with its mirror
opposite, the Sell-in-May effect, named after the old English maxim—

141

"sell in May and go away, but remember to come back in September"—these epithets describe a general tendency—noted by the authors of the *Almanac*, Ned Davis Research,[3] and others—for share prices to underperform during the warmer months and outperform in the cooler months that follow. Although widespread holiday cheer, optimism about prospects for the upcoming year, the crystallization of corporate spending plans, and nonstop promotional efforts by retailers and other businesses have probably played a part in stoking a bullish cold-weather bias, a key structural difference seems to be that there has usually been more liquidity sloshing around during the winter than in the summer. As a result, this has often provided considerable fuel for investment from November through April.

There have also been other interesting calendar trends observed over the course of the past century that have likely been influenced by the same seasonal factors. The first, widely known as the January effect, refers to the fact that mean returns—excluding dividends—have tended to be greater during the first month of the year than in any of the 11 that follow. The second, based on calendar quarters, revolves around the fact that, since 1928, the period from October through December has produced the strongest average gains in the S&P 500 index. Though researchers have been hard-pressed to identify the specific causes of these anomalies, it seems a good bet that heightened liquidity, among other things, has played an important role. Nonetheless, in recent years—for large capitalization issues, at least—there are signs that shifts in the timing may be occurring. For one thing, as Figure 6.1 suggests, the best average month seems to have moved forward from January. Indeed, based on its standout performance during the last decade, it would appear to be more accurate to speak in terms of an *October* effect nowadays.

Aside from that, if one looks at the distribution of average returns—again, without taking into account dividends—for the three months that comprise the seasonally strong fourth quarter, there appears to be a similar pattern unfolding. Over the course of the entire 75-year span, the mean gain during that period has been skewed towards November and December, with the pair accounting for over 75 percent of the total in uncompounded terms. During the past decade, however, as the data in Figure 6.1 indicates, the bulk of the quarterly rise has come during the first two months, with the average December return for the most recent three-year time frame actually in the minus column. While, statistically speaking, there are flaws in this analysis—the number of data points in the recent reference periods is relatively small, for example—along with the fact that the modern era includes an extraordinary boom and bust, it does seem

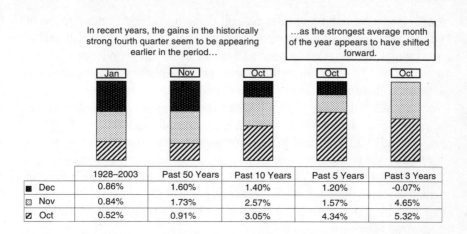

In recent years, the gains in the historically strong fourth quarter seem to be appearing earlier in the period...			...as the strongest average month of the year appears to have shifted forward.	
Jan	Nov	Oct	Oct	Oct

		1928–2003	Past 50 Years	Past 10 Years	Past 5 Years	Past 3 Years
■	Dec	0.86%	1.60%	1.40%	1.20%	-0.07%
▨	Nov	0.84%	1.73%	2.57%	1.57%	4.65%
▧	Oct	0.52%	0.91%	3.05%	4.34%	5.32%

Figure 6.1   Anticipating the Future? Percentage Distribution of Mean Monthly Returns During the Historically Strong Fourth Quarter and the Month with the Strongest Average Return During the Year (S&P 500 Index, Excluding Dividends, 1928–2003) (Source: Bloomberg LP).

to jibe with anecdotal evidence that the accepted wisdom about seasonal tendencies may be somewhat off the mark. What is more, assuming that such a shift is not just a mirage, it does not appear to have been caused by a dramatic change in the nature of longtime structural factors.

Historically, much of the extra cash in circulation during the winter months has come from businesses by way of year-end employee bonuses, dividends, profit-sharing payouts, and other distributions. Some additional stimulus has also been provided by the anticipation and implementation of institutional investment strategies and tax-advantaged savings mechanisms. Many conservative large-scale investors, for instance, have long made it a policy to review available options, determine allocation preferences, and initiate fresh buying and selling activity at the start of each year and quarter, for various reasons. Individuals, on the other hand, by virtue of the rules and statutory limits associated with deferred compensation plans, have usually found themselves in a position where a significant proportion of the total they could set aside annually from earnings for retirement has been skewed towards the early part of the year, especially during the past three decades.

There are two reasons for this. Most tax-advantaged investment schemes, such as employer-sponsored 401(k) plans,[4] have percentage and dollar limits on the amounts that can be deducted from gross compensation and socked away on a tax-free basis. Consequently, with many employees establishing regular payroll deductions based on a portion of salary, and New Year's Day resetting the clock, so to speak, on allowable maximums, there has often been a tendency for the aggregate level of earmarked flows to peter out as the year wears on, only to rev up again when January rolls around. This is because many people, instead of spreading the allowable total over 12 months, maximize their percentage deductions to put more money to work as quickly as possible. In the case of higher-paid employees, who tend to be better savers overall, such a strategy has invariably led to considerable front-loading. In addition, numerous plans have provisions that only allow first-time enrollees to start participating in January. Taken together, these factors have usually boosted the flow of funds coming into the market from individuals during the first quarter, as compared to prior months.

Action Point

Although markets have always been affected by activities that revolve around certain days of the week, month, or year, the modern investing environment has seen a range of new and often arbitrarily determined timetables brought into the mix. Many exchange-traded derivatives, for example, stop trading at the close of business on the Friday before expiration, which often triggers a flurry of activity. New index additions and deletions, which can take place at any time—though often at the beginning or end of a month or quarter—can also boost turnover. The dates when convertible bonds or other equity-related products expire, or when "lock-up" periods—times when certain large shareholders are restricted from selling stock—end, can also stimulate increased trading activity. For more information on stock-specific factors, check with a broker or the companies themselves; alternatively, tap into the news search functions at *http:// finance.yahoo.com, http://moneycentral.msn.com, http:// cbs.marketwatch.com*, and other market-oriented Web sites.

In addition, tax-advantaged Individual Retirement Accounts (IRAs) have also become a significant factor in the private savings market since they were first authorized in 1974. Although the annual deductions allowed by these plans, which have expanded to include three different options—Roth, traditional tax-deductible, and traditional nondeduct-ible—can usually be taken at any time from January of the relevant calendar year through April 15 of the following period, the tendency for many individuals has been to use annual bonuses and other lump-sum distributions to fund those retirement vehicles. Indeed, this seems to correlate fairly well with data on mutual fund inflows, where April has been the best average month since 1978, and the January totals have not trailed far behind.[5] Consequently, much of the associated funding activity has generally taken place somewhere between November and the IRS filing deadline. Most likely, the overall timing has also been influenced by tax-related uncertainty, which tends to diminish somewhat as the year end approaches. No doubt procrastination has played a part, too.

In contrast, events taking place in the fall have often created conditions that have primed the market to begin rallying sometime after the start of the fourth quarter. The majority of mutual funds, for example, usually start focusing in October—because of tax-related deadlines at the end of the month—on the capital gains distributions they will be making at year end. In practical terms, this has meant that managers would typically take part around that time in portfolio activities that were intended to balance out gains and losses and raise cash to fund any upcoming payouts. Some would also use the opportunity to tidy up their investment mix—or engage in window-dressing[6]—in preparation for the next 12 months. Not surprisingly, with December 31 looming, many other investors would often be doing the same. As a result, the year's losers—and frequently the winners—would often end up being sold off for reasons that had little to do with company-specific analysis, and prices would tend to move towards the lower end of contemporary valuation ranges. This would invariably create bargains that were ripe for the picking.

Hence, with numerous stocks having been knocked down to relatively attractive levels and an influx of fresh funds coming into the market from individuals and institutions, the combination would regularly create a bullish technical situation. There would usually be some level of anticipatory and hedge-related buying by market-makers and speculators as well—some of it driven by short-covering by those who had jumped on board the initial selling jaunt—that would add further fuel to the fire. In fact, because many operators generally scale back activities and limit exposure as the year end approaches, the financial equivalent of "hot potato" would often ensue, spurred on by the activities of bargain hunters. Regardless, a pattern of rising share prices would tend to play out, starting sometime in late October or November and carrying on until April. And, because the action was usually taking place in a wide cross-section of securities, the advance would typically be reflected in broader market measures.

Arguably, such activities have sometimes called into question the view that markets are inherently efficient—where stocks would be unlikely to be knocked too far out of whack for the "wrong" reasons. Moreover, the regularity of some cycles and seasonal tendencies, at least during previous decades, has occasionally served as a rebuttal of sorts to the argument that stock price behavior is a "random walk." Of course, there are those who would argue that correlation does not equal causation and that the factors apparently influencing overall supply and demand were merely coincidental. Whatever the case, there are indications that some patterns appear to be shifting forward and others are becoming more variable. This is making for a modern equity environment that is less predictable than the long-term tendencies would seem to indicate, and one that is becoming more difficult for participants to come to grips with.

Part of the reason, ironically enough, most likely comes down to the fact that there is more widespread awareness of historical seasonal tendencies. It is a reality of life in financial markets that when patterns and relationships are identified—"learned," as some would say—participants invariably try to make the most of that knowledge. At the initial stages of recognition, when a relatively small number of players are involved, such efforts are often successful. Eventually, the winning formulas become more broadly known, which draws in a host of other operators who look to follow in the footsteps of the early adopters. Once the scale of participation reaches a critical mass, however, the combined efforts of all those who are attempting to profit from the strategy begin to sow the seeds of self-correction. Margins get squeezed, and potential imbalances quickly get neutralized by the anticipatory actions of the trading crowd. Eventually, various aspects of the trend begin to change, and the outcome becomes more uncertain.

Because of the vast quantity of information that is now available through a variety of modern sources, as well as continuing media commentary and the educational efforts of the financial services industry, professionals and amateurs alike are increasingly familiar with many of the cycles and seasonal tendencies that have revealed themselves in the past. As a result, countless market participants now take steps, directly or indirectly, to adapt to what they perceive the supply and demand picture will be in the future. In doing so, it seems that many have even de-emphasized individual valuation assessments or have not given enough thought to what underlying conditions actually are at present. One result, interestingly enough, is that it tends to alter, collectively at least, the very behavior that played a part in creating the patterns in the first place.

In many respects, this present-day response mirrors the reaction of individuals who, upon hearing others take exceptional note of their manner or appearance, suddenly act in ways that downplay those unique aspects of their own identity. Whether driven by such factors as a desire to be accepted by others, an urge to be successful, or a fear of making bad decisions, a variety of behavioral influences are usually at work when it comes to how people deal with finances and interact with the stock market. And, as is the case with life in general, when individuals are consciously aware of some new piece of information, it is difficult for them to avoid being affected by that knowledge, especially if it has substantive value. When enough people start making adjustments, however, it can create new paradigms. In the case of some longstanding cycles, for instance, widespread recognition seems to be influencing the way that events unfold.

One apparent result has been a tendency, as suggested earlier, for the seasonal strength that has historically peaked in January to shift forward towards the end of the third quarter. A key reason seems to be that while a number of structural influences have remained the same—most investors, for example, are tied to a calendar-based tax year, and tradition dictates that annual disbursements are paid out during the winter months—there has been a substantial pickup in speculative and anticipatory behavior, as players jockey for advantage ahead of expected moves. Consequently, because participants "know" that share prices have tended to rally around the turn of the year, and November is the beginning of a historically strong six-month period, it seems that many have apparently decided to change their behavior to discount this knowledge. They do this by engaging in some measure of buying beforehand or by holding off on making sales until much later in the period. Even mutual funds, most of which are obliged to follow certain year-end portfolio management practices, appear to be tweaking their strategies by varying trading patterns or sacrificing some measure of tax efficiency.

Action Point

It is relatively easy to make the assumption that share prices will continue to move in ways they have always done, that previously employed strategies will carry on producing the same set of results, and that certain developments will follow along a similar path as they have done in the past. In reality, the market is a tricky animal, with a nose for capitalizing on complacency and taking advantage of those who think the investing game is easy for anyone to master. Many people assumed, for example, that the old rule of thumb about the stock market always being higher 18 months after the Federal Reserve begins cutting rates would be the inevitable outcome when the central bank began an aggressive easing campaign in January 2001. Needless to say, this time it was different. Generally speaking, it always makes sense to allow for that possibility.

As it happens, this observation also serves to highlight a more widespread change in the discounting outlook that appears to have taken place in recent years. For one thing, it is evident that time horizons are somewhat shorter than they once were. Whereas most market operators once preferred to look out at least six months or more when formulating investment views or contemplating the economic future, it seems that a quarter or even a month is the more relevant framework for many nowadays. Part of the reason, of course, is the increasingly widespread focus on near-term catalysts, as numerous participants adopt a more speculative approach to making money in the share-trading arena. However, while the immediate effect is relatively obvious, it does appear to have narrowed investors' sights with respect to the broad outlook as well. In addition, the uncertain and unsettled environment since the Bubble burst, together with the overriding sense that the world is changing much more rapidly than it used to, has likely reinforced the shift

There also seems to be a greater element of superficiality with respect to how people assess what is going on around them. Many market operators, for example, appear to have little interest in exploring why things are happening in any great detail, and they often seem anxious to move from analysis to action. For numerous individuals, the strategy of distilling complexity down to simple, bite-sized chunks invariably implies a narrowing of the time window. And even in the case of those who are more analytically inclined, the speed and volume of information coursing through the marketplace makes it difficult to take the time to stand back completely and analyze what is going on without worrying about missing some critical detail in the process. Moreover, with constant time pressures undermining the quality of decision-making, countless participants are focusing on those aspects that tend to give them a relatively high degree of confidence. More often than not, they are the near term factors.

To be sure, the transformation has not only come about because of changes in attitudes and perceptions. A less than robust economic environment since the go-go days ended, together with faltering employment trends—as companies have either downsized staff or outsourced functions overseas to boost margins—has played a part in disrupting the timing of flows into and out of the share-trading arena. Yet, what seems to matter more is that the devastating bear market in equities after the Bubble burst affected tolerances for losses and appetites for risk, altering some established patterns of behavior. Many market participants, for instance, are less willing to stick with recently acquired losers for too long, or are more inclined to trade in and out of shares on relatively short notice. Aside from that, a significant proportion of fourth-quarter activity during the previous two decades was directed towards minimizing taxes on capital gains. No doubt this circumstance was much more common during the secular upswing than in the choppy markets of recent years.

Other modern influences have played a part in distorting seasonal trends and making them less predictable. In general, there are far more forms of automatic, market-neutral, technically driven, or derivative-related flows affecting equity prices on an ongoing basis than there were even a decade ago, and many appear to bear little relationship to traditional investing activities and strategies. For instance, up until the passage of the Revenue Act of 1978, which included a provision allowing for the creation of 401(k) deferred compensation arrangements, most employees were provided for in their twilight years by Social Security payments or employer-sponsored "defined benefit" plans. The latter programs usually fixed a set payout at retirement, and employers and trustees generally determined how the underlying pool of supporting assets was managed and when it was funded. For the most part, there was usually some sort of link between economic circumstances and relevant decision-making.

However, with the significant expansion in the use of "defined contribution" plans—which, along with IRAs, account for around 44 percent of the total retirement market, as noted in Figure 6.2—that has occurred since then, especially during the past decade when companies sought to aggressively reduce future pension obligations by shifting some of the burden to employees, the rhythm of activity associated with retirement investing has changed. Rather than setting out a predetermined schedule

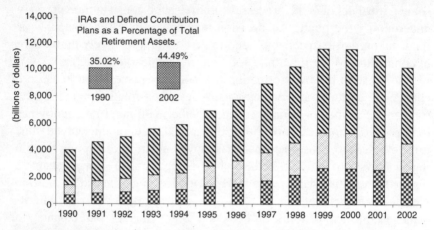

Figure 6.2　U.S. Total Retirement Market (Source: Investment Company Institute, Federal Reserve Board, National Association of Government Defined Contribution Administrators, American Council of Life Insurers, Internal Revenue Service).

of pension disbursements in advance, these programs typically delineate only the amounts that can be socked away every year on a tax-advantaged basis. This leaves timing decisions—as well as the risk of underperformance—in the hands of the covered individuals themselves. Consequently, because of the structural elements cited earlier, this has led to a situation where substantial sums are regularly pumped into equity or other financial markets—often based on fixed-percentage allocations—that are largely unaffected by day-to-day or even month-to-month changes in the fundamental backdrop.

As it happens, a significant proportion of those contributions have ended up in pooled investments, such as mutual funds, many of which are either directly or indirectly linked to the performance of broader market measures. What is more, numerous individuals have also favored having at least some proportion of their taxable savings invested in products tied to one benchmark or another. At the same time, increasing numbers of investors have elected to direct funds towards equities as an asset class or to target "themes" rather than choosing between individual shares. Hence, although countless participants seem to have become more active in recent years, placing a greater emphasis on short-term trading and aggressive speculation, substantial amounts of money are nonetheless tied to

passive investing strategies. In these instances, the programs often attract
recurring monthly inflows that mirror the funding patterns associated with
deferred compensation plans.

Apart from the obvious impact that such rhythmic activity can have
on prices, the process of index-related investing, in particular, can also
affect market dynamics. It does this by "forcing" some investment dollars
to be allocated on the basis of capitalization rather than analysis. Most
well-known indices—the Dow Jones is a notable exception[7]—are
weighted according to the size of their constituent members. What this
means in practical terms is that the funds that pour into products based on
these broad measures flow disproportionately towards shares of companies that are already large to begin with. In other words, the big get bigger
and the small shrink, often leading to a self-feeding momentum that can
seriously distort relative valuations. It can also create situations where
stock-specific assessments are overshadowed by basket-driven or mechanized investing routines, unsettling traditional supply and demand
considerations.

Action Point

To make fully informed investment decisions, it makes sense
to dig deep when doing the necessary research. That means
exploring not only the fundamental factors, but a wide range of
technical issues as well to get the big picture. For example, if it
is late in the year, try to determine if the security being evaluated has significantly outpaced or underperformed the market.
If so, it may be hit with tax-related selling prior to the end of
December. Has the stock pulled back towards its 200-day moving average? If that is the case, it might trigger some buying
from technical traders or bargain hunters. Are other shares in
the sector lagging the performance of the stock in question?
Under those circumstances, players might step in and sell the
security as part of a long-short arbitrage trade. Has the S&P
500 index approached a widely watched resistance level? If the
answer is yes, nervous profit-taking may lead to selling in a
wide range of issues. Finally, are outstanding options expiring?
If that is true, it could lead to a noticeable increase in short-
term volatility.

It is not only index-related trading that can affect seasonal tendencies—so, too, can certain strategies, such as "pairs" or sector trading, which have become more popular as the influence of the alternative investing sector has grown. For the most part, these methods attempt to take advantage of situations where individual issues are seen as mispriced relative to peers, or where groups of stocks are perceived to be trading out of line with others. Although they often incorporate an element of subjectivity and active engagement that most mechanical investing approaches lack, they nonetheless create "couplings" that can have a different impact on underlying conditions than straightforward substitution. Historically, the latter has been the method most often used by long-only investors, who once dominated the investment landscape. When they identified mispricings or perceived risk to be higher or lower than expected, they subtracted funds from or added them to the market, or they swapped one or more securities for others.

Nowadays, however, with many institutional operators having substantial analytical and technological resources at their disposal, as well as the willingness and ability to sell securities short or hedge existing positions with derivatives, there are more options available to them than there once were. To capitalize on valuation discrepancies, for example, it is no longer necessary for players to get out of one position in order to take on another—the two can coexist, as a long and a short. Whether it is a single security or several, a cash instrument or a synthetic hybrid, it has become easy—and preferable in some cases where liquidity or taxes are an issue—to play both sides of the investing fence at the same time, rather than relying on the classic one-dimensional approach. As a result, this has introduced a diffusing influence that can dissipate or redirect supply-and-demand pressures.

Overall, it seems that numerous traditional money managers are also changing their investing behavior. Whether they are attempting to reduce the risk of underperforming their peers or are choosing, for one reason or another, to strictly adhere to certain mandates, many are not adopting traditional defensive measures when circumstances seem to warrant. Rather than increasing the percentage of cash in their portfolios, for example, because they perceive that macroeconomic conditions are negative or valuations are excessive, they are remaining, as a group, fairly fully invested—as Figure 6.3 seems to make clear. However, to protect themselves, anecdotal evidence suggests that no small number are operating with actual or mental stop-losses, apparently counting on the fact that they will be able to get out when the time is "right." Others are acquiring

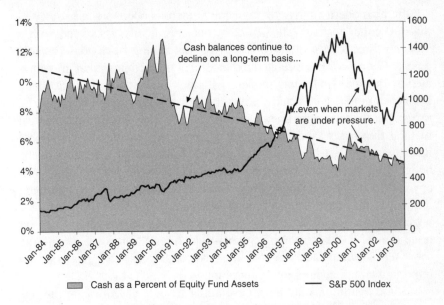

Figure 6.3   U.S. Equity Mutual Fund Liquidity Ratio vs. S&P 500 Index (Source: Investment Company Institute, Bloomberg LP).

put options or are setting up "collars"—writing calls and using the proceeds to buy puts—to try and reduce the risk of losses instead. Taken together, these alternative strategies and approaches have unleashed a uniquely modern—and potentially unsettling—influence on share prices.

Similarly, on the back of the post-Bubble bear market and the dramatic expansion in the alternative investment sector in recent years, many operators are much more willing to use short-selling tactics to hedge risk or speculate on lower prices than previously. This, too, has likely unhinged a number of historical tendencies. Generally speaking, the plain vanilla approaches once favored by traditional buy-side firms tend to create a lopsided dynamic in the share-trading arena. One where dramatic selloffs reach greater relative extremes than rallies before significant countertrend reactions set in. It is not hard to see why this was often the case in the past: There was much less shorting going on, an activity which tends to create an expanding reservoir of pent-up demand as declines unfold. Nowadays, however, with the parity between longs and shorts in a broad range of individual issues undergoing a structural shift in favor of the latter, it has begun to affect the supply-and-demand balance of the entire market.

In the modern equity environment, numerous operators use strategies that are either technical in nature or not specifically associated with a view on direction. Some involve buying and selling stocks based solely on chart signals or price-related indicators, or on recommendations generated by quantitative trading models. Although such approaches have long been seen in the share-trading arena, historically they have been less of a factor in their own right than they appear to be now. Another mechanical method that has waxed and waned in terms of popularity in traditional investment circles, but which has gained a number of adherents in the hedge fund world, is momentum investing. In practical terms, this strategy distills down to a simple formula the wide range of crowd-following influences that have been a feature of financial markets from the very beginning. Still, while it is not a uniquely modern way of capitalizing on price trends, the current applications—which tend to revolve around the short term—often lack the measured responsiveness that has been an important component of equity investing in days gone by.

Some institutions are even developing models that draw on the science of artificial intelligence. They feed a host of inputs into a processor and it automatically churns out buy and sell recommendations. Many such systems function without users necessarily having a handle on the basis for each choice or the patterns that have been detected. Of course, not all modern approaches go to such technological lengths, but mechanical decision-making processes have clearly taken hold in today's equity marketplace. Many program traders, for example, rely on systems that constantly monitor levels of relative valuation, which can automatically set arbitrage processes in motion with little or no human intervention. Although these tactics may seem to provide nothing more than a rebalancing offset with little net impact, they do, in fact, alter the share-trading landscape. In essence, they eliminate many anomalies that would likely have influenced the behavior of fundamentally driven investors in the past.

Aside from that, a number of specialist operators are employing strategies driven by derivative valuations, which are often far removed from the traditional estimates of worth associated with the underlying securities. Such approaches tend to focus mainly on variations in options pricing or perceptions about future volatility. These are essentially just a subset of the universe of variables that straightforward equity players concern themselves with. And, as noted previously, the limited lifespans of these instruments and the regular expiration cycle of exchange-traded options and futures have laid down a backbeat on markets that can affect historical patterns—something that an expansion in the adoption of regular monthly investment plans has also likely done. Arguably, these manufactured phases may create new opportunities in and of themselves, but bear in mind that they represent one factor among many that can influence share values.

Action Point

In the new world of derivatives, program trading, and arbitrage, certain shares are likely to be left out of the action because they are not part of any actively traded bundle of securities. Other stocks may be ignored by analysts or institutional investors because they are too small or are in out-of-favor industries or sectors. Certain securities may even be left high and dry because they are conglomerates or are spin-offs that professionals find too confusing or difficult to categorize. Situations such as these can provide ideal prospecting grounds for investors who are seeking out potential diamonds in the rough. One way to screen for such anomalies is to use filters that can identify low average dollar or share volume securities. These tools can be found at Web sites such as *www.fool.com* and *www.marketscreen.com*.

The post-Bubble collapse in equity prices and the economic uncertainty in recent years have done their part to change some of the perspectives that became ingrained during the secular bull market. One result of this transformation has been a decline in available trading liquidity because participants are less willing to supply the marginal funds that often served to dampen volatility and smooth out trends, as was the case when prices were working their way higher. The current big-picture environment has also had a significant impact on overall investor psychology, with the prospect of geopolitical disruption boosting skittishness and impairing some players' confidence and judgment. Heightened worries about what the medium-to-long term future holds, in an era where traditional fiscal and monetary stimulus has seemingly failed to produce the full range of expected benefits, has also raised anxiety levels, leaving many individuals hesitant about making long-term commitments.

It seems that the pace and complexity of the modern age has also altered the dynamic of the stock market by inhibiting, rather than promoting, consensus-building. Vast quantities of information coming from a variety of sources have made it difficult for people to get a consistent and cohesive sense of where things are headed, or even where conditions actually are at present—not to mention the continuous corrections, revisions, and updates of public and private sector statistics that help to keep overall perceptions about the economic outlook in a state of flux. The hectic and increasingly jumbled nature of the news and data streams that regularly hit players from every angle can also be disconcerting. For one thing, they boost the prospects for information overload, which can distort normal decision-making processes. In addition, with potentially relevant facts and figures coming from any number of directions—whispers in the crowd, shouts over the PA, a scrolling headline on a terminal—the cacophonous effect can sometimes make it difficult to separate the wheat from the chaff.

Interestingly, data does not necessarily have to arrive in a downpour to trigger false starts and unsettled trading conditions. Various flow patterns can cause important details to fall by the wayside, as when a steady rain over the course of a few days saturates the ground and eventually creates a muddy runoff, or when a sudden slight pickup in intensity challenges the capacity of the thirstiest soil to absorb the extra volume. Under those circumstances, some critical information is invariably excluded from the investment decision-making process, and potentially unwarranted buying and selling ends up taking place. Such activity may even cause further instability and add to overall confusion as short-term speculators pounce on the moves, oblivious to the reality that they may have not been kicked off on the basis of an appropriate measure of analysis beforehand.

Of course, the fact that huge amounts of data can flow quickly through the market is made all the more relevant because increasing numbers of participants have acquired itchy trigger fingers and have the ability to take on substantial positions at relatively short notice. Combined with the widespread availability of efficient, state-of-the-art dealing technologies, this makes it easy for operators of all shapes and sizes to react almost instantly to what they perceive is going on. As a result, it can create concentrated bursts of activity that overwhelm attempts at more measured responses. In past decades, when communications networks were less advanced and execution methods depended on multiple links in a chain, information was absorbed and acted upon more slowly. That seemed to promote a more consistent and orderly rhythm in share price movements than seems apparent in today's equity environment.

A change in the speed at which information is disseminated also implies that there is less consistency of opinion in the prospective investor population at each stage of the investment cycle. In the old days, for instance, the pattern of interest tended to evolve from a small number of savvy operators to a large number of less sophisticated individuals. Typically, the first group would get the inside scoop and would start taking positions on board. After that, they would spread the word to others through a variety of channels, and so on and so forth. While this process clearly left latecomers at a disadvantage, one small consolation was that it seemed to act as a "governor" of sorts that facilitated smooth-flowing price action. Now, with a wide range of participants poised to pounce on potential moneymaking opportunities at every step along the way, there is more noise and less gradualism.

Psychology has always played a critical role in influencing investor behavior, of course, but one factor that has frequently cropped up since the 1990s ended seems to be intermittently confusing the picture. Despite unsettled economic conditions and the anxieties triggered by the post Bubble-collapse, numerous market participants still have an underlying sense of exuberance that quickly reveals itself when there are any signs that share prices may have turned a bullish corner. As a result, many seem quite willing to drop apprehensions about valuations and future business prospects without thinking twice, even if the supporting data is tenuous at best. Having experienced the headiness and excitement of the go-go years, they appear overly amenable to the idea that the situation can return to the way it was during the dot-com days. While anything is possible, history suggests such a turn of events is extremely unlikely.

Another aspect of the modern environment that has disturbed traditional buying and selling patterns is the intense competition that has come to the fore in the financial services industry. While nearly every business has been subject to such pressures in recent years, the powerful upswing of the last decade spared brokers, money managers, and similar institutions some measure of the associated pain. This was because the gusher of money that was flowing into the equity market left plenty of food on the table for everyone. Since the Bubble burst, however, excess capacity has become a significant concern, and many operators have aggressively sought ways to gain an edge over rivals. At the same time, the share-trading landscape has seen a dramatic rise in the influence of the alternative investment sector, where managers generally lean towards a flexible and aggressive approach to wheeling-and-dealing.

One tactic in particular that many operators have adopted is an increased willingness to trade without necessarily having enough relevant facts in hand, aggressively second-guessing others in a bid to jump ahead of the pack. Consequently, they seem to be buying and selling shares in various sectors, such as cyclicals, financials, or utilities, prior to the point in the business cycle where such activity has usually taken place in the past. This has led to choppy price action and created confusion about what particular outlook investors are discounting. In some ways, the effect resembles the foamy churn produced when two opposing waves come together and trigger a gurgling eruption on the beach. Combined with the fact that many economic variables appear to be out of synch with historical precedents and the sense that traditional policy measures seem to have lost some of their punch, share prices are subject to a considerable amount of noisy cross-currents nowadays.

Action Point

Although it may seem like a necessary evil in the modern investing age, think long and hard before getting caught up in a seat-of-the-pants style of anticipatory trading. All investing, of course, involves some measure of expectation about the future. However, to minimize the prospects of getting blindsided and to gain a consistent advantage in fast-changing markets, investors need to gather more information, not less, before making critical decisions. The right way to go about this is to collect as much background data as possible ahead of, say, an earnings release, so that when the results are actually made public, it is only a matter of making a few quick checks to verify that circumstances are as expected or are significantly out of line. That way, any views taken and decisions made are more calculated than speculative—which can make a significant difference when it comes to boosting bottom-line performance.

In addition, based on the longstanding belief that successfully playing the market depends on being in the right group of securities at the right time, it seems that many operators are almost constantly on the prowl for the next fad or trading theme. This has fed a sort of hyperactive sector rotation that frequently inspires an extreme element of anticipatory behavior. Aggressive traders, for instance, appear quite willing to step in front of expected moves before there is even a modest indication that the timing is appropriate. That seemed to be the case, for example, when some institutional investors were eyeing late-cycle sectors such as pharmaceuticals in the fourth quarter of 2003—although the economic recovery had only "barely begun."[8] Alternatively, players appear to be exiting positions before trends have fully developed or shown signs that they are waning. What is more, there seems to be an increased willingness to countertrade unexpected developments—such as profit-warnings or earnings releases that beat estimates—before the dust has actually settled.

Ironically, even when participants are operating in synch with one another, the impact on markets can still be disruptive. This is because of overcrowding, which is discussed in more detail later on. With many more players, such as hedge funds, willing to adopt an aggressive dealing posture and to take on substantial positions without engaging in a great deal of time-consuming analysis, it is increasingly leading to a rapid build-up of unstable short-term technical imbalances. Moreover, as trading ideas course through the investing grapevine, aided by instant and broadcast messaging and various "promotional" efforts, the excesses get compounded when additional operators join the fray. The lack of transparency in some segments tends to make matters worse, of course, because it often leaves everyone unaware about the true scale of the aggregate exposure—until it is too late. What happens then is that a number of those who are exposed will suddenly realize that many others are positioned the same way, which sets off a major rush for the exits.

Holding periods have been shortened as numerous participants have adopted a more active approach to investing, which has altered supply-and-demand relationships, too. Many players, for instance, are making the conscious choice to take profits quickly. Alternatively, they are going home flat every day, or at the end of each week, month, or quarter. This preference shift, in fact, may have accounted for the change that took place during the 1990s, when Mondays stopped being the statistically weakest day of the week for large capitalization issues. Although the exact reasons are unclear, anecdotal evidence suggests bullish speculators feared being exposed to potential weekend disruptions in markets that were clearly floating on air. Hence, they tended to scale back positions on Fridays. Once the next regular session rolled around, however, they were only too happy to wade back in.[9] Apart from that, significant numbers seem to be putting more mechanical measures, such as stop-loss orders, in place to limit risk, and are more inclined to cut and run than long-term investors traditionally have been.

Another factor that has likely played a role in reshaping historical patterns is the ease with which capital can flow between sectors and markets. Index-related products, such as futures and ETFs, make it a cinch to move in and out of equities at a moment's notice, and the decision does not necessarily have to be based on some form of elaborate analysis. Indeed, with one telephone call or click of a mouse, participants can switch substantial sums from fixed-income securities into stocks, from money market instruments into commodities, or from one group of investments into another. Increased interest in thematic trading has also had a significant impact on the equity landscape, particularly when major geopolitical influences are present. For example, amidst the rising tensions over Iraq, investors apparently began to anticipate a rally similar to that which had taken place during the first Gulf War, and they "started buying without waiting for hostilities to break out. Stock prices rebounded on March 13, 2003, six days before the war began, and continued to soar"[10] in the early days of the conflict. This seemingly self-fulfilling process also inspired unusually strong correlations between shares, overshadowing other influences.[11]

Interestingly enough, this phenomenon highlights another behavioral influence that seems particularly acute in the modern age: availability bias. In essence, it appears that a broad cultural shift has taken place, one which characterizes the relevance of history based on the amount of multimedia material that is available. While past generations have always viewed contemporary developments in a more significant light than ancient events and circumstances, the distinction nowadays seems especially striking. Moreover, with the population at large having less patience and more limited attention spans than their forbears, it is not surprising that market participants are quick to draw on the approaches and experiences they are most familiar with, regardless of whether or not that is the most appropriate course of action. In hindsight, it seemed that investor response to the second Gulf War was almost predestined, at least in the short run. Under these circumstances, traditional fundamentals can be easily undermined.

It is not only the financial world that has seen changes, of course. There have been important developments taking place in the real economy that have had an impact on equity markets, too. For one thing, intense global competition and the overhang of excess capacity in industries ranging from automobiles to telecommunications have muted some measure of response to stimuli such as sharply lower rates. For another, the structure of the operating environment has been dramatically transformed in recent decades. In the U.S., for example, the makeup of the economy has shifted from production-oriented activities towards those which are more service-related. This has had a significant influence on spending and investment patterns, and has altered some of the money flows feeding through to shareholders and employees. Many lower-paid customer service workers, for example, can ill afford to sock funds away for retirement, while those at the higher end sometimes receive production bonuses on a quarterly or more frequent basis.

In addition, many companies have adopted just-in-time production methods and point-of-sale tracking systems that shorten feedback loops and make operations more efficient. This has created more opportunities for chief financial officers and treasurers to effectively manage their firms' cash holdings by considering a wider range of investments than bank deposits and short-term instruments. In some instances, the funds are finding their way into capital markets that have not seen such flows before, adding a new wrinkle to supply-and-demand considerations in arenas that may have at least an indirect impact on equities. Taken together, these developments have likely affected a variety of traditional parities and financial relationships, making it more difficult to piece together a top-down assessment of where things are headed. Under such circumstances, aggregate buying and selling activity is probably infused with greater uncertainty.

Although many historical relationships are being affected in one way or another by modern developments, some patterns could remain relatively intact. One such example is the Presidential Election Cycle, which describes a tendency for the stock market to strengthen in the third year of a four-year term. Generally speaking, the move takes place in response to stimulative measures fostered by the incumbent administration in a bid to boost re-election prospects the following November. Typically, the upswing follows a period of relative weakness in the early part of the term, when the newly elected chief executive promotes changes designed to clear the decks and put the excesses of the previous officeholder out to pasture. Arguably, significant budget and trade deficits and increasing voter apathy could end up neutralizing the availability and effectiveness of some policy measures down the line. Nonetheless, it seems likely that politics will remain as potent an influence on share prices as it has always been.

Indeed, despite an abysmal historical record of success, it is a good bet that governments around the globe will, for the most part, continue their attempts to intervene in markets to dampen volatility, counteract undesirable short-term developments, and achieve a variety of political and other ends. While many such actions will prove to have a limited impact in the long run, the near-term effect will tend to play havoc with traditional supply-and-demand influences—as it has done on occasion in past years. Consequently, seasonality and cyclical patterns will likely end up being distorted, not only by the actual implementation of such activities, but by market anticipation of when they might next occur. No doubt, the effect will be most pronounced when it comes to countering price declines, given the natural tendencies of politicians and bureaucrats.

Finally, it is worth noting that throughout the history of the equity market, natural evolutionary processes have always played a key role in influencing price trends. As dramatic events unfold, economic circumstances change, and technological advances come to the fore, there will always be companies and industries that will benefit from or lose out on the new developments. Moreover, in a world that is growing increasingly fast-paced and complex, it seems likely that investor perceptions about future prospects will be even more variable than they are now. Taken together, the reality is that much of the accepted wisdom about historical tendencies may fall by the wayside. In an era where sectors such as utilities have become riskier and more volatile, where beverage shares can act like growth stocks, and where the shares of the largest technology companies can trade like defensive holdings, nothing can be taken for granted.

Action Plan

One of the most important rules for any investor is to remain anchored in reality. In a world where many individuals prefer nonstop action over in-depth analysis, superficial appearances over hardcore substance, and conventional wisdom over contrarian thinking, it is easy to fall into the trap of believing that the stock market will carry on as before—or as the "majority" believes it will. Avoid the urge to substitute the word "should" for "may" or "will" for "could." While it is possible—maybe even probable—that events could turn out as expected or as before, the key to consistent long-term success is to remain alert to the possibility that they may not. In addition, when you make an investment decision, evaluate your choice in a real-time framework, not a hypothetical one. Although it is fun to dream about the future, when it comes to investing, it is foolhardy to fantasize about the present.

As in the world of sports, do not take your eye off the ball for too long when considering your next step—otherwise, errors will invariably crop up. It clearly makes sense to contemplate what the future may hold and weigh potential outcomes, particularly during the initial stages of the decision-making process. However, if you focus too much on where you see things headed, you may miss the critical fact of where they actually are at present. It may sound strange, but it does seem as though Mr. Market always "knows" when investors are not concentrating on current developments, and the result is often a financial disaster. Whatever happens, banish the urge to picture what you will do with the money "after" you have taken your profits. In fact, if you hear yourself thinking in those terms, it is usually a sure sign that you should immediately exit the position. Remember, while it is the results that ultimately matter, it is the concrete steps along the way that get you there.

Many investors spend an inordinate amount of time trying to minimize their tax liabilities. Although this perspective clearly has a bottom-line benefit, do not lose sight of the fact that it is successful investing that will ultimately make the need for this strategy a reality. Ironically, it seems that more often than not, if you attach too much importance to how much you will owe in capital gains taxes by taking your profits now, the market invariably finds a way of ensuring that you will not have to worry about that problem in the future. Again, as is the case with goals and anticipated outcomes, the reality is that if you spend too much time paying attention to anything other than what you have and what the prospects are as they stand at the current point in time, you may end up with little to show for your efforts.

If you get a sense that it is the right time to buy or sell equities, dissect that urge in detail. Is it based on popular opinion, or is there some other reason for the assessment? If it is not conventional wisdom, who is promoting the concept and what are their motivations? If you decide that the view may have substance, try to determine whether or not you may potentially be the last one on board—the greater fool—who will be buying from—or selling to—those who became aware of the trend at a relatively early juncture. Identify the source: Has it come from the mass media? One quick way to see if you are on to something important is to do a search of the Internet and investment newsgroups, using different combinations of keywords that give an appropriate context for determining whether others have been exploring the concept. Although it is not always easy to tell, of course, whether people have put their money where there mouths are, if you see a lot of relevant online chatter, that is often a good sign that many are already positioned that way.

Introspection is a valuable strategy when it comes to investing. When contemplating any decision to buy, sell, or hold, incorporate a regular reality check about the state of your mind and of your emotions. Ask yourself why you are looking to take whatever action you feel is necessary. Are you being influenced by your own free will or the pull of the crowd? Is there a compelling reason to do something now, or does it make sense to wait for more data? Once you have made your decisions, one of the biggest risks is losing sight of why you actually got involved in the first place. Engage in a regular review of your holdings, and ask yourself if it still makes sense to stick with what you have got. Do the fundamentals and technicals remain intact, or are you hanging on in hope? Could it be complacency, unrealistic expectations, or fear of losing money because the positions are underwater? If you stick with them for the wrong reasons, the market has a way of making you wish you had not done so.

Finally, if you are considering making purchases on margin, incorporate the full extent of the potential risk into the equation. This means taking account of the anticipated time frame as well as the prospective interest rate on your margin loan. Unlike unleveraged investments, there is an actual cash outlay that can seriously dent the economics of the whole concept if it takes too long to come to fruition. As with all investments, you should always factor in the prospective costs in terms of dealing spreads, slippage, and commissions—on both the way in and the way out—as well as what you may be giving up in terms of other opportunities. A six-month leveraged investment in a thinly traded security, for example, may entail a minimum absolute hurdle cost of 5 percent or more of the face value, with the possibility that a significant decline in value could trigger an unwelcome margin call.

CHAPTER 7

Imbalances and Upheavals

Aggressive approaches and tactics are leading to more unstable short-term imbalances.

In the physical world, there are self-correcting mechanisms at work that provide a natural offset to asymmetric and unsustainable growth. Whether referring to cell division in a developing organism or the ratio of predators to prey in a closed population of animals, all are governed by feedback loops that help to keep unhealthy excesses in check. Many counteract imbalances through chemical signals or similar means. Often, though, the limiting force is some sort of involuntary culling, such as mass starvation, that typically kicks in after substantial disparities have arisen. Indeed, systems can sometimes remain unsettled for a considerable period of time, or parities can shift far out of whack, before equilibrium is restored. Nonetheless, unless outside influences relieve the pressure, nature usually ends up bringing the situation squarely back into line.

When significant short-term imbalances develop in the share-trading arena, a similar sort of adjustment process takes place. Historically, such upheavals have been an occasional fact of life for investors. In recent years, however, the sharp corrections set in motion by "crowded trades" seem to be occurring more often than in the past. Moreover, when they do arise, they often appear suddenly and unravel with little warning. Part of the reason can be traced to the dramatic expansion and growing influence of the hedge fund sector, which uses aggressive tactics such as short-selling and leverage—up to 10 times capital in some instances, as Table 7.1 illustrates—to boost returns. Other contributing factors include the modern trading approaches many players rely on, as well as numerous technological developments. Combined, they are producing regular instances of overcrowding that frequently trigger, as in the animal kingdom, severe reactions and volatile conditions. Unfortunately, those who fail to take account of these new realities risk getting caught out by the spontaneous bloodletting.

Table 7.1 Typical Leverage Used in Different Hedge Fund Strategies (Source: Financial Risk Management)

	Gross Long[4]	Gross Short[4]	Net Exposure[4]	Typical Leverage
Security Selection[1,3]				
Long Bias	50–200	20–120	+40 to +80	1.5–2x
Short Bias	0–40	30–120	-40 to -100	0.5–1x
No Bias	50–150	50–150	+20 to -20	1.5–2x
Specialist Credit[2]				
Distressed Securities	80–120	0–20	+60 to +80	0.8–1.2x
Credit Trading	60–80	60–80	+20 to -20	1x
Relative Value[2]				
Arbitrage (Convertibles)	300–800	300–800	0	3–8x
Statistical Arbitrage	100–400	100–400	0	1–4x
Merger Arbitrage	80–200	80–200	0	1–2x
Arbitrage (Fixed Income)	500–2000	500–2000	0	10x
Directional Trading[2]				
Systematic Trading	300–800	300–800	+300 to -300	3–8x

1. Leverage is defined as the sum of long and short positions, divided by capital.
2. Leverage is defined as gross long positions, divided by capital.
3. Funds operating under U.S. "Reg T" have an effective maximum leverage of 1.8–1.9 times.
4. Figures are percentage of assets under management.

Generally speaking, stock markets have always been prone to temporary supply-and-demand imbalances, but certain influences have tended
to minimize the prospects. To begin with, it is worth noting that there are
a wide variety of players in the market, with different attitudes, styles,
expectations, and time frames. Some are passive in their approach, others
active. Most traders, for example, tend to seek consistent short-term
gains, while traditional investors usually focus on opportunities that can
generate significant long-term returns. Then there are the arbitrageurs,
who depend on systematic strategies; the contrarians, who bet against the
crowd; and the technicians, who follow the charts. The point is, individuals buy and sell for a number of reasons at different times, and even in
those instances where all the signs seem to point in only one direction, it
is relatively rare to discover that no one is willing to take the other side of
a trade.

One benefit of this diversity is that it often serves as a moderating
influence on prices, at least in the short term. In essence, market-makers,
arbitragers, and speculators who decide to sell—either an existing holding or one resulting from a newly created short position—help keep values relatively stable when new buyers enter the fray; when new sellers
appear, the opposite holds true. Regardless of whether they are looking to
take a quick profit, capitalize on fleeting inefficiencies, or place a temporary bet against prevailing levels, short-term countertraders' actions tend
to offset the potentially unsettling influence of fresh supply and demand.
Obviously, it is not possible for both sides to be correct, but for reasons
that have to do with transaction costs, trading styles, and investor psychology, most market participants will accept varying degrees of adverse
movement before they will consider throwing in the towel. Up until that
point, it is almost as if those on the "wrong" side of the trade enable those
on the "right" side to do their thing.

Occasionally, though, this offsetting activity creates a large measure
of pent-up supply or demand that, like the compressed air in an over-
stretched balloon, is unstable and susceptible to shock. Though it is hard
to say exactly why, natural complacency and a lack of transparency with
respect to overall speculative interest probably play a part. Regardless of
the reasons, when unexpected catalysts, or additional buying or selling,
tip the balance too far, it can unleash a burst of energy that triggers a one-
sided frenzy. Under those circumstances, the influence of the dominant
group expands significantly, forcing participants who are positioned
incorrectly—short-term countertraders, among others—to reconsider
their exposure. Invariably, many will cut and run, joining sides with those

who have, temporarily at least, gained the upper hand. Once that happens, the lopsided pressure overwhelms the routine two-way flow, setting off a sharp move in prices. Only when supply and demand are again back in balance does the market settle down.

Another factor that can lead to unsettling disparities is a relatively fast and concentrated push into or out of a stock, sector, or index, particularly when it involves the use of leverage or derivatives. In the past, technological limitations, institutional mores, and other factors associated with traditional investing approaches tended to foster price moves that, generally speaking, followed a slow and steady progression. In the case of a bullish trend, for example, the unfolding pattern would often originate from a point where certain insiders or astute investors had become aware of some potentially positive development on the horizon. As a result, this would usually lead some of them to take positions on board, and in the days and weeks that followed, they would gradually spread the word to others. After a while, there would be outward signs—such as a pickup in trading volume—that some sort of accumulation was taking place, which would help to draw in additional buyers. Over time, the continuing purchases would begin to put upward pressure on the share price.

Eventually, other operators, especially those who pay attention to technical factors, would pick up on the scent, and they, too, would do some nibbling. In the meanwhile, word would continue to spread through the market grapevine about the prospective news, and many fundamental investors would begin to sit up and take notice. Following that, the growing chatter and increase in activity would inspire even more players to jump on the bandwagon, adding to the momentum. All the while, the shares would grind higher, gradually at first and then at a faster pace. For the most part, any short-term imbalances that developed along the way would tend to dissipate naturally, especially during the early stages, as traditional investors would often lean towards passive acquisition strategies. Ultimately, the stock would reach its peak, as a range of buyers stepped in and the good news became largely discounted. Then, the pendulum would start to swing back in the other direction, and the next phase—a bearish cycle—would get underway.

Action Point

Many investors look at stock tables or focus on reported lists of the most active shares to get a sense of where the "real" action is. However, this can often be misleading, as securities that are members of an index or serve as trading vehicles for speculators will often have lofty turnover levels despite a lack of long-term investor interest or fundamentally driven developments. Sometimes there are valid reasons for the unusually high volume, of course, so it does not make sense to completely ignore the traditional signs. Nonetheless, for useful insights on which stocks are seeing a potentially significant pickup in activity, try zeroing in on those which are generating volumes greater than, say, their weekly or monthly averages. For useful screening tools, Web sites such as *http:// moneycentral.msn.com* and *www.incrediblecharts.com* can be a good place to start.

In the modern equity environment, however, the processes of accumulation and distribution often appear to evolve more rapidly and less smoothly than in the past. One result of this is that they frequently create sizeable short-term buildups that seem to overwhelm the ability of the markets to efficiently absorb the buying and selling pressure. Interestingly, in a market simulation that introduced narrow dealing spreads and increased participation by active traders—much like what has been seen in the U.S. share-trading arena in recent years—modelers saw evidence of heightened speculation and "the very distant beginnings of a bubble."[1] When these situations occur, it sets the stage for sudden and dramatic moves that can abruptly discharge the pressure. Although there are likely several factors behind recent developments, substantial improvements in communications networks have probably had a great deal to do with it. With fatter, more efficient voice and data pipes, as well as vast increases in the density of contacts between various participants, news travels far and wide in fairly short order. Even in those instances where intelligence is theoretically available only to a select group of individuals or at a significant cost, certain links in the modern connectivity matrix ensure that information flows freely over dealing desks and onto trading floors.

One explanation for this comes down to the fact that market intelligence has evolved as a valuable form of "currency" in the Information Age. Nowadays, analysts, hedge fund managers, reporters, and others are often swapping facts and figures to garner a variety of benefits. While such exchanges have, to a certain extent, always taken place, intense competition in the financial services arena since the Bubble burst seems to have boosted the relative value of high-impact data to a broad cross-section of interested parties. Moreover, the growing emphasis on active investing and short-term speculation has stirred a constant craving for up-to-the-minute insights. Whether they are seeking a trading edge, looking to attract client business, or attempting to promote an agenda—or, in the case of those who are doing the sharing, trying to create knowledge "reserves" that can be tapped at some later date—everyone seems to want in on the information action. What invariably happens, however, is that much of it—including the most exclusive insights on what people are saying and doing—ends up spilling into the vast electronic data pool, where it becomes readily accessible to all and sundry.

In fact, although the largest and most astute operators have retained some measure of the advantage they have always had in terms of early access to valuable intelligence, two relatively recent developments seem to have shrunk their lead-time edge and turned this spillage into something of a flood. First, a variety of modern operators are not only willing to discuss recent trades and strategies with prospective competitors, they seem much more aware than their conservative forebears of the positive impact such efforts can have on their bottom line. Ironically, while traders and hedge fund managers have a reputation for being close-mouthed with respect to proprietary methods and overall market exposure, many are nonetheless keen to share information that can serve a valuable marketing purpose or garner payback knowledge about what others are up to. Whether through instant messaging to peers, selective updates to reporters, or whispers to colleagues, sensitive data is constantly being pushed out into the marketplace—and ultimately into widespread circulation.

At the same time, it seems that many of those who are coming up with the intelligence to begin with are not averse to releasing details to the media and other parties with only minimal delay from when the data is sent out to subscribers or clients. Partly as a defensive measure—to control the flow of information that is leaking out anyway—and partly as a marketing strategy, numerous providers appear unwilling to keep even the most valuable information under wraps for too long in the current environment. The end result of all of this active dissemination on both sides is that potentially profitable investment ideas tend to race through the marketplace like wildfire. When that happens, a range of individuals—from established fund managers to short-term traders to hedge fund operators—are invariably drawn into trying to make money on the back of that knowledge. Even if they are hesitant about charging in, when confronted with worries about competition, performance, and other stresses, players frequently find themselves trapped in "informational cascades," where they essentially dismiss their reservations and trade along with the herd.[2] With today's efficient dealing technologies, that is, of course, as easily done as said.

Indeed, for many market players, the gap between assessing ideas and taking action has shrunk dramatically over recent years. A great deal of that change, as noted earlier, has to do with the impact that the alternative investment sector has had on equity investing. Generally speaking, the newer operators tend to have a different mindset than the traditional managers. They often adopt, for example, an aggressive and flexible posture when deciding on a course of action. They also seem more comfortable with risky maneuvers than established buy-siders, and are willing to use leverage, aggressive pyramiding, momentum trading, and other high-octane strategies to boost returns. Combined with the fact that they are usually evaluated on the basis of absolute, rather than relative, performance and tend to be measured over shorter time frames than their conservative counterparts, these players naturally gravitate towards opportunistic situations that offer near-term potential and major-league upside.

Action Point

Individual investors occasionally find it quite difficult or feel fairly frustrated when trying to compete in the same arena as sizable institutional operators, given the substantial resources and market intelligence those players have at their disposal. Rather than going head-to-head, however, why not look elsewhere? In other words, why not focus on sectors and shares where there is unlikely to be much competition from the pros, and where the possibility of inefficient mispricings is all that much greater. To identify such opportunities, try filtering out stocks that are index members, have relatively high daily turnover, or comprise part of an institutionally overweighted sector, such as financial shares. The stock screener sections of Web sites such as *http://moneycentral.msn.com* and *http://finance.yahoo.com* can be useful starting points. Bear in mind, of course, that securities that are less widely followed and more thinly traded can have their own unique set of risks.

Not surprisingly, heightened competition in the fund management industry and unsettled economic and market conditions in recent years have spurred some traditional managers to rethink their approaches and emulate, at least partly, those of their modern-day rivals. Rather than remaining wedded to the idea of analyzing opportunities over time and vetting them by way of regularly scheduled investment committee meetings, some established operators are trying to become more flexible and responsive to day-to-day flows and developments. In several instances, firms have streamlined certain internal structures, allowing details about block trading interests, for example, to be passed virtually straight through from sell-side dealers to buy-side managers. Then, when interesting situations arise, they look to assess the fundamentals on a fast-track basis and immediately decide whether to get involved and at what price. In the modern share-trading universe, many old-timers have accepted the premise that change is for the better in an ultracompetitive institutional marketplace.

New attitudes about equities in the wake of the post-Bubble malaise and a related decline in customer business have also spurred a sea change on the sell side of the industry. In order to make up for the contraction in commission revenues, many Wall Street firms have expanded their proprietary trading activities and adopted a more aggressive stance to market-making under certain circumstances. In essence, they appear to be moving away from the traditional agency brokerage model towards the principal-driven approach that is common in the foreign exchange and fixed-income markets. Moreover, because of their existing risk management and regulatory structures—and somewhat ironically, shareholder sensitivity to quarterly earnings variability—many have shifted in favor of short-term trading at the expense of long-term position-taking. Consequently, as has increasingly been the case with those on the buy side, they are emphasizing action over analysis and data points instead of data trends. With such a perspective, they, too, are quick to pounce on any interesting ideas that come wafting along. Indeed, across the investment spectrum, institutions are finding it easier to instantly analyze and react than ever before.

Along with an improved read on what is going on, increased flexibility, and a more active approach, market participants also seem willing to employ the full range of tactics and instruments available to them in the modern share-trading environment. Whether seeking to magnify returns through leverage, to capitalize on changes in volatility by trading derivatives, or to capture broad-based moves by buying and selling index-

related products, aggressive operators are looking to exploit market inefficiencies in ways that few would have even contemplated 10 years or so
ago. What is more, in many instances, the up-to-date approaches allow
players to quickly place concentrated bets without thinking twice, and the
depth of available liquidity in some newer instruments has tended to be
fairly large. With many participants also using options and futures as
compounding "kickers" for suddenly popular investment themes or as
leveraged proxies for less liquid securities, it seems as though the stage
has been set for even more short-term imbalances in the future.

One increasingly popular mechanism that also appears to be playing
a major role in stimulating unstable overcrowding—and the dramatic
upheavals that often follow—is short-selling. Widely adopted as a defensive measure in the wake of the post-Bubble collapse, this technique has
attracted a range of individual and institutional supporters in recent years,
many of whom have had little previous experience. Not surprisingly, the
tactic frequently serves as a means of betting on falling prices and as a
tool for hedging portfolios. However, short-selling is also used in the various market-neutral strategies that have been adopted by many hedge fund
managers, traders, and others in recent years, which are designed to capitalize on discrepancies in relative valuation, among other things. Regardless of how or why it is employed, though, short-selling has had a
pronounced effect on the supply-and-demand dynamics of the modern
equity marketplace. With unique attributes that some operators have not
thought through clearly, the tactic seems to have come to the fore in spurring unexpected price moves and spontaneous feeding frenzies.

In general, the short-seller's lair feels very much like a place that
Lewis Carroll might have had in mind if he had decided to write a story
about a bear trader instead of a little girl named Alice. At first glance, it
is a topsy-turvy world—one where up is down, rising prices are costly
and painful, and the grimmest of developments can trigger feelings of
elation and greed. Indeed, for outsiders, the process of wagering on failure can seem completely alien, and occasionally it appears as though
there is a sinister shadow cast over those who engage in the tactic. In
fact, history has often portrayed those who sell short as an unsavory lot,
prone to wearing black and talking in dark, cynical tones. Moreover,
when equity prices are falling—in individual shares or in the market as
a whole—those who capitalize on such trends have often found themselves labeled as convenient scapegoats. Rightly or wrongly, because
the approach has been known to cast an uncomfortably bright light on

foolishness and skullduggery, it has often triggered feelings of anger and resentment in those whose interests have been targeted.

Another reason why short-selling occasionally raises considerable ire pertains to its history. Going back many decades, when the regulatory regime was fairly light and financial markets were subject to a host of abuses by insiders and unsavory operators, it was relatively easy for determined short-sellers to create a panic through well-orchestrated bear raids. They did this by aggressively dumping shares onto the market, often on a "naked" basis—without borrowing them from existing owners first—and simultaneously spreading rumors that created fear and uncertainty among existing shareholders. In an environment where insiders and sharp operators usually became aware of negative developments well before they were made public, such attacks were often successful in triggering a downward spiral fed by the panic selling of weak longs. Although the introduction of "tick" rules and other regulatory measures that accompanied the Securities Exchange Act of 1934 helped to limit abuses going forward, the inherent fear of such ghoulish tactics has nevertheless lingered on.

To this day, there is a broad sense that short-sellers are often the first to know when things have gone wrong within a company. Partly because bear traders tend to be especially cynical types who usually view the glass as half empty, and partly because those who specialize in the technique tend to dig deep and look well below the surface when assessing how matters really stand, the ranks of those who favor the downside often have a considerable number of maverick operators—individuals who are willing to buck conventional wisdom and ignore the efforts of the stock-promoting crowd. Many noted short-sellers, for example, were the first to raise alarm bells about the fraud at Enron and were instrumental in bringing the company's various misdeeds to light. Nevertheless, for various reasons, the perspective of those who prefer being short generally remains at odds with the mentality of most equity players.

Action Point

If for no other reason, the practice of short-selling should be viewed as useful because it is a good way of getting over the common psychological hurdle that assumes rallies are "good" and selloffs are "bad." Historically, there has always been an ebb and flow to the financial markets, and the world at large does not necessarily seem the worse for wear because of it.

Generally speaking, keeping an open mind about the prospective path that any investment might follow in future, despite its apparent directional prospects at the outset, leads to a more balanced and practical analysis—the kind that tends to produce the most consistent and satisfying investment results in the long run. Although the compounding mathematics of bullish trends is compelling, it may not necessarily reflect the reality of the moment.

While it is not too difficult to understand the concept of benefiting from a decline in share prices, the actual mechanics of the process are not so easy to come to grips with. What is more, the decision to go long happens to square nicely with the natural optimism most individuals appear to be born with, which is not the case, of course, when it comes to short-selling. In general, the traditional bullish bias seems to satisfy a basic human belief that good times invariably lie ahead. And, whether they choose to dabble in stocks, real estate, precious metals, art, antique cars, or what have you, most people usually find themselves in a position where they stand to benefit most from an increase in values. In contrast, selling something one does not own with the idea of buying it back later at a lower price seems to violate all sorts of inalienable truths. It also seems to probe at an unfamiliar underbelly that few are really keen to explore in any great detail.

As it happens, it would be extremely difficult to undertake such an activity outside of the traded markets anyway because the process depends on having ready access to fungible, or easily interchangeable, substitutes that can be borrowed at relatively short notice. Trying to short a home or a car, for example, would almost certainly be an exercise in futility because it would require the short-seller to locate an owner willing to lend the identical asset for some reasonable period of time. In all likelihood, it would be next to impossible if the holder knew what the seller's actual intentions were. Indeed, it seems rather ironic that operators who take the bear tack in the share-trading arena depend, to a considerable extent, on the good will of bullish strangers who readily lend out their stock—for a fee, of course. Despite the seeming paradox, significant conflicts usually only develop after share prices have been under pressure for some significant period of time.

At first glance, selling short might seem to be the mirror opposite of going long. However, in practical terms, there is a world of difference between the two. Apart from issues noted earlier, there are inherent structural disparities and unique emotional pressures. When an operator establishes an outright short position—in other words, one that is not hedged with an equivalent derivative, convertible bond, or other security—it effectively alters the equilibrium of the marketplace. That is not the case when operators acquire shares held by others or liquidate positions they already have. In those instances, the counterparty's interests are simultaneously offset in an equal and opposing manner. After a short-sale, however, the net market exposure of both the bullish and bearish camps increases. As a result, this expands the universe of those who stand to benefit from a rally in prices, potentially solidifying a vested interest that may work against the seller.

There are practical considerations as well. For one thing, unless shareholders have bought stock using borrowed money and are faced with the prospect of a margin call, there is theoretically no market-related reason for them to liquidate their positions, even if the shares fall sharply or their interest becomes worthless. Of course, substantial losses might induce them to sell, but practically speaking, they cannot be compelled to do so unless the securities are collateral for another obligation. Apart from that, there seems to be a curious anomaly that comes into play when prices fall "too far." Because of what can be best described as a "lottery ticket" or option effect, many individuals routinely avoid selling stocks trading in the low single-digits, even if, for all practical purposes, they have no intrinsic worth. Whether out of hope, denial, or naïveté, they seem to discount the possibility of locking in the remaining value and instead hold out for the prospect that the shares might rebound and eventually produce a substantial gain. Similarly, it appears that many people would rather buy a security that has doubled than sell—or go short—one that has halved.

Short-sellers, on the other hand, face the ongoing prospect of having to unwind their positions at some point in the future, unless of course, they have targeted shares in a company that eventually goes out of business. That is because when they initiate the transaction, they borrow shares to deliver to the buyer that ultimately must be returned.[3] While it is conceivable that those who lent out the stock may never ask for it back, as a practical matter that is unlikely. Consequently, this introduces an element of time pressure that is not necessarily present in other circumstances. Moreover, if the seller has bet incorrectly, it opens up the possibility that the losing position may have to be bought back quickly to prevent losses from getting totally out of hand. Unlike long positions, which put holders at risk for the market value of the shares alone, short positions expose sellers to a substantially greater potential loss. This is because they usually must pay whatever the asking price is when it comes time to close out the transaction.

Another problem that short-sellers face is that they may have to unwind their positions prematurely because they can no longer borrow the shares or the cost of doing so becomes prohibitive. Indeed, this is frequently the case when overcrowding comes into play. It may also occur when certain shareholders withdraw their shares from the securities lending market in an attempt to make life difficult for the bears. Under those circumstances, short-sellers may be forced to act even if they believe it is totally the wrong thing to do. This is one reason—among others—why even the shares of bankrupt companies sometimes trade at levels that seem to make little sense. If the securities cannot be borrowed, short-sellers are out of luck. While such a development can occur for a number of reasons, it essentially reflects a supply-and-demand imbalance that weighs against keeping the exposure in place. In other words, high borrowing costs or limited availability usually signals that existing owners are unwilling to support the bears' efforts or that too many players are engaging in the same behavior.

There are a variety of factors that can influence the technical situation. First of all, the tactic depends on borrowed securities; as a practical matter, this can be affected by how much supply, or "float," is actually available. For tightly controlled and some thinly traded issues, the quantity of stock that is free to trade—potentially accessible, in other words—may be substantially less than the shares outstanding. This can happen, for example, when some proportion is tied up as collateral for a bank loan. Apart from that, availability is subject to the same forces of supply and demand that affect most markets. Hence, if there are already a large number of shorts in existence, it becomes more difficult to locate the shares. Some insights on this can usually be found in the monthly Short Interest statistics put out by the various exchanges. These reports detail not only the total number of shares sold short for each security, but also give the amounts relative to average daily volumes, otherwise known as the Short Interest Ratio. Expressed in terms of days, this figure describes, in theoretical terms, how long it would take to cover outstanding bear positions based on normal turnover patterns. The higher the value, the greater the risk short-sellers face of getting caught in a painful squeeze.

Action Point

Generally speaking, there are three prospective sources of supply that should, at a minimum, always be noted when analyzing investment opportunities: corporate executives, large shareholders, and the company itself. Arguably, in all three instances, it is possible that the transactions represent views on the overall market that may be as good or as bad as those of anyone else. In a powerful bull run, for example, where "the rising tide lifts all boats," even the most astute operators can often end up bailing out of sizable positions at relatively cheap levels. Nonetheless, despite apparent motives and public comments to the contrary, when those who should know best about a company's prospects—the "insiders"—decide it is time to raise cash, it is unlikely that they are doing so because they believe the stock is cheap. For more information on these sorts of transactions, check out Web sites such as *www.argusgroup.com,* *http://finance.lycos.com,* and *www.insiderscoop.com.*

While such statistics help to describe the scale of the activity taking place in the short-selling arena, they do not necessarily highlight how skewed the risk-reward profile can sometimes be against those who engage in the practice. To begin with, those who make such trades face the possibility of limited upside and unlimited downside. In other words, they can only benefit to the extent of any proceeds they receive from the original sale. Even if they get it perfectly right and target the shares of a company that eventually goes belly-up, the initial transaction price is the maximum they can realize for their efforts. However, if the position goes awry, the sky is the limit as far as their potential losses go. Of course, that is the worst-case scenario, but the mathematics can be quite daunting nonetheless. For example, if a stock is sold short at a price of $20, and it subsequently rallies to $41 without being bought back in the interim, the sellers face the prospect of losing more on the transaction than they could ever have hoped to have made if it had worked out perfectly.

In addition, unlike what happens when one is long a security, the more successful a short-sale transaction is, the less benefit each interim percentage increase brings to the seller's bottom line. To use a simple example, if a $50 stock rallies 20 percent in the first year and records a similar gain in the following period, it will be trading at $72. That is an absolute return of 44 percent for the existing shareholder based on the $50 starting price, excluding any dividends paid. If, on the other hand, the value falls by 20 percent in both year one and year two, a short-seller's overall gain will be 36 percent. In the latter case, the amount may vary depending on whether the seller receives interest on the cash generated by the original sale, less any stock-lending fees or dividends reimbursed to the owner of the shares while they are out on loan. Although the strategies can make sense if attractive opportunities with near-term downside potential are identified, the asymmetric economics of short-selling adds a further element of time pressure.

Apart from technical issues, another reason why selling short can be so treacherous is because many of the companies that are targeted turn out to be those with stock valuations that depend more on assumptions and expectations than historical performance and hard data. As a consequence, these securities, which are often constituents of volatile sectors such as technology, tend to be more prone to delusion, excessive optimism, and manipulation than those whose prospects have been more clearly identified. Under those circumstances, there is usually a strong emotional component as well, and the attitudes of those with a positive vested interest tend to be hard to shake with logic alone. Often, such situations represent the epitome of what economist John Maynard Keynes referred to when he noted that, "markets can remain irrational longer than you can remain solvent." And because many supporters, promoters, and insiders tend to be vociferous advocates of the "cause," short-sellers sometimes stir up great feelings of animosity, which can lead to an aggressive backlash, such as a publicly orchestrated bear squeeze.

Nevertheless, as Figure 7.1 appears to indicate, the number of operators who employ the tactic has increased in recent years, despite the obstacles. One reason, as mentioned, is that the substantial growth of the alternative investment sector has been matched by a parallel expansion of interest in market-neutral, arbitrage, and relative value strategies, which often involve some element of short-selling. Another explanation is the fact that spectacular frauds like Enron emboldened many bear traders, giving credence to the view that even the largest companies can turn out to be a house of cards. In addition, relatively high valuations since the Bubble burst have induced many practitioners to stick with the tactic, reassured by the view that PE multiples would eventually revert back towards historical averages. No doubt the results achieved by short-sellers in the wake of the post-2000 collapse have also contributed to a reluc-

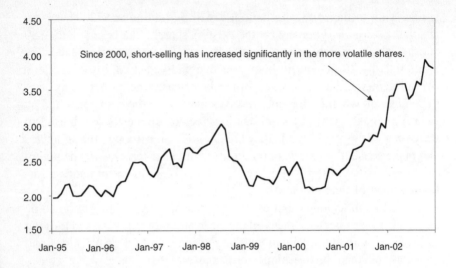

Figure 7.1   NASDAQ Value-Weighted Short Interest Ratio (Source: Owen A. Lamont, Yale University; John M. Griffin, University of Texas; NASDAQ).

tance to give up the bearish ghost. However, with a similar sort of determination seemingly evident in the bull camp—where dreams of a return to the go-go days often seem to crop up—attitudes on both sides appear to be hardening. This has fostered an emotional tension that can quickly come to a boil.

As noted earlier, helping to compound the recurring problem of crowded trades is the increased use of leverage by both sides, along with the influx of relatively inexperienced operators to the short-term trading game. Generally speaking, modern trading tactics and investing approaches seem to include much less margin for error than the conservative strategies of old. Combined with greater use of automatic risk-control measures, such as stop-loss orders and rapid position-cutting, often all it takes to set off a short-term stampede is a mildly unexpected catalyst, a slight shift in prices, or a sudden awareness about the true extent of a lopsided speculative interest. Once that happens, the consequences can be dramatic. Sometimes, in fact, the upheavals can trigger moves that grow legs and develop into something much larger than a temporary correction.

Even in those instances where short positions seem to be matched up against comparable or equivalent longs, creating a theoretically neutral market exposure, current dynamics sometimes foster a large measure of what can be labeled as "basis" risk, or an unevenness in relative price swings that turns out to be somewhat asymmetric—that is, more extreme on the upside. What happens under those circumstances is, during a broad market rally, shares with a relatively large short interest tend to rise at an accelerated pace compared to those with somewhat less exposure. As a result, operators may be forced—for risk control purposes, if nothing else—to unwind arbitrage trades before they have had a chance to pan out, adding further fuel to the fire. Arguably, the increased use of automated trading methods and simplistic statistical models may be playing a part, as strategies are put in place that do not take full account of stress-related irrationality.

Action Point

It almost always makes sense to keep an eye on short interest, particularly when it is high relative to the number of shares outstanding or, better yet, the available float. As with any indicator, though, it is important to look at it in the context of other data before drawing any definitive conclusions. It may, for example, represent a near-term technical situation related to derivative hedging or takeover arbitrage that has little relevance for longer-term investors. Of course, it may also be highlighting the fact that there is a significant degree of bearishness associated with the stock. If the latter applies, try to explore the rationale of the short-sellers in greater detail before wading in with a buy order. Following that, if the investment arguments still seem compelling and all of the bases have been covered, then the pent-up demand can offer a powerful additional incentive to get involved. For more information on the statistics associated with specific shares, head to *www.nasdaq.com* or *www.nyse.com*.

In the modern share-trading environment, there is a broader range of avenues available to prospective short-sellers than in previous decades. In fact, many are easier to put into effect and require less processing than is necessary when targeting individual shares. Selling index futures short or buying put options, for example, does not require securities to be borrowed beforehand, and neither tactic depends on having a certain price tick go through before orders can be executed. The same holds true for exchange-traded funds. In addition, there are other products that allow individuals and institutions to wager on the downside, even when the methods just described are not permitted or are otherwise unavailable. Mutual fund groups such as Rydex Funds and ProFunds, for example, offer products that are inversely linked to the performance of major U.S. indices, while portfolio managers overseeing investments at the Prudent Bear Fund are permitted to engage in significant short-selling. Overall, market participants have more reasons, more ways, and more willingness to go short than in earlier decades.

One result of this development has been a change in the relative balance of longs and shorts in the marketplace. What is more, instead of being associated with certain market conditions or being used mainly in isolated circumstances, the practice is being employed on a more frequent, widespread, and sustained basis. Consequently, the overall dynamic of the equity market has been considerably altered, which has, in turn, fostered an undercurrent of time pressure, a rise in underlying emotional intensity, and an element of uncertainty that readily spurs a quick build-up of unstable market electricity. At the same time, with more players adopting an active investing approach, engaging in a strategic swapping of intelligence, and relying on aggressive tactics such as leverage and pyramiding, short-term imbalances can quickly develop. Taken together, the combination seems to be facilitating an environment where events can unfold quickly and just as quickly reverse course, often with little or no warning.

In fact, occasionally all it takes to set off an upheaval is something innocuous. For example, sometimes the "trigger"—following a sharp decline that has been accompanied by significant short-selling—is a minor oasis of steady prices and light volume. Once that happens, it seems that the time pressure effect begins to weigh on the bears, and fleeting worries start to crop up that the worst may be over. Consequently, a few nervous operators will begin to do some buying, gently pressuring prices, and before long, the shares are ripping higher for no apparent reason. Similarly, sudden gaps in available liquidity can also prompt mini-stampedes where there has been a recent pickup in speculative interest on either the long or short side. Again, a few players will be looking to pare down their exposure, and they will enter fairly nondescript orders to buy or sell stock. Their interests, however, will be just enough to prick a temporary air pocket that unsettles prices and causes others to pounce on the action. By then, the spontaneous momentum will start to gain pace, and those who had piled in during the preceding trend will become quickly unnerved by the countermove. Suddenly, what began as minor profit-taking will degenerate into a wholesale rush for the exits.

This effect seems to be particularly pronounced at selected times of the year, as well as during certain days of the week or hours of the day. During December, for example, there are often occasions, especially in the latter half of the month, when a small flurry of orders can set off a round of "pass the parcel," as market-makers and others look to keep positions and overall exposure at a minimum going into year end. The same holds true around certain holidays, such as Independence Day, Thanksgiving, Christmas, and Easter, when volumes naturally tend to dry up and illiquidity increases, especially when the holiday occurs just before or after a weekend. There have also been occasions in recent years when quiet, relatively low-volume midday share-trading activity has been punctuated by sharp short-term swings, as various traders and speculators exaggerate the impact of incoming flows. Under these kinds of circumstances, players with significant exposure, tight stops, and itchy trigger fingers can end up overreacting to what is essentially noise.

Of course, sometimes an actual catalyst, such as a profit-warning or positive earnings surprise, will set the upheaval in motion, but even then, the event may not necessarily be as dramatic as the turmoil unleashed when an unstable technical imbalance exists. Undoubtedly, the contagion effect that seems more evident nowadays can sometimes make matters worse, as well as the emotion stirred up by fear that others may have better insights into what is going on. It does seem that, more often than not, when crowded longs or shorts unravel, the situation is much like that of the old Roadrunner cartoons, when the coyote, seemingly hovering on air after running too far out over the edge of the cliff, takes a look down and discovers how precarious his situation is. At that point, the bottom suddenly drops out, and the poor creature crashes to the ground. For players who have rushed into a short-term speculation without first looking around, similar sentiments can sometimes arise when they begin to notice all the company they have.

Interestingly enough, even the minor stampedes call to mind a recurring reality of the financial markets, one that is similar to the problem that failed hedge fund Long Term Capital Management faced when it was confronted with unexpectedly large moves in some of its "hedged" portfolio holdings. What sometimes occurs, and what many analytical models do not necessarily take full account of, is that in times of market stress—even on a relatively minor basis during the course of a trading session—liquidity can sometimes dry up as a panic response takes over, spurring those who would normally buy dips or sell rallies to back off. In other words, when the emotional balance is tipped too far, normal relationships reverse—at least temporarily—and higher prices can drive sellers to the sidelines while lower prices can frighten away buyers. Although relatively rare on a broad scale, such circumstances could become more common-place in a world where unstable situations increasingly crop up and where the emotional intensity can surge with little warning.

One additional point worth noting is that because increased short-selling has probably played a role in eliminating many market inefficien-cies, competitive forces seem to have induced some bearish practitioners to veer off into riskier territory. They, like their counterparts on the long side, appear to be anticipating outcomes sooner, taking more directional bets, and operating with larger sizes than they might have been comfort-able with previously. Arguably, these efforts, along with the more wide-spread increase in short-selling that has taken place in recent years, were probably significant contributing factors in the sharp rally that began in March 2003 on the heels of the U.S.-led invasion of Iraq. As *The New York Times* noted in September 2003, in a story headlined, "Bull Market 2003: The Worse the Company, the Better the Stock,"[4] the shares that per-formed best during the year were those that had the weakest fundamen-tals. While there may have been any number of reasons why, the one thing that many of the outperformers had in common, as suggested in Figure 7.2, was a significant level of short interest.

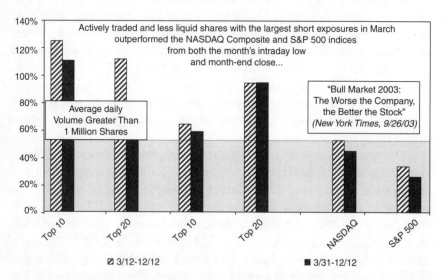

Figure 7.2   Performance of Shares with the Highest Short Interest Ratio in the Wake of the March 2003 "War Rally" (Source: *www.trading-deas.com, www. bigcharts.com*).

Overall, of course, there are still far more operators who play the long side than the short side, which is likely to be the case no matter what happens in the future. Nonetheless, whichever way they operate, it seems that rapid information flows, continuing advances in technology, a shift towards shorter time frames, a preference for a more active investing approach, and a flurry of competitive forces will induce greater numbers to pile in to positions when potentially profitable opportunities arise. Under such circumstances, the prospects for further unsettling imbalances—and the sudden upheavals that follow—are likely to increase.

Action Plan

If a stock appears to be trading out of synch—repeatedly underperforming expectations despite a string of positive developments, regularly rallying on days when most other shares are lower, suddenly becoming active during sessions when the overall market is sluggish and all is relatively quiet on the news front—that can often be a sign of a crowded trade. Under those circumstances, the stock is likely to remain overshadowed by short-term supply-and-demand considerations until at least some measure of the imbalance has dissipated. Such a situation can present an excellent opportunity for patient long-term investors who are comfortable with their assessment of what the security is worth to accumulate a position at unexpectedly advantageous prices. For those with shorter investment horizons, however, the frustrations associated with such quirky and unsettling moves probably means it is better to focus on other possibilities.

While it is not always obvious, of course, one general rule of thumb you should keep in mind when exploring investment alternatives is to try and get a sense of how a security or sector—or even the overall market—responds to what appears to be unexpected information. If shares rally on seemingly bad news or sell off on apparently positive developments, that frequently indicates the data is more or less in the price. For investors, that would also seem to imply that perhaps it makes sense to discount those particular facts and focus on other issues. However, if a security or index seems to react both ways during a relatively short period of time, that sort of schizophrenic price action is often a sign that unstable technical forces are distorting the picture. If so, you should be especially wary about drawing too many conclusions from near-term trading patterns.

Short-selling is a useful tool, but it is not for everybody. For a start, it usually requires a financial relationship that is a bit more complicated than a straightforward share purchase in a cash brokerage account. More important than that, though, are the mental attributes that are required. Do you have the nerve, the discipline, and the resolve to employ this particular technique? For many investors, it seems that their scariest inner fears become magnified when they have a short position on. Maybe this is because it runs counter to intuition or stirs up some sort of vague sense of right and wrong. Whatever the reasons, if you are unable to keep a strong grip on your emotions, then short-selling is probably not an appropriate strategy to consider. Of course, as in all investing approaches, it is crucial that you do whatever is necessary to rein in unhelpful emotions that can unduly influence rational decision-making.

Again, if you decide to adopt the practice, it usually requires a bit more specialized due diligence and planning than some other strategies. In the case of individual shares, for example, arrangements must be made in advance to borrow the stock. If it turns out to be difficult or costly, that can send a message in itself. Along with a high short interest ratio, it is frequently a sign that many other market players have had the same idea. Unfortunately, history suggests that when it comes to the bear tack in particular, the more company you have, the riskier the proposition. Keep in mind as well that the economics of short-selling are not all that favorable. Some brokerage accounts, for example, do not pay interest on the credit balances generated from the original sale, even though they might assess a fee for lending you the securities. On top of that, the short-seller is responsible for reimbursing the owner of the shares for any dividends that are distributed during the period.

Another alternative, of course, is to use derivatives to accomplish your goals. Again, it depends on your tolerance for risk, your understanding of how markets work, and your available resources to determine whether or not this is a viable alternative. Although there may be a number of instruments that can do the trick, remember that each has its own advantages and drawbacks. For example, what a put option gives you in terms of flexibility and a relatively low up-front cost is sometimes more than offset by timing risk and the magnitude of the move in the underlying security that is required in order to break even. And, as far as shorting naked options goes, that can be an extremely risky maneuver that is best left to those who do it for a living. However, one somewhat conservative approach that some investors use is covered call writing. This involves a short sale of an option against a long position in the underlying stock, to generate extra income. The risk, of course, is that if the market rallies, the stock may be "called away." In any case, whatever you do, make sure you engage in substantial due diligence beforehand, and choose a strategy that is appropriate for your individual circumstances.

CHAPTER 8

Form and Fantasy

*Substance and reality increasingly give
way to form and fantasy.*

The stock market is something of a paradox. On the one hand, it is a place where numbers rule, where people generally know where they stand, and where the consequences of poor decision-making can be financially devastating. On the other hand, it is a world where dreams can seem real, where emotions can overshadow rationality, and where those who can talk—or trade, if Figure 8.1 is any guide—often have more influence than those who can think. Although this bipolar reality has long been a feature of the share-trading arena, the Bubble years seemed to have been both a trigger for and a reflection of a general shift in favor of the chimerical. In many respects, that period brought out the worst of irrational behavior, with some excesses still lingering despite the devastating bear market that followed. Indeed, though much of the speculative froth now appears almost surreal in hindsight, many players nonetheless seem quick to suspend judgment and assume those days can return again. Sadly, investors who fail to take account of today's flights of fancy risk getting caught out when the pieces come tumbling to the ground.

One of the reasons why such dichotomies exist at all has to do with the fact that there are, in reality, relatively few absolutes with respect to equity investing. Take the concept of value. To a great extent value is what

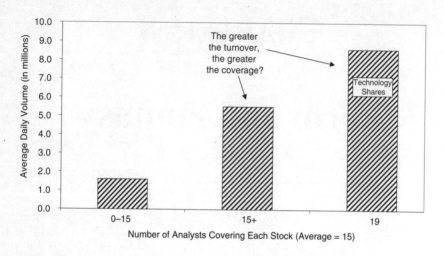

Figure 8.1 S&P 500 Index Analyst Coverage Relative to Average Daily Volume (Source: *The Wall Street Journal*, Reuters Research).

people say and believe it is. Investors could credibly argue, for example, that a stock with a price-earnings ratio[1]—or PE—of 18, the 40-year median for the S&P 500 Index, is either cheap or expensive, depending on a variety of often conflicting factors. These could include the multiples of other similar shares or the market as a whole, the "quality" of the earnings, the time of the year when the reference price is chosen, whether the number is based on historical or estimated data, and so on and so forth. While classic Graham and Dodd[2] analysis has attempted to categorize what "real" value is in some sort of objective sense, at the end of the day it remains largely a matter of opinion. The one exception—though some might disagree—is that value is what investors would willingly pay for an asset at a given point in time.

Another reason why the stock market can often seem like many things to many people has to do with the richness of human language—in both its spoken and written form—and the fact that brevity is often viewed as a necessary evil when it comes to discussing the intricacies of the share-trading arena. For example, if a group of individuals were to argue that they are "bullish," it would seem on the surface that they were looking for prices to move higher. However, that may not necessarily be enough detail, especially given the democratization process that has taken place in recent years, when millions of people from within the U.S. and around the globe became involved in equity investing in one form or another. Depending upon their perspectives, they could be talking about today or three months from now, they could be referring to the universe of stocks they follow or the market overall, they could be speaking in terms of either absolute or relative performance, or they could be noting the fact that they are invested and are therefore hopeful that prices will rise. It is not so easy to get the precise meaning under those circumstances.

Listeners' perspectives can also play a role in muddling meanings. In the case of the statement above, they might "hear" all sorts of things. Some might interpret the utterance at face value and assume that it represents a collective point of view—and nothing more. Many professionals take it for granted, however, that what people say usually reflects their actions or their intentions. In other words, if they are positive on X, they most likely have a position in the shares of X. Or, the language reflects a desire that will ultimately be translated into action. Optimists might conclude that if that crowd is positive, maybe they should be too. Pessimists might try to look through the statement, assessing whether it reflects a scheme to draw in "fresh blood" to boost demand—and hence the price— or to serve as greater fools upon whom the group's shares could be unloaded. Contrarians might interpret such views as a sign that too many are long and nobody is left to buy. Whatever the case, the language of the market has many subtle shades that are not always apparent.

Action Point

The English language is rich and varied, and it usually makes for more interesting reading when writers and speakers introduce an element of variety into the text. However, in the investment world, substitution of terms and concepts can also serve as a way of changing the basis and painting a picture that does not accurately reflect reality as a reasonable person would understand it. If brokers or analysts use a certain standard of measurement to define value—operating earnings growth, for example—ask whether there are other valid barometers that might be less supportive of their stated point of view. If forward earnings are the focus, is that because past results do not give as great an impression? If sector comparisons are used, what happens when other benchmarks are substituted? Generally speaking, try to get an accurate definition of the terminology as well as their reasons for using it.

The curious thing is, while most people have tried to take account of this complexity through the years by assuming that the world is better described in shades of gray than black and white, the Information Age seems to have created a conflict. In a world where much data is digitized or has otherwise been made to conform to a relatively rigid framework, modern developments have often fostered a structural preference for concise concepts and single points of reference. This seems especially true in the financial markets, where earnings estimates, for example—which might encompass the views of 15 or more analysts—are regularly distilled down to a single average for reporting and comparison purposes. Admittedly, the variations in this particular series tend to be relatively small, but in many instances the spread of opinions about all sorts of fundamental measures ends up as one number. This has been helped along, no doubt, by the shift towards a more active investing approach—with its emphasis on trading catalysts—as well as a growing preference for simplicity among numerous market participants nowadays.

Ironically, while some might have argued that the transformation would lead to more consistency of opinion and a greater understanding of fundamental conditions across the investment spectrum, in fact, it often seems to produce the opposite effect. By allowing nuance and diversity to fall by the wayside, expectations now revolve around focal points that provide little in terms of overview, but create a powerful discharge when the relevant data is released. As a consequence, there seems to be less reason and more emotion flowing through the market on a regular basis, causing confusion rather than clarity. The noise makes it difficult for even disciplined long-term investors to sort though the chaos and determine what is actually going on. What is more, while there has always been an element of variability with respect to which indicators are in fashion and which are out of favor—usually depending on current economic conditions or political concerns—it seems that shifts now occur more randomly and frequently than they once did, as literal significance becomes secondary to catalytic value.

As it happens, the Bubble years did seem to set the stage for a rise in the emotional state of the share-trading arena as compared to prior decades. While there were any number of factors behind the increase, the fact that many unsophisticated players with little clear understanding of market dynamics were drawn in was certainly important, as was the fallout from the breathtaking run that had even seasoned professionals projecting explosive growth going forward. However, once prices peaked, rather than declining in strength, the energy seemed to be refocused by the changing conditions. Nowadays, the current tends to pulse in synch with the ebb and flow of data to a greater degree than before. While the overall level of emotional intensity seemed higher during the go-go era, the peaks and valleys appear more extreme under current circumstances. In many ways, this seems to have exacerbated the behavioral foibles of many market participants, making it harder to gather a balanced and consistent assessment of what is going on.

Generally speaking, all people have some sort of individualized view about how the world works and which particular factors are the most relevant. They tend to base their understanding on the knowledge they have gained through education and experience, as well as that acquired through the words and actions of others. Because of variations in genetic makeup and the fact that each person's pattern of development is fairly unique, this can often lead to differences of opinion about what even simple concepts mean. At worst, it can provoke the sort of reasoning put forth by former President Bill Clinton during testimony about his relationship with a White House intern while he was still in office. That is when, in response to a pointed question from a grand jury interrogator, he answered, "It depends on what your definition of 'is' is."

Along with this personalized world view, most individuals seem to be influenced in one way or another by idiosyncrasies that appear to be a common element of the human condition. In general, people are prone to all sorts of subconscious filtering mechanisms that automatically sift and evaluate information in various ways. These processes, some of which have been labeled as behavioral biases, probably developed in our primal ancestors as a means of creating order out of life's chaos. It seems a good bet, in fact, that many evolved as hardwired strategies designed to help early humans react quickly and appropriately to the dangers of an uncertain and often terrifying world. As is generally the case with respect to influences of the inner mind, though, these responses can vary considerably from one person to the next. Nonetheless, despite the individual differences, when it comes to investing, they often provoke actions, reactions, and interpretations that can negatively affect anyone's performance.

A few of the more common susceptibilities—identified by behavioral finance experts—that can lead to poor investment decision-making include anchoring, availability bias, and confirmation bias. Anchoring describes a phenomenon whereby people base current views on some previously linked—though not necessarily relevant—measure. One example is when investors make the argument that a stock is "cheap" because it is trading at half of its peak price. Never mind that traditional valuation methods might indicate that the shares are still extremely expensive. Availability bias reflects an over-reliance on facts that are readily accessible or that come easily to mind, as when individuals decide not to invest in a particular company because the last time they did it turned out to be a disaster. The third type of behavior, confirmation bias, is one that many share traders have probably experienced—that is, buying a stock and then keeping an eye out for only those facts which justify the decision.

Action Point

Few investors are fortunate enough to be unaffected by the sorts of biases that can turn good investment decision-making into bad judgment. Many will be tempted, for example, to rely on what is already known or immediately available to make their financial choices, regardless of whether or not that information accurately reflects the true picture. And, once they decide on a particular option, they will repeatedly be drawn towards data that will confirm that the appropriate option has been selected. To offset these natural urges, establish a routine that requires information to be gathered from a wide variety of different sources, both before and after selections are made. Under these circumstances, even the strongest counterarguments will often provide a useful measure of insight and validation.

Sometimes the distorting tendencies only crop up under certain conditions, influenced, perhaps, by short-term market developments, temporary mood swings, or transient attitudes. One way of looking at it is to use the water-filled glass analogy. For some individuals, their perspective always leans in a particular direction—whether half-empty or half-full—when interpreting information and events. In those instances, it usually takes a dramatic change in the amount of liquid to transform their view. For others, their perspectives might shift randomly or rhythmically, or as a result of subtleties that are not apparent at first glance. For many people, though, such factors as changes in climate, feelings about personal relationships, attitudes about work, or a variety of other issues can set the tone, and as a result, the state of the glass can vary considerably. On the first frosty day of winter, for example, it is not uncommon to see New

York–based traders automatically bidding up the price of energy shares, despite the fact that a single low-temperature reading may not necessarily signal that a harsh winter—and higher oil prices—lies ahead.

Occasionally, another sort of filtering process takes place—one that is subject to more of a conscious influence, though not necessarily twisted by intent. This is the case when individuals, their perspectives distorted by either attitudes or emotions, choose to view information through rose-colored glasses. Cognitive dissonance is one such variation. In essence, people will be aware of information on one level that is at odds with their established view of things, but they will mentally override the conflicting data. Generally speaking, they either rationalize the divergence away or they repress unsupportive details through some form of denial. In either case, despite what appears to be an element of willfulness, it seems to be more an issue of self-deception than one directed at others. Arguably, many investors probably suffered from such contortions when they accepted the premise that technology stocks could keep rising forever during the Bubble years.

The last category of distortions, which can be a particularly danger-ous circumstance for investors, are those that involve some element of deliberate deception. In other words, there is a clear intent to influence others, either by expressing views that are false or misleading or by taking actions with the sole intention of inducing others to respond in a certain way. While some ploys are harmless—giving your spouse a kiss in the hope that he or she will take out the garbage, for example, is unlikely to raise serious alarm bells—many times they cause people to do things they might have avoided in the absence of the deceit. This approach can involve all sorts of manipulative tricks, running the gamut from withhold-ing relevant information to the production of wholly fabricated evidence. Whether or not malice is involved, when it comes to the investment world, such efforts can make for a potentially unhealthy relationship. As it happens, though, one factor that often plays a pivotal role is the rewards involved.

Incentives exert a powerful influence on behavior. The classic exam-ples of this, of course, are experiments where animals are trained using food to produce a variety of responses. While it is a bit of a stretch to say that humans react like dogs that salivate when a bell is rung or like rats that know how to push a bar to make a pellet drop, there is nonetheless some element of truth to the idea. Researchers have long noted, in fact, the persistent human urge to satisfy a variety of needs, and whether it involves basic necessities, love, recognition, or some other craving, people tend to learn fairly quickly what steps they must take to fill the void. Sometimes, of course, individuals do not really know what they want, or if they do, they discover that there are no easy solutions. Alternatively, they may choose to satisfy one need at the expense of another. Regardless, most usually have some sense of what it is they must do to gain a measure of satisfaction, whether in their personal relationships, social lives, or working environment. Not surprisingly, for those who are employed in the financial services industry, the same usually holds true with respect to what it takes to get by.

Although it is not quite as simple as it sounds—after all, humans are more complex creatures than rats—the relatively generous compensation practices of the sector, as well as the above-average bonus-to-salary ratio—especially for those who are "producers"—has traditionally defined a fairly straightforward relationship between what people do and how they get paid for it. Even in those instances where a discretionary element is involved, the economics have generally been uncomplicated. Of course, this is not confined to the investment world—it is a common feature of nearly all sales-oriented cultures. In fact, it is probably safe to say that the concept of directly linked financial incentives is at the heart of what makes business and the economy tick, and is possibly a key reason why capitalism seems to work reasonably well. Under such a system, people tend to focus on what they do best and seek out situations where they will be rewarded for doing it. In hypothetical terms, at least, everyone stands to benefit.

Action Point

There are two questions one should never forget to ask when contemplating a financial decision or relationship. The first is: "What's in it for me?" More important, perhaps, is the second question: "What's in it for you?" In either case, if there is no financial gain or other stated concrete benefit, it may be time to stand back and reassess the situation. If investors are acting for the wrong reasons—out of boredom, for example, or to satisfy a speculative urge—that is almost certainly grounds for immediately stopping what they are doing. If others are disguising their true motives or are claiming to be operating on the basis of altruism alone, it is likely that they are not being totally upfront about their intentions. If that is the case, how great can whatever it is they are offering turn out to be?

Of course, it is the specific structure of the incentive system that tends to matter most in influencing day-to-day behavior. If employees are rewarded for bringing in revenue, then that is where they will direct their efforts. Although people have widely varying skills, standards, motivations, and circumstances, most will nevertheless share a natural tendency towards focusing on the important parameters at the expense of others. What that means is, at worst, they may end up bringing in low-quality business that is relatively unprofitable. Alternatively, if individuals stand to benefit from their cost-cutting efforts, then that is what will drive them, even if, at its silliest extreme, it means slashing overhead to zero and turning away new customers. Finally, if they are evaluated on the basis of production, than that will be their mantra, regardless of whether there are any buyers in sight. Indeed, that was frequently the way things evolved in the centrally planned economies of the old communist regimes, where factories often cranked out mountainous stockpiles of goods that nobody really wanted.

For most of those who work in the securities industry, there has usually been relatively little doubt about goals and incentives. The research community, however, has always been in sort of a quandary in this respect. A few decades ago, when commission rates were relatively high and Wall Street firms were largely focused on agency business, analysts produced research tailored to the needs of long-term investors. In general, they were rewarded on the basis of track records or qualitative surveys. Then, when brokerage houses evolved into multiproduct behemoths and the various new issue booms came along, many were drawn into the investment banking side—pulled over the Chinese wall,[3] so to speak. As a result, they started getting compensated according to how effective they were at creating IPO demand and bringing in new corporate clients. Finally, when the Bubble burst and the scandals erupted over research practices, analysts once again shifted their focus. This time, their efforts were directed at the increasingly influential hedge fund sector, and their pay often became linked to how much turnover they generated.

At each stage, they were under the gun to produce what was expected or risk not getting paid—or worse. What made it all the more challenging, of course, was that because of the various businesses their employers were involved in, they often had to wear many hats. Under these circum-

198 — The New Laws of the Stock Market Jungle

stances, some were not even sure whether they were coming or going. On top of all the internal demands, analysts faced a wide assortment of other strains, too. For example, because of the influence and visibility they have had within the investment community, they, more than most, were constantly faced with having to conform to any number of expectations. While there are various reasons why, peer pressure certainly played a major role. To be sure, many people have an innate fear of being singled out, especially if it is for the wrong reasons, and the siren song of the crowd can be very comforting. What makes the problem worse for analysts, however, is the fact that their thoughts frequently end up on public and permanent display, leaving them especially vulnerable to scorn and ridicule. Given that, many have been quick to fall back on the premise that there is safety in numbers.

Indeed, it is not really all that surprising that so many eventually went along with some of the absurd pronouncements of the Bubble years. While they may have believed on one level that things had gotten crazy, it was difficult for anyone to stand pat against the tidal wave of money that poured into the market, especially when they were being told to toe the line—and were reaping financial rewards from it to boot. On top of that, many analysts were confronted by additional pressures that had them constantly walking on eggshells. For example, if they were too negative, they risked being cut off or cold-shouldered by the senior executives of the companies they covered; if they were too positive, they faced the prospect of being totally marginalized in the investment community. Consequently, many adopted euphemistic language, relativistic comparisons, and multitiered analysis as a sort of defensive measure. Unfortunately, as with the opening of Pandora's Box, these distortions tended to give rise to a host of others.

Action Point

For all its benefits, one of the dangers of a measured and rational approach to investing is that it invariably inspires the formulation of a hypothesis, which can sometimes trigger a subconscious attempt to make the data fit the model. While it is difficult—and, in fact, probably unwise—to avoid having any preconceived notions about how the investment world works, it usually makes sense to ask "What if?" questions all along the way to avoid giving weight to dubious and financially precarious assumptions. Moreover, if the odds of a

"worst case" scenario are small, avoid the natural urge to eliminate that possibility from the range of options. It is exceed-
ingly rare to discover investment choices where exceptional
returns can be achieved without risk; to believe otherwise
because it is consistent with a streamlined view of things can
be a recipe for disaster.

Modern day research is filled with caveats that make it hard to know
where people really stand. However, what has made it worse is the fact
that regulatory constraints, competitive pressures, and internal cross-
currents have put analysts in a position where they must either say many
different things to many different people or use methods of evaluation that
are, to a great extent, dependent on shaky foundations or relationships
outside the researcher's control. In the first instance, what has evolved in
recent years is the use of various types of formal and informal communications to convey different messages. Often the written research reports
represent the watered-down versions of what analysts are thinking, especially in the case of those that are targeted to both individual and institutional investors. Part of the reason is the fact that they are usually vetted
by a number of interests, including compliance departments and senior
managers, which naturally sways the final presentation in the direction of
the lowest common denominator.

While recent attempts to grant analysts more independence in the
wake of the research practices settlement have taken some of the pressure
off, the reality is that few can ever truly operate free of restrictions. For
one thing, most are employees of firms that tend to be somewhat sensitive
about their public image, with the majority generally fearful about upsetting the wrong constituency in case they might represent a potential threat
or opportunity somewhere down the road. There are also clear rules about
what can and cannot be said from a regulatory point of view. Overly confident statements about the future, for example, are usually a big no-no.
Finally, while there has always been some sort of disclaimer on published
research noting potential conflicts of interest, the rules are stricter now
with respect to all sorts of communications, and analysts generally have
to disclose such details in virtually any public forum.

Aside from the fact that the report usually represents a compromise
of sorts, the structure often serves to satisfy a variety of interests. Generally speaking, most published research has three elements: the financial
analysis, the written commentary, and the rating. While one might natu-

rally expect the pieces to be consistent with one another, that is not necessarily the case. In essence, by capitalizing on the fact that each component
can, orally at least, be stripped of nuance or looked at separately, many
analysts have been able to play to different constituencies, and even
rationalize away inconsistencies. What they have done in many instances
is to create documents where the number-crunching parts could be as
close to their real-world view as practical, but where the text components
could be dumbed down or softened up to make the research more palat-
able to a greater number of readers. Not surprisingly, the process usually
requires a measure of doublespeak, especially with regard to the stock rating. Consequently, while the financial data might paint, say, a relatively
bearish picture, the overview could be somewhat diluted, in the interests
of "balance." Meanwhile, the stock's rating could be something as innocuous as "Hold."

More often than not, in fact, the lowest rankings that most securities
would have garnered in the past, especially at the height of the Bubble,
were those depicting a neutral rather than a negative stance. According to
Thomson First Call, the historical rate for "Sells" is just one percent.[4]
Aside from that, even if one takes the word "Hold" at face value, it is still
essentially a mildly positive recommendation. The problem is, while
many professionals could read through the lines by looking at the financial details or by gathering additional color from analysts, salespeople,
and traders, the investing public had a hard time getting any sort of consistent insights. Frankly, some did not appear to want too much detail
anyway, especially given the structural shift that digitized data was fostering and the increasing focus on trading catalysts. All many individual and
institutional players seemed to care about was whether the rating was a
"Buy," a "Hold," or a "Sell," and whether that represented a change in
view from a prior outlook. What is more, it seemed to suit the interests of
numerous constituencies to have only one measure to focus on, whether it
was the companies being evaluated, the reporters breaking the story, or
the brokers looking for interesting fodder for a 30-second sales call.

Still, many could not quite leave well enough alone, and sometimes
other interests came into play, such as sales and marketing. Measures
were tweaked or rebased to create categories that were supposedly "new
and improved." Instead of a sticking with a simple three-tier system, ver-
bal pluses and minuses were added, with such variations as "Weak Hold"
and "Strong Buy" cropping up. Alternatively, analysts occasionally
adopted number rankings—with a "5," for example, being the highest and
a "1" being the lowest. Over time, a variety of other friendly sounding

descriptives also drifted into the language, including "Accumulate" and "Market Perform." Even speculators got their own categories, with terms such as "Trading Buy." Despite the range of new labels, the system continues to revolve around a High-Middle-Low scale, though with the sort of grade inflation found in the American education system remaining firmly in evidence. Also providing further support for the simple terminology has been the increased emphasis on short-term trading, as operators react strongly to such feverish developments as a broker upgrade from "Hold" to "Buy." How, though, are investors supposed to go from a "Sell" to a "Hold"?

In an environment that generally favors conformists over mavericks, it is not surprising that many recommendations and rating changes are frequently behind the curve, especially at critical turning points. While there have always been some psychic and financial rewards associated with being first out of the gate, the fear of falling flat and the various cross-currents that analysts face have nonetheless fostered a considerable degree of follow-the-leaderism. On the whole, it is rare to see a researcher aggressively downgrade a stock that has been shooting skywards, and nearly as odd to see an upgrade in the shares of a company that is in the midst of a freefall. In most cases, the rankings will tend to bunch up near a similar point along the rating scale, which is admittedly likely to have more "Sell" recommendations nowadays than in the past because of the research practices settlement.[5] Nonetheless, the ratio of positive to negative rankings still remains strongly skewed to the up side, and there seems to be little willingness to buck the status quo. In most instances, in fact, that perspective seems to have extended across the operating landscape. Many researchers, for example, continue to rely on an assessment technique, relativism, that when used improperly, serves as an analytical variant of the greater fool theory.

Simply put, relativism defines the relationship between two or more trends or concepts. If a stock rises at a faster rate than the S&P 500 Index, for example, one can say the individual share is outperforming the market on a relative basis. In that context, the measure often gives useful clues about the technical underpinnings of a stock, sector, or market. However, in its most basic form, the ratio reveals little about the appropriateness of using either point of reference. Unfortunately, in the research world, such comparisons are frequently employed as methodological sleights-of-hand that can help to facilitate rationalization and a blurring of the truth. While the relationships cited can be valid and the underlying premise seemingly reasonable, the strategy often appears to serve merely as a way of skirting awkward questions. Typically, problems crop up because the baseline measure is somewhat questionable. However, the line of defense that analysts will repeatedly fall back on is that everyone else is currently making the same comparisons, or that such relationships have been accepted in the past. At an extreme, of course, this sort of logic allows for the possibility that the earth is flat or that the business cycle no longer exists.

In more specific terms, analysts often justify the valuation of a company by comparing it to a group of similar businesses or the overall universe. For the most part, the thinking goes something like this: If the PE ratio of the market is 30, for example, then the stock of a steadily growing company with a multiple of 25 is cheap—even if the aggregate measure is rich in historical terms. Alternatively, the view might be that a stock priced at a multiple of 50 is inexpensive because it is trading at a 25 percent discount to its "peers"—despite the fact that the sector valuation itself is based on a peak, or unsustainable, level of earnings. Under these circumstances, analysts are effectively avoiding the question of whether the reference measure is valid or are indirectly making the case that it is without clarifying the reasons why. As such, the approach seems to reflect a combination of peer pressure, intellectual laziness, and the influence of numerous behavioral biases all rolled into one. It can therefore be quite misleading, which makes it a questionable basis for making investment decisions.

When the reference value is shaky, in fact, it can call the entire argument into question, creating an analytical structure akin to that of a house built on quicksand. The semiconductor sector, for example, often provides a glimpse of some of the dubious assessments that researchers make. For one thing, the constituents are often evaluated relative to each other, rather than to the broad market or even other technology shares. Consequently, the reason given for rating a certain chip stock as a "Buy" is not that it is inexpensive compared to most companies, but that it is out of line with respect to the rest of the sector. Never mind that the group's fundamentals may have been deteriorating, many of the companies may have been cutting jobs, or rivals' shares may have been driven to ridiculous heights by a major bear squeeze. In a way, it is a bit like arguing that a McDonald's hamburger is cheap at $10 because Burger King's version is $11—while the cost of dinner at a four-star restaurant is $8. Sure, some people might be willing to pay extra for junk food but, practically speaking, the parity is out of whack. What is more, it is illogical to think that because the burgers—or the shares—may be priced at some fraction of what they used to be, it makes them any more of a bargain.

Sometimes the reference value is not based on an established relationship or hard data, but merely reflects wishful thinking or the use of questionable proxies. This was especially the case during the Bubble years, when new-era analysis meant relying on such financially unquantifiable measures as "eyeballs," "page-views," and "click-throughs" to promote or rationalize views and valuations that could not be supported with traditional fundamentals. Nowadays, however, the distortions that take place are subtler, but often crop up as a result of spurious forecasts about future sales growth that can depend on any number of questionable assumptions. These include expectations that are, by definition, speculative and have a wide margin of error, such as those involving trends going out five years or more. At the other extreme, they may have some link to a reasonably stable growth indicator such as GDP, but with a multiplier that is colored by excessive optimism. Frequently, though, the outlook is simply based on a fanciful projection going forward.

Action Point

When it comes to making important financial decisions, investors often ignore or dismiss the impact that emotions, attitudes, and the environment can have on the process. Recent successes or failures, feelings associated with personal relationships, attitudes towards money, and issues on the job front often influence judgment and color the prism through which the investing world is viewed. To minimize the unhelpful impact that unrelated factors can have when choosing a course of action, always engage in a healthy dose of introspection. Then, take steps to ensure such influences do not hold undue sway. If life has been on the upswing, temper enthusiasm with skepticism and cold-blooded logic. If anxiety is high, step back and wait for the energy to dissipate before jumping in. If recent events have been disheartening, write down the pluses and minuses and take an objective look at the facts before making a final decision.

In general, such efforts fall under the heading of another type of behavioral quirk called extrapolation bias, which describes a tendency towards giving undue emphasis to recent patterns when making assumptions about the future. In some ways, it reflects a measure of the sentiment underlying the old trading adage, "The trend is your friend." Although there is some evidence to suggest that recent share price momentum may be a viable indicator of prospective near-term moves, such thinking can frequently be a source of error and confusion in the case of longer-term fundamental analysis. It may also be a factor behind why many analysts—and other market operators, for that matter—have a difficult time calling turning points. In practical terms, researchers either exaggerate the significance of temporary developments or fail to pay heed to the fact that markets, historically at least, have tended to "revert to the mean." In other words, they swing back from both the bullish and bearish extremes.

Some analysts, for example, seemed not to take full account of the fact that U.S. economic growth during the third quarter of 2003 reflected an extraordinary combination of one-shot fiscal policy maneuvers, which came into effect as part of the pre-election year stimulus package orchestrated by President George W. Bush. These included a $3.8 billion reduction in withholding taxes in July, as well as a child tax credit paid out then and in August, to the tune of $4.6 billion and $9 billion, respectively. Consequently, when they saw the brisk pace of expansion, with GDP coming through at an 8.2 percent annualized rate, no small number were only too happy to revise long-term revenue growth projections upward for a wide assortment of companies. While it is not necessarily illogical to make certain assumptions about the future—in fact, most investment analysis requires it as a matter of course—momentary exuberance and the associated compounding errors that result can lead to significant investment missteps.

Another bit of monkey business that researchers sometimes engage in is to shift the comparison basis or highlight only those time frames, values, percentages, and other aspects that tend to cast data in the most favorable light. To be sure, it clearly does not make sense to offer up only conflicting facts and figures when undertaking and presenting an analysis. The risk, though, is that the alternative can easily develop into a serious case of confirmation bias, reflecting either naïveté or intellectual dishonesty. For example, an analyst might make the point that since company X's recent growth rate was greater than that of the market, that would justify a premium multiple. What some fail to note, however, is that the share price and PE ratio are both higher than they were a year ago and the longer-term profit trend has been on the decline. Or, the comparison makes reference to a baseline measure that includes a one-time write-off or other aberration. Alternatively, analytical rationalization may lead to a back-fitting process, with researchers screening for data that justifies current prices or valuations without taking account of cyclicality or other historical fluctuations.

In fact, such approaches often seem to be a factor when research specialists set and adjust "price targets," which tend to be primarily associated with "Buy" recommendations. Although they ostensibly reflect a measure of calculated value derived from the financial analysis, it is not all that unusual for analysts to work in reverse. What that means is they may already have a reference price in mind, which they based, for example, on parities with other shares in the sector or the market as whole. Under those circumstances, they will weigh any number of possible configurations of raw data to come up with a figure that fits. It may even be a blended valuation based on real or forecast earnings, cash flow, book value, or whatever other plug-in happens to be handy. Then, it is simply a matter of dropping the data into a spreadsheet to come up with a forward projection. The real fun seems to occur on those occasions when the shares actually hit the bull's eye. More often than not, instead of adjusting the rating, many researchers will simply plug in "revised" values and calculate a new target.

Perhaps the most controversial practice that has cropped up during the past decade, which was raised to an especially fine art during the Bubble years, has been the wholesale recasting of results in a more favorable light. Basically, analysts stopped focusing on reported results, calculated according to GAAP[6] standards, and directed their efforts instead to "pro forma," or operating, earnings. In theory, the latter are meant to convey a better understanding of how the underlying business is performing; in practice, like many of the seemingly beneficial insights that were promoted during the 1990s, allegedly good aspirations often turned into relatively bad outcomes. Rather than reflecting reality, as was intended, the pro forma results invariably represented attempts to show that the business was healthier and more profitable than it actually was. It did not help that there was little agreement on acceptable standards with respect to the final presentation and any associated accounting "adjustments" that were made.

What made it worse, of course, was the fact that the reported figures were already "massaged," with corporate accounting rules allowing for certain items and actions, such as the issuance of incentive stock options, to be excluded from—or included in—the bottom-line results. Nevertheless, it probably comes as no surprise to learn that operating earnings are almost always higher than the official results—indeed, Figure 8.2 clearly says as much—though in recent years, the differences between the two

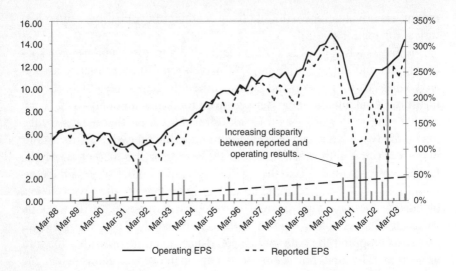

Figure 8.2   S&P 500 Reported (GAAP) vs. Operating (Pro Forma) Earnings per Share, with the Differences Expressed in Percentage Terms (Source: Standard & Poor's).

have been particularly striking.[7] While the post-Bubble scandals have fostered widespread efforts to boost analytical independence, to make companies more accountable, and to ensure that financial data is more realistic and helpful to investors, it has, nonetheless, suited a wide variety of interests—including the companies themselves—to draw attention away from the negatives.

Clearly such a situation could not exist without the influence and cooperation of corporate America, and managers appear to have done their part to keep some of the analytical fantasies going. In fact, it is arguable whether the general decline in research standards that seems to have taken place in recent years might have occurred at all if the subject companies had not enthusiastically played along. However, with regulators becoming more vocal and regulatory mechanisms such as Regulation FD and the Sarbanes-Oxley Act putting pressure on executives to tighten up their act, the nature of the game has shifted somewhat. Nowadays, the emphasis is on "managing" expectations. Essentially, this strategy involves a two-tier marketing approach that is designed to stimulate a continuing momentum in the share price by walking a fine line between straightforward promotion and the subtle downplaying of investor expectations.

The top-level or overt message is generally directed at customers, suppliers, the media, and others that operate outside of the Wall Street arena. It tends to paint a picture that suggests matters are progressing smoothly and the future remains promising. The background or covert strategy, however, is aimed at the investment community, and it focuses on fostering a measure of muted optimism by encouraging analysts, traders, portfolio managers, and others to remain positive, but to avoid making assumptions that are overly optimistic. In some respects, it is a sort of come-on designed to create a positive technical situation in the underlying shares, as various speculative interests either refrain from going long ahead of the results or get lulled into placing near-term bets on the short side. Consequently, when the actual results are released, they often turn out to be better than expected—a positive earnings "surprise"—and create a burst of energy and activity that ratifies the top-level message. It also energizes the market like a triple-shot espresso. As Figure 8.3 suggests, growing numbers of companies have caught on to this approach in recent years. Indeed, *The Wall Street Journal* noted in July 2003, that "the earnings-management game is alive and well on Wall Street."[8]

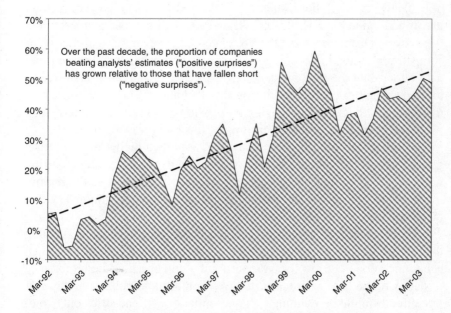

Figure 8.3 Earnings Management? Quarterly S&P 500 Positive–Negative Earnings "Surprise" Differentials (Source: Standard & Poor's Index Alert, Bloomberg LP).

What makes it particularly effective, of course, is the increasing focus on the near term, as well as the shift towards a more speculative approach that seems to be taking place in the share-trading arena. Together with the impact that digitized data has had on all sorts of modern evaluation measures, it appears to have made life easier for everyone involved to direct their efforts towards single data points. Still, in the wake of the post-Bubble letdown, companies have not given up on other feints entirely, though they have had to shift their emphasis somewhat. During the go-go days, managers were under pressure to produce results that justified the already-high share prices. Nowadays, their efforts go towards delivering outcomes that will justify higher share prices in the future. In either case, as Warren Buffet suggested in his 2003 annual letter to Berkshire Hathaway shareholders, "Managers that always promise to 'make the numbers' will at some point be tempted to make up the numbers." In some respects, such a perspective appears to be somewhat in evidence based on recent practices.

Although the methods have changed from what took place during the dot-com days, it seems that many companies are still doing what they can to create momentum based on massaged results or an Orwellian reshaping of bad news as good. For instance, one Baby Bell[9] made much of the fact that it had gained wholesale access lines; in reality, those gains resulted from losing customers—and the associated higher-margin retail lines—to competitors. Another technology company has begun emphasizing net debt rather than the total outstanding,[10] a financial sleight-of-hand seemingly designed to create the illusion that its balance sheet was somehow improving. Others are capitalizing on pension accounting rules to realize what are, in essence, phantom arbitrage gains by borrowing money at one rate of interest to fund pension plans that assume a higher rate of return going forward.[11] Some are relying on continually occurring nonrecurring write-offs to keep their dreams alive.[12] Many, of course, are still employing the "old faithfuls"—the various forms of accounting gimmickry that managers have always had access to.

Unfortunately, it is not only analysts and companies that are playing the numbers game. Government officials seem to have cottoned on to an economic version of pro forma reporting by emphasizing the importance of data with an "ex" in front of it. Never mind that monthly measures of price trends might be pointing to higher inflation—if one strips out "volatile" components, such as food and energy, there is no cause for alarm. Of course, most people would love to lead a life where all they had to pay was the "ex-food and energy" cost, but the reality is otherwise. Some mutual fund groups have not been entirely innocent in this respect either. Because they tend to be rewarded on the basis of assets under management, there is often a tremendous incentive to "game" the system to bring in additional investors—along with their savings. Whether by operating at the extreme limits of allowable risk parameters or by focusing on short-term results at the expense of stated long-term objectives, no small number have clearly gotten caught up in the same sorry state of affairs.

To be sure, it has not all come down to the individuals involved—modern communication methods frequently end up turning good data into bad. With considerably more information being cranked out informally, much of it passing through many hands, it invariably leads to errors and distortions that were not necessarily intended at the outset. Moreover, the one clear advantage that written research has is that it tends to force a measure of clarity and a bit more objectivity than words dashed off when markets are in a funk. Alternatively, though analysts are under endless pressures to conform, a different kind of expectation sometimes gets factored in during personal interactions, when people often have a natural tendency to shade their message towards the viewpoint of the other side. On top off that, the phenomenal growth of the Internet, along with a wide range of modern sources of news and information, has churned up a host of perspectives that frequently lack even a minimal measure of analytical reserve.

For many investors, the market has always been mainly a mixture of hype, hope, and hearsay. However, in recent years, the emotional noise seems to have become more pronounced, and for numerous operators, there seems to be considerable confusion about where fantasy ends and reality begins. Occasionally, as the various scandals since the Bubble burst have revealed, some in the financial services industry clearly stepped over the line and made the wrong choices. As a consequence, a growing number of individual and institutional players have become disillusioned with the analysis and data that permeates the equity landscape. While regulatory changes might make the situation easier to read going forward, for most of those who venture in to the share-trading game, it will unfortunately remain a case of caveat emptor.

Action Plan

The first rule of operating in any environment is, of course, to know the terrain. For investors, that means understanding the terminology and the analytical underpinnings upon which many in the investment world are basing their assumptions. The next step, though, which involves looking ahead and trying to anticipate what might happen down the road, usually requires more digging—to discover facts and trends that are not necessarily relevant now, but which might be in the future. One useful starting point is to explore whether current approaches are the best ways to evaluate the risks and opportunities. Is the marketplace looking at all the relevant factors and time frames? Arguably, this is a tall order, and one could easily assume that those who get paid to do this for a living have already done the dirty work. Nonetheless, as in the Hans Christian Andersen fable, "The Emperor's New Clothes," sometimes those who are caught up in the status quo cannot—or will not—see the realities of the situation.

This brings to mind a whole range of questions that investors can—and should—ask. For example, is the investment community actually using "metrics" that matter? While the term took on ridiculous connotations during the Bubble years, it nonetheless describes a range of possible measures than can be used to assess value and investment potential. It makes sense, of course, to get rid of any half-cocked clutter, such as "eyeballs," that clearly does not show a consistent degree of correlation to hard-dollar activities. Once past that, though, explore the analytical slant of the professional crowd more closely. Are they focused on revenues, earnings, or capitalization? Depending on the industry, all of these attributes play some role when it comes to evaluating potential risks and rewards. However, an excessive emphasis on one to the exclusion of others can occasionally mask a fundamental weakness that might have negative consequences later on.

Indeed, it usually makes sense to look at data in its entirety, not just selectively. As in the case with the old joke about a blindfolded individual who concludes that he is surrounded by a variety of animals after touching various parts of an elephant, it is easy to make mistakes when evaluating financial data in isolation or without reference to historical patterns. Sometimes it is the combination that provides the most interesting insights, offering a measure of confirmation that stand-alone indicators may lack. Certain pairs of data, for example, can provide useful intelligence about the "quality" of earnings a company may be reporting. Are revenues declining at the same time that earnings are rising? This can be a sign that a company is benefiting from cost-cutting while its basic business is under pressure. Are both sales and the average number of days that accounts receivable are outstanding on the increase? This could indicate that growth is occurring primarily as a result of easy credit—if so, is that because customers cannot really afford the products and services?

Also worth remembering in the modern communications era is that published estimates and opinions may not necessarily represent the inside scoop as far as the institutional community is concerned. With much more research and commentary being pushed out though various informal channels, such as email, instant messaging, text messaging, and even the telephone, financial information is often in flux, changing as it is picked over and acted upon by those who are closest to the action. Consequently, like the flurry that takes place at the racetrack in the moments leading up to the starting gun, when the tote is rapidly fluctuating to take account of last-minute bets—presumably incorporating up-to-date assessments and dealings of the "smart money" operators—information circulating around the market sometimes evolves in a similar fashion. With such data—sometimes found at market-oriented online bulletin boards and at Web sites such as *www.whispernumber.com*—it is occasionally possible to gain an enhanced understanding of trader psychology and prospective short-term supply-and-demand considerations.

In the modern share-trading environment, of course, market intelligence can come from a variety of sources. Individual investors will be well served to remain flexible and retain a degree of "information trolling" in their approach to investing. Sometimes this will require adjusting strategies to incorporate a degree of lateral thinking. For example, take time whenever possible to analyze the action written about and discussed in commodity columns, futures Web sites, and options-related articles in newspapers such as *The Wall Street Journal*. Sometimes they reveal insights about the big picture before any company-specific understanding filters through to the equity markets. At the very least, information that seeps out of other spheres can often add to your understanding of the broader state of affairs.

CHAPTER 9

Market Indicators

Many traditional market indicators are becoming less reliable.

Since ancient times, travelers have relied on a variety of signals to guide them on their journeys. At night, mariners used the stars to make their way forward; during the day, nomads kept an eye out for landmarks that would ensure they were on course. In similar fashion, stock market players have traditionally monitored a variety of indicators to assess the future direction of share prices. Fundamentally oriented investors have focused on PE ratios, dividend yields, and growth rates to formulate their views; technical analysts have scrutinized price trends, chart patterns, and sentiment measures to gauge what might happen next. Experienced operators would often take both kinds into account, looking for one to confirm the other. In the modern share-trading environment, however, it appears that some traditional guideposts—as Figure 9.1 seems to indicate—are no longer as reliable as they once were. Consequently, those who continue to believe otherwise risk being stranded in the investment wilderness.

One of the interesting things about the stock market is the fact that people naturally take it for granted that the best way to figure out what might happen next is to study what happened before. Generally speaking, that perspective follows along the lines of what George Santayana noted when he wrote, "Those who cannot remember the past are condemned to

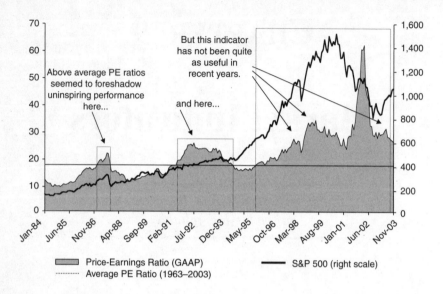

Figure 9.1   S&P 500 Trailing 12-Month Reported Price-Earnings Ratio vs. Price
(Source: Bloomberg LP, Standard & Poor's).

repeat it." Many chart watchers, for example, will argue that the patterns found in the 50-year old classic by Edwards and McGee, *Technical Analysis of Stock Trends,*[1] are as relevant today as they were when the book was first published. From their point of view, the configurations are a reflection of basic human behavior; as such, they are influenced by emotions, attitudes, and beliefs that have changed relatively little through the years. For these specialists, factors such as fear and greed are essentially the only "fundamentals" that really matter.

Most fundamental analysts, on the other hand, appear to have a slightly different perspective. They might not disagree with their technical brethren about the irrational influences that can affect share prices, but their overall view tends to be that it is the hard financial data—the "numbers"—that ultimately win out in the end. Often, they will highlight the long-term success of value investors, such as Warren Buffett and other followers of the disciplined approach advocated by the late Benjamin Graham, to emphasize their point. As they see it, whether markets are overbought or oversold in technical terms is largely irrelevant—once enough rational investors start to come around, the security will invariably move towards a price that reflects its underlying worth.

Unfortunately, despite the convincing arguments on both sides, it seems these days that things often do not pan out as expected. Ironically, one reason why is likely the fact that many modern players are well aware of those two perspectives. That is somewhat facetious, of course, because knowledge does not necessarily translate into action. However, history has shown that when it comes to the financial markets, once people realize that a particular strategy or indicator has been successful in the past, that information invariably colors their behavior. In fact, some operators will have almost a compulsion to act on the knowledge, while others will simply incorporate it into their thinking to some degree. Whatever the case, the awareness of what "works" usually remains in memory, ready to be called upon when needed. Once enough people learn about it, though, the combined response often leads to an outcome that is different from, or even wholly the opposite of, what might have been anticipated.

This seems to be a common problem in an age where the volume and sophistication of information coursing through the marketplace has increased dramatically, and where an efficient and far-reaching communications network ensures that many players are quickly informed of what is going on and what others are up to. In the past, the valuable intelligence that seeped into the mainstream typically followed a slow and steady progression—that is, it often began with a relatively small group of savvy operators, usually insiders and institutions with size and analytical advantages, and worked its way down the equity food chain from there. Over time, the knowledge would gradually flow outward until it reached the wide delta of public awareness. Interestingly enough, though part of the reason why such insights tended to be slow in coming was because people naturally wanted to keep the good stuff for a while, the reality was that many players were not necessarily keen to hang on past the point where the information had been acted upon.

In fact, once they had done most of their buying—or selling—there was often no longer any real incentive to keep the intelligence under wraps. On the contrary, it made sense to let everyone in on the secret as soon as possible, especially if the investment decision was based on a one-off development or a strategy that others would probably discover on their own. In practical terms, however, the communications infrastructure was simply not there and, at least in pre-Bubble days, neither was the demand. For, unlike the pervasive presence of 24/7 business news coverage that exists today, there was a time when financially oriented reporting was a relatively small segment of the news-gathering universe. Back then, many individuals depended upon newspapers and magazines for the bulk of their market-related content, at least with respect to day-to-day developments. That changed, however, with the 1981 unveiling of the Financial News Network (FNN), which featured 12 hours of business news programming a day. Later, following the 1989 launch of CNBC—which acquired FNN after it went bankrupt in 1990—nonstop mass-media coverage began to have a major impact on the quantity of potentially useful intelligence that was in circulation. These services were later supplemented—some would even say supplanted, in very recent times—by the wide variety of resources that became available with the rise of the Internet as a primary information medium.

What really seemed to get the flow of business-related intelligence going, however, was the Bubble that developed in the late 1990s. While it is a matter for debate whether the euphoria in share prices would have reached such a fever pitch if it had not been inextricably linked to the Information Age, the relationship between the rapidly expanding global communications infrastructure and the rapidly rising stock market was symbiotic nonetheless. Regardless of which was the dominant influence, both seemed to feed off and depend on each other. Along with the increase in the ranks of newly enlisted shareholders that was taking place came an additional thirst for knowledge about the equity world that seemed to grow in leaps and bounds. Overall, both the interest and the output rose dramatically, with each seeming to stoke the other in a sort of virtuous circle. Essentially, the more people were actively involved in the market, the more they wanted to know about it.

Action Point

When a formerly reliable technical signal does not produce worthwhile results, or a fundamentally driven investment method does not work out the way it used to, the first inclination is to discard it out of hand. This can be a mistake. Often such failures reveal unique insights about the character of the market, which players are dominating the action, or what influences seem to matter most in the contemporary investing environment. Ironically, sometimes measures that once helped to identify potential buying opportunities turn out to be even better indicators for deciding when to sell. Before switching tracks on any particular gauge or method, look carefully to see if there is any value left in it first. If not, so be it; otherwise, it may help to minimize the potentially costly learning curve associated with identifying, testing, and adopting new approaches.

Though the boom did eventually turn to bust, forcing the most exuberant practices and pronouncements of the financial media to be toned down, a substantial business reporting framework remains in place. This is not all that surprising, as historically at least, many of the changes ushered in during previous periods of euphoria did not necessarily disappear when the music stopped. As a result, individuals at all levels have almost constant access to resources that can keep them reasonably well-informed about what is going on. Within the institutional investing community, there is an even greater array of communications links available. From continually scrolling Bloomberg and Reuters headlines to the ocean of data that gushes through informal channels, valuable intelligence is regularly coming in from all angles. Under these circumstances, it usually does not take long before people have some idea about what strategies others are using and which trades seem to be making money. At that point, some will invariably have a flutter. If too many do, however, the market usually ensures that most will end up being frustrated.

Another factor that is likely playing a role in muddying the waters owes much to the aftereffects of the bursting Bubble. In essence, the once-in-a-lifetime bull market turned out to be a powerful people magnet that drew vast numbers into the investing world over the course of a fairly short period of time. While the going was good, the environment proved resilient enough to absorb the influx, and for a while at least, many were able to get ahead by just going long and hanging on for the ride. Once the boom ended, however, it revealed a problem much like that which exists in many technology-related industries—that is, excess capacity in the trading and investing ranks. What made matters worse was the dramatic expansion that had taken place in the hedge fund sector, which brought out a host of aggressive operators who were looking to profit from the choppy market conditions. Taken together, the two developments turned up the competitive heat and forced many individuals to veer away from the straightforward investing approaches they were most familiar with.

To be sure, the share-trading arena has always had operators engaging in a wide variety of activities, but many of those who suddenly felt compelled to embrace riskier, more active, and more complex money-making strategies found themselves in an awkward position. In essence, they adopted approaches for which they were poorly trained, entered niches that were increasingly overcrowded, and employed tactics that often required a rare combination of flexibility, discipline, and stamina. On top of that, the stock market had become more volatile and difficult to get a handle on since the spring of 2000. Overall, conditions in the wake of the bursting Bubble had laid the groundwork for an increasingly schizophrenic trading environment, and it did not help that unusual geopolitical developments and various macroeconomic uncertainties were constantly lurking in the background. Under these circumstances, it is not surprising that there have been increasing instances when participants act in unpredictable ways and move prices in unexpected directions.

Action Point

It is relatively easy for anyone to get caught up in the emotional frenzy of wild, noise-driven trading or the aftershocks of surprise developments, but many investors have long regretted actions taken in the heat of such moments. More often than not, a five-minute pause for reflection, a short walk around the block, or even a move to a quiet room—away from the hurly-burly—can strip away emotional elements that can cause confusion and needless doubts, thus helping to facilitate a calm and measured assessment of the situation. Of course, that is not an excuse to sit idly by when action is called for. If, in fact, the outlook associated with an existing investment has clearly taken a turn for the worse, then steps must be taken to exit the position. Avoid the urge to procrastinate. Under those circumstances, it is usually best to pay heed the old market adage, "the first cut is the cheapest."

Yet even when individuals are clearly focused on what they are doing, the wide range of market-neutral, arbitrage, derivative, and alternative investing strategies that many are involved in often provide a historically unique counterbalance to the traditional forces of supply and demand. In today's market, in fact, there is an assortment of operators with seemingly little interest in placing directional bets. Sometimes they have little choice in the matter anyway because the decisions are being made automatically. That is the case with statistical arbitrage strategies, where software programs analyze small fluctuations in the prices of thousands of shares and send buy and sell orders directly to electronic trading venues in an attempt to profit from the discrepancies. Alternatively, large players might use computerized models that search for minute variations in the prices of hundreds or even thousands of derivatives. When they are identified, the transactions that result often impact the underlying shares when market-makers or traders on the other side hedge their risk.

Others may operate with motives and approaches that, while ostensibly benefiting from a swing in one direction or another, are not necessarily oriented towards absolute moves in price. Instead, they use strategies that compare current relationships to prior ones or are otherwise based on some form of relative value analysis. The simplest examples are pairs trades, which feature a simultaneous or near simultaneous purchase and short sale of two or more securities that have historically had some measure of correlation between them. The process itself might involve looking at something as simple as the ratio or the difference—the spread— between the prices of the shares. Alternatively, it may revolve around a statistical model that highlights when the mathematical connection varies by some calculated degree, often a multiple of the standard deviation from moving averages. Whatever the case, these methods have helped to foster a state of equilibrium that varies from that which was seen in earlier times.

On the flip side of the modern investing coin are those who look to profit in a more traditional manner, but who do so using instruments and methods that are tailored to the present. Placing a bullish bet, for example, no longer requires much knowledge about the individual equities being bought or sold. In fact, if it involves the use of an index, it is possible that those who are doing the trading may not even know which underlying securities they are effectively dealing in, except in a general sense. When investors acted on thematic views in the past, they usually exercised some element of discretion as to which stocks were selected and how the funds were apportioned. Sometimes they made their decisions on fundamental or technical grounds; at other times, they might have divided amounts up equally. In the case of today's exchange-listed derivatives and ETFs, however, the specifics have already been determined in advance by someone else. Under those circumstances, it is possible that the issues of companies with the poorest prospects will end up garnering the lion's share of the associated inflows because they are the most heavily weighted constituents of the sector or index.

There are also many operators who look at equities purely in aggregate terms, as merely one of many different asset classes, along with bonds, currencies, and precious metals, among others. A substantial number of theses managers are commodity trading advisors, or CTAs, who reportedly oversee around $57 billion,[2] most of which is invested in the futures markets. Often they rely on arbitrage strategies, black-box models, and trend-following approaches that do not require much human input once the methodology is developed and the systems are up and running. Interestingly, although the programs are frequently optimized to reduce whipsaws, they are generally not affected in the same way that flesh-and-blood money managers sometimes are when these abrupt short-term reversals do occur. For example, unlike the mechanical systems, it is not unusual for people to lose confidence when they go through a rough patch where they realize a string of losses, despite the fact that such setbacks are an inevitable part of the process. Regardless, automated and momentum-driven macro approaches are another relatively modern wrinkle of the supply-and-demand equation.

The tactics modern participants use can also vary somewhat from what most share-traders once relied on. Markets have always had players, of course, who operate within a variety of time frames and who employ an assortment of investing styles. Nowadays, though, it seems that changing perceptions about risk are altering at least some collective behavior patterns. Historically, for example, there has been more of a connection between size and approach than there seems to be now. More specifically, many operators are less fearful about—or more confident in—their ability to trade out of potentially unwieldy positions than their conservative forebears were. In the past, those who invested substantial amounts of money in equities usually took the view that potentially large transaction costs and the prospect of unleashing a self-defeating momentum meant that a longer-term perspective was really the only viable option. In the current environment, aided by optimistic views about available liquidity in certain derivatives and index-related markets, many equity investors have the willingness and wherewithal to take massive "punts" for periods as short as a few hours.

Action Point

Although unreliable technical signals and market indicators might seem to be a curse, for long-term players such situations can sometimes offer up interesting opportunities. Following an extensive review of the merits, and with a clear understanding that a prospective investment makes sense in its own right, using execution strategies that capitalize on whipsaws and "false breakouts" can sometimes enhance returns. If markets are near visually important lows, or reports suggest that short-term traders believe a move through a particular level will likely trigger further selling, try establishing orders with limits that are 1 to 3 percent below the presumed breakdown points. In other words, if a price of $50 appears to be "support," enter a request to buy the shares around the $49 level. Under these circumstances, the frustrations of others may turn out to be somewhat fortuitous.

Many modern operators are especially keen on leverage as well. Generally speaking, most individuals and some institutions have always been permitted to use borrowed money to boost equity returns, typically by arranging margin loans through brokers. While conservative money managers have often frowned on the practice, and analysts have regularly tracked the aggregate level of margin lending to get a sense of whether speculators were getting in over their heads, the multiplier effect that gearing can have on investment performance does have a potent allure. In fact, this is probably the most important reason why the technique appeals to the new breed of aggressive player. For one thing, they tend to be paid on the basis of absolute performance; hence, all else being equal, they have a natural incentive to maximize returns as best they can. For another, many arbitrage and market-neutral approaches are predicated on high-volume, low-margin strategies that can be enhanced with the aid of other people's money. To top it off, the prime brokerage community realizes considerable value from its financing activities and regularly promotes the benefits that borrowing can bring to its hedge fund clientele.

Nowhere has the influence and impact of leverage been more apparent, of course, than in the derivatives arena. While it is possible to take a conservative approach to that market, evaluating risk in terms of the face value of the underlying assets, many of those who trade synthetic securities capitalize on the fact that exchanges usually require buyers and sellers to stump up only a fraction of their theoretical exposure. So what often happens is, instead of thinking in terms of how much they control when they acquire a position equivalent to X, operators will focus on how much can they control if they have X to spend. Taken together, the more widespread use of credit and the growing influence of the derivatives sector seem to create an intensifying dynamic that can easily unsettle markets and foster a quick build-up of short-term imbalances. What further complicates matters is the fact that many strategies have nothing at all to do with a view on direction, but are instead focused on narrow aspects such as time value and share price volatility. One way or another, it seems likely that these various factors have distorted the relevance and significance of indicators that may have been useful in the past.

An increased appetite for risk also appears to be stimulating a growing interest in trading volatile instruments and individual shares that have a high beta—the degree of movement relative to the market as a whole. In other words, many operators are directing their attention to those issues that tend to rise and fall more rapidly than others. Undoubtedly, this interest in speculative high-fliers reflects a measure of the broader shift towards a more active investing approach that appears to have taken hold in recent years. It also serves to underscore the fact that the usual way to achieve above-average returns is to employ riskier strategies, a perspective likely to come to the fore on the heels of the evolution taking place in the investing world. In general, the combination of unsettled markets, heightened competition, increased regulatory pressures, and the phenomenal growth of the hedge fund sector has spurred a shift away from relative performance comparisons and fees based on assets under management towards evaluation methods and compensation formulas linked to absolute performance.

While many of the developments that are occurring owe much to the impact that relatively modern products, strategies, and players are having on the marketplace, a variety of traditional fund managers have also been updating their tactics and approaches. Part of the reason, of course, is that frustrations tend to flare up when long-only portfolios lack the performance-boosting tail winds of an ongoing bull market. It also does not help that the uproar over the unsavory practices that some mutual funds allegedly engaged in has caused investors to look around and explore other options. Whatever the reasons, many established buy-side firms seem to be taking steps to adapt to the new realities. Historically, for example, they have tried to disguise the nature and extent of their activities. They have done this by using a variety of trading tactics designed to defuse the effects on supply and demand of their potentially market-moving order flow. They have also sought to uncover hidden or alternative sources of liquidity that could help them to offset their interests with minimal fallout.

Action Point ─────────────────────────────────────

For many professionals, the countermove that takes place following an initial sharp swing in a share or index on the back of
unexpected news often provides more useful intelligence about
the state of the market than the original flurry. In some
respects, the follow-up action appears to reveal a measure of
"hidden" supply or demand that has been poised to react when
a fleeting opportunity presents itself. Although it is more art
than science, one general rule of thumb worth keeping in mind
is if the recovery bounce that occurs within the first hour of a
catalyst-driven slide fails to recapture at least two-thirds of the
initial move during that time, then there is a reasonable chance
that at least a short-term retest of the initial lows—or worse—
will soon unfold. The opposite often seems to hold true following an initial upside surge.

Through the years, buy-side traders and portfolio managers have typically employed techniques that limit the prices paid or the proportion of
market volume executed—or both—when accumulating—or even when
exiting—a position. For the most part, those who classify themselves as
value players have tended to emphasize the former approach, though not
necessarily exclusively. This is not surprising, given that these managers
generally operate on the basis that they are seeking out bargains that fit a
set of rigorously defined fundamental criteria. As it happens, the evaluation process usually leads to the identification of some sort of intrinsic
value for the security, which invariably serves as a primary reference
point when it comes to executing the order. Although it is often the case
that such analyses produce a range of prices rather than one single number, historically at least, conservative investors such as these have adopted
the "smart money" view that it is important to acquire a stock at the
"right"—or lowest possible—price. Otherwise, they simply walk away
and explore other opportunities.

For growth-oriented investors, however, the often volatile nature of
the shares they favor has frequently supported a strategy linking the
amount they buy or sell to what is trading in the market. While percentages vary, institutions have typically used ratios somewhere between a
quarter and a half of the reported turnover. Hence, where a firm is looking
to acquire 100,000 shares, for example, they might restrict their maxi-

mum participation to 25 percent, whether by doling the order out piecemeal, by using automated systems, or by passing the appropriate
instructions along to their executing brokers. Under those circumstances,
the transaction would not be fully completed until the cumulative volume
hits at least 400,000 shares, which might take some time if it involved a
relatively illiquid security. Whether or not a price limit is used as well, the
rationale is that the approach is somewhat passive, leading to less slippage and, theoretically at least, lower transaction costs. Arguably, while
any dealings in a security may ultimately affect the supply-and-demand
balance, the goal is to minimize short-term disruptions.

Apart from these methods, many institutions have often tried to get
their business done by looking for "the other side." In other words, if they
are buyers, they seek out natural sellers who have revealed their interest
through brokers, electronic trading systems, and other methods. Of
course, on those occasions when there are broad-based swings that move
most shares up or down, the stampede can make it difficult to find a match
if the buyer or seller is on the wrong side of the herd. Interestingly
enough, though, given the range of different trading styles, investment
objectives, short-term cash flow requirements, and other attributes that
influence investor behavior, it is not all that unusual for two or more buy-
side operators to strike a bargain at prices near existing levels. One reason
is that while negotiations are always affected to some degree by existing
conditions and the sense of urgency each side has with respect to executing their orders, many traditional players have historically shared a common desire to reduce the market impact of their activities and to transact
their business as efficiently as possible.

Up until about 25 years or so ago, buy-side firms mainly relied upon
brokers and their network of contacts to try and meet their execution
needs, partly because of tradition and partly because there were few viable alternatives. Back then, the interaction was usually based on a
straightforward agency relationship, with the intermediary mainly overseeing orders at the relevant exchange. Sometimes the stock would be
traded "upstairs," where it was matched up or "crossed" against offsetting
purchases and sales by other clients. During the 1980s and 1990s, however, the growth of well-capitalized investment banks with relatively
sophisticated risk management structures brought a significant change to
the equity landscape. Instead of always going out in search of natural
counterparties, many sell-side firms became interested in taking on the
exposure themselves. With considerable financial resources at their disposal, finely hewn trading capabilities, and access to a substantial net-

work of investors, they took the view that they could satisfy the needs of commission-paying clients and manage the position until the shares could be distributed to or acquired from other accounts, or otherwise traded at a profitable price.

Not surprisingly, this increased emphasis on large-scale principal-oriented block trading activities played an important role in altering the stock market's supply-and-demand dynamics throughout the period, helping to shift the balance of power towards the sell side. Suddenly, it was no longer just a question of what the traditional end clients were up to that mattered, but what a whole group of other, generally more aggressive operators were doing that might affect the day-to-day action in the share-trading arena. Of course, the ongoing activities of the institutional clients remained a critical aspect of the bigger picture, but until very recently at least—in the wake of the emergence of the hedge fund sector as a dominant force, as well as the dramatic expansion in the availability of direct access trading platforms—the Wall Street broker-dealers were a force to be reckoned with.

Action Point

Although many technical indicators appear to have lost some measure of their usefulness, one particular chart formation, the bullish "key reversal," still seems to provide a useful buy signal on many occasions. As with all technical patterns, it is not infallible, but experience suggests it usually reflects a state of seller exhaustion that is consistent with the view that the worst is, or is nearly, over. What typically happens is that following an extended sell-off of perhaps 10 percent or more, there will be a day when volume surges and the price of a stock touches a new low for the move—triggered, perhaps, by the release of ostensibly bad news. At the end of the trading session, however, the security finishes unchanged or even closes higher on the day. Under those circumstances, it generally means that many of the bears have succumbed and the bulls have gained the upper hand, signaling that at least a short-term rally is at hand.

Unfortunately, some of the consequences of this evolution did not turn out to be so client-friendly. For a start, when brokers act in a dual capacity, it tends to create a natural conflict of interest between their needs and those of their clients. Although many representatives and firms genuinely try to strike a balance, it seems that one of the side effects of this particular transition was that it spawned a host of bottom-feeders on the sell side who looked to profit from the sizable order flow of the traditional fund managers. This issue became particularly pronounced during the latter half of the 1990s, when torrents of money poured into professionally managed investment portfolios. With the frenetic pace of trading and the heady advances that the bull market was making on a regular basis during that time, more often than not the emphasis was on getting fully invested, even at the expense of poor executions and self-defeating instability. The overriding view seemed to be that as long as the market was heading to the moon, it made sense to focus on volume rather than price.

Consequently, with all of the flows that were coursing through the market, the increasing chatter across expanding communications networks, and a host of individuals—many of them new to the game—looking to jump on board the gravy train, institutional buying and selling activities became a primary focus of attention. Whether they were legitimately detected through such methods as technical analysis, or were picked up by way of winks and whispers across trading desks and exchange floors, the data inspired a growing number of operators to try and step in and position themselves ahead of the end clients. It became a bit of a daisy chain, with knowledge about what the larger players were up to being passed around by various individuals, and eventually began to have a negative effect on some investors' performance. On top of that, many traders had begun to adopt more of the anticipatory approach that has become increasingly common nowadays, and it almost seemed as though they knew what fund managers were going to do before the fund managers themselves did.

Eventually the environment changed, however, especially in the wake of the bursting Bubble, and the hedge funds started to become a major factor in the equity world. With a flexible and generally more aggressive approach to wheeling-and-dealing, those players learned quickly—like the American revolutionaries who outwitted the British Redcoats over two centuries ago—that it was necessary to adopt guerilla-like tactics to remain on top in difficult circumstances. While approaches vary, one strategy that some have used is to convey a sense that they are doing one thing while actually engaging in another. Sometimes the ruse takes the form of a "head fake," where an operator might enter a relatively small purchase order with a broker known to be at the forefront of information leakage and, at the same time, leave offers with intermediaries such as ECNs that would likely be taken out by those reacting to the initial feint.

Alternatively, operators might be somewhat upfront to begin with, but would subsequently hide the true scale of their interest from sell-side counterparties. They would do this by buying or selling blocks of shares around the same time through different dealers without letting any of them know what was going on away from them. This would often have a twofold effect: It would enable them to take on large positions in relatively short order, and once the brokers became aware of the suddenly unfavorable technical picture, the resulting scramble would tend to move prices in the client's favor. What is more, once other short-term traders pounced on the action—which was frequently the case—it would stir up additional anxieties about the full extent of the demand, further exacerbating the situation. Not surprisingly, such tactics have proved to be unpopular with dealers, but since many of those who used them were typically large commission payers, most times the associated losses were grudgingly accepted as a cost of doing business. Not every institution engages in such practices, of course, but even traditional long-only managers have become aware of the advantages of occasionally playing games with the Street.

Indeed, it sometimes seems that their goal is to force a specific market reaction that can boost the value of existing positions or otherwise help to get difficult business accomplished. For example, it is not all that strange to see operators aggressively purchase call options or place similar types of upside bets after seemingly bad news is announced, with the apparent intention of unsettling others and inducing them to follow suit out of fear that they might have missed something. At other times, institutions might temporarily drive up the price of index-related instruments such as S&P 500 futures in the hope of triggering arbitrage-related program trades that can help them to sell a range of less liquid individual share positions. While such manipulative techniques rarely offer any long-term benefits, they can, if properly timed, provide a small performance boost that can make a significant difference in a highly competitive marketplace. Moreover, because short-term traders react more quickly and temporary air pockets appear more often than they used to, the tactics occasionally produce generous windfalls. Nonetheless, they can also cloud the supply-and-demand picture and throw off potentially misleading signals in a variety of indicators.

In fact, it appears that no small number of modern operators have taken matters a step further by employing strategies that try to capitalize on the popularity of certain technical and fundamental analysis methods. In essence, they "game" the system by instigating false breakouts or by aggressively trading against widely expected outcomes. While no one is bigger than the market, of course, there does seem to be more occasions nowadays when emotions in the crowd hang in the balance or liquidity momentarily thins out. When that happens, it often does not take much to kick start a sudden sharp swing, especially when various speculators are quick to join in. No doubt one reason why it works at all is that so many players know what the "important" price levels and evaluation measures are. In the Information Age, even those who do not use certain types of analysis cannot help but be aware of what others are focusing on, and that knowledge frequently has at least a subliminal impact on their actions. Moreover, at a time when people are wary of what rivals are up to, it has become increasingly common to find fundamental analysts looking at stock charts and technicians scrutinizing earnings data. As a result, the market gets fixated and charged up when there is a consensus about certain prices or data, making it vulnerable to an intentional and well-timed assault.

Apart from that, some of the irrational elements that are helping to unsettle markets on a day-to-day basis also appear to be affecting the investing environment in a broader sense. Although there are numerous reasons why—the huge influx of relatively inexperienced investors in recent years has likely played a major role—it seems that during and after the Bubble, short-term emotions have often fluctuated wildly within a broad range of extremes. There have also been sudden and unpredictable shifts in feelings and attitudes taking place on an almost regular basis. Combined, these elements and others appear to be distorting the relevance of many sentiment-based indicators. Over the years, technicians and contrarian investors have accepted the premise that if there are "too many" bulls, the market is vulnerable to a setback; if there are too many bears, it is primed for a rally. While the question of what represents excessive optimism or pessimism has typically been more of a judgment call than a strictly defined parameter, history has often shown that when a clear majority believes one thing, that is often a warning sign that circumstances are set to change. Generally speaking, participants have relied on a variety of measures to gauge those views, though most have admittedly been more helpful in identifying risk levels than as timing tools.

It is worth remembering, of course, why attitudes even matter at all: Historically at least, people have tended to put their money where their mouths are when it comes to investing in the stock market. Although some will bluster about what they did last night or occasionally dream up stories that make their lives appear more exciting than they actually are, it seems that when it comes to buying and selling shares, the patter has traditionally had some basis in truth. Consequently, when individuals claimed to be bullish, that was usually a sign that at least some significant proportion were exposed on the long side—if not directly, then as advocates promoting the cause to others—and the odds were good that prices had risen to a level that discounted some element of those positive expectations. Once enough market participants were positioned that way, however, it was likely that at least some would be looking to take profits or pare down positions to capitalize on other opportunities. At the extreme, as contrarians are fond of saying, there would be "nobody left to buy."

In addition to anecdotal evidence and press reports, people have used a variety of measures to gauge sentiment through the years, though the signals have usually been somewhat consistent at important turning points. Perhaps the most widely known varieties are the survey-based indicators, such as the weekly Investors Intelligence poll of newsletter writers, as well as those produced by Market Vane, Consensus, and the American Association of Individual Investors.[3] Generally speaking, these polls attempt to quantify the degree of bulls, bears, and neutrals—those who either have no view or who are bullish but looking for a correction—to help subscribers discern whether attitudes have swung too far in either direction. Two other indicators that many operators look at take their cue from the derivatives market—more specifically, the exchange-traded options pits. The first is the put-call ratio, a measure that compares the turnover in puts to that which takes place in calls. In this case, there is an assumption that those markets have traditionally been driven at the margin by speculative interests, who tend to trade most aggressively after a sustained run or when emotions have gotten the better of them. Hence, if too many are wagering the same way, then Mr. Market tends to step in and make sure few actually come out ahead.

The second derivative-based indicator that has become popular in recent years is the Vix index. Essentially, this gauge reflects participants' aggregate bets about future volatility, an annualized percentage value calculated using the last prices paid for put and call options on the S&P 500 Index.[4] While it may sound complicated, the essence is that it represents the cost of insurance associated with uncertainty over the future direction of share prices, which tends to be somewhat asymmetric by nature. In other words, when people are nervous or fearful about the prospect of the market heading lower, they frequently buy puts, which pushes the premiums on those options higher. However, when they are bullish or even

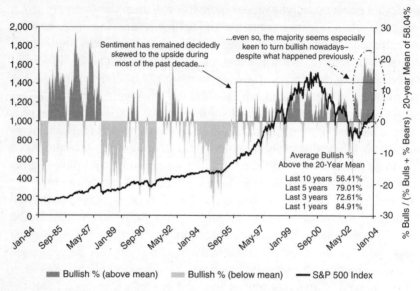

Figure 9.2   S&P 500 Index vs. Advisory Newsletter Bullish Sentiment (Source: Investors Intelligence, Bloomberg LP).

complacent, they usually do not have the same degree of interest in purchasing calls, as many are long-only players, who are naturally exposed to the upside. Aside from that, fear—and the prospect of losses—tends to be a much more powerful motivator than greed when it comes to financial matters. However, because there is an arbitrage relationship between both types of options, the overall level of implied volatility tends to rise when aggressive put buying takes place, while aggregate premium values usually drift or decline when the opposite is true. As a consequence, moves in the Vix index have, in the past, often provided useful insights about investor attitudes.

Recently, however, it seems that sentiment-based indicators have lost a measure of their usefulness, as Figure 9.2 seems to suggest. Although the wide range of market-neutral and volatility oriented strategies being employed in the derivatives arena are probably the main reasons why the latter two gauges have not worked so well, other factors also appear to be at play. For one thing, the volume of information flowing though the marketplace and the intensive surveying that takes place on a regular basis may be causing some participants to offer up canned responses or recycle perspectives picked up through the various communications channels. No doubt efforts by the financial services industry, the government, and the media to reinvigorate faith in equities and optimism about the future in the wake of the collapsed Bubble have exerted an influence on attitudes as well. Practically speaking, it is hard for anyone to make a decidedly negative case in the face of such a massive public relations onslaught, even if logic tells them otherwise. In addition, the fact that individuals are constantly being told what others are thinking may implant subliminal views that do not necessarily jibe with their own assessments of the situation.

Another development that is likely having an impact on the relationship between sentiment and market direction is the fact that the equity environment is much more splintered than it used to be, especially given the democratization process that has taken place over the past decade. Not only are people with a wider range of experiences, educational backgrounds, cultural differences, and resources at their disposal playing the game than before, many more are engaging in a variety of strategies that have little to do with traditional investing activities. As a result, the group being polled may not necessarily be the ones who are exerting a dominant influence on the existing supply-and-demand situation. This seemed apparent during the latter half of 2003, when the market rallied—without pulling back—in the face of widespread bullishness on several fronts, which in historical terms at least, was somewhat surprising. While fresh funds did come into the market through the mutual fund arena, what seemed to have provided a substantial amount of the early buying power was the hedge fund community, which had built up substantial short positions during the early part of the year. Generally speaking, their pessimistic views were not really represented in the well-known surveys.

The increased risk profile that many institutions have adopted since 2000 is likely playing a role, too. It seems that traditional money managers, for competitive reasons or with the perspective that they will be nimble enough to react at exactly the right moment, are not adjusting portfolios to reflect market conditions in the same way that they used to. Whether it relates to the percentage of cash they hold, the types of instruments and strategies they are involved in, or the assumptions they are making about the future, they appear to be introducing uniquely modern barriers between what they say and what they do. Ironically, even in those instances where they seem to recognize that prices are out of line, some have adopted a bizarre form of second-guessing. Essentially, if they perceive that "everyone" is positive, their response is to do the opposite of what experienced investors would tend to do under those circumstances—that is, they take a bullish tack—because of the belief that their sophisticated peers would be reacting the same way. In other words, they have

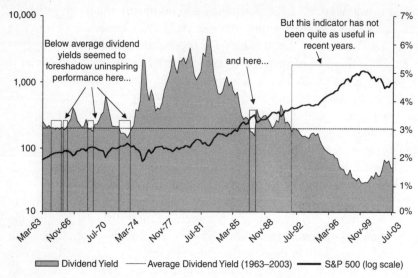

Figure 9.3   S&P 500 Index Quarterly Dividend Yield vs. Price (Source: Bloomberg LP, Standard & Poor's).

become contrarian contrarians. All of these factors have probably begun to foster a novel divergence in the historical relationship between stated views and actual market exposure.

To be sure, fear and greed are still the primary factors that influence investor behavior, so it seems unlikely that the most basic elements associated with buying and selling shares have changed all that much from earlier times. In addition, it is a good bet that how much companies actually earn and what their shares yield will ultimately remain a critical method for separating out the good from the bad—despite what Figure 9.3 seems to suggest regarding the pattern in recent years. Still, in an era where many investors are constantly trying to gain an edge by anticipating, second-guessing, and digging below the surface of what others once relied on, and where unusual macroeconomic conditions and the realities of a post-Bubble era have not been fully taken into account, it should not seem all that strange for indicators that appeared to work before to no longer function the way they used to. One way or another, though, it is likely that both the fundamentalists and the technicians will ultimately find their way back to a world where expectations about the future can be narrowed down to a more manageable range of outcomes. The odds are that at least some of the signposts they will be employing then will be different than what they use now—at least until everyone learns about the new ones and forgets about the old ones.

Action Plan

One of the advantages of operating in an environment where indicators do not perform as well as they once did is that it invariably brings to mind one of the cardinal rules of investing: Avoid the urge to take the easy way out. Whether that means engaging in halfhearted superficial research instead of doing the requisite amount of due diligence and homework, taking on a seeming "lay-up" trade before exploring why it might not necessarily work out as planned this time around, getting out of a winning position in an actively traded security instead of shedding an illiquid loser, adding to losses—averaging down—rather than cutting them outright, or laying the blame on others for investment decisions that are, at the end of the day, all your own—all of these actions will invariably lead to poor investment performance. In fact, they can do potentially significant harm to your personal bottom line—the one you have today and the one you may have to depend on tomorrow.

Interestingly, while certain indicators have turned out to be less than reliable in recent years, one of the basic realities of the share-trading arena seems to have remained intact. That is, most shares go up when "the market" is moving higher, while the opposite holds true when it is heading lower. Simply put, it is better to be long than short when money is flowing into equities and indices are in an uptrend. While there are any number of available gauges to look at, one approach that, broadly speaking, provides a good guide with respect to whether shares are in a bull or a bear phase is to examine whether benchmarks such as the Russell 2000 or the S&P 500 are trading above their 50-day and 200-day moving averages, with the smaller average also above its longer-term counterpart. If that is the case, it will usually lead to more promising results and cause fewer headaches if you focus on potential buying opportunities rather than short-sale candidates. Of course, these are general tendencies, and if numerous signs clearly indicate that you have identified the next Enron-like disaster, it might be worth taking the risk of shorting the shares in spite of a broad-based advance.

To obtain valuable insights on where the real action is, one measure that many professional investors often focus on is relative performance. In essence, they look for stocks that tend to rise more than the market on rallies and decline less than other shares on selloffs. While there can be a number of reasons for the disparity, especially in the short term, the strategy nonetheless remains a good way of identifying situations where securities are being accumulated or distributed by institutional investors. In its most basic form, it involves looking at how a share reacts during a major swing—does it tend to underperform or outperform? For a quick snapshot, take a look at a graph of the stock price divided by the value of a selected benchmark, such as the S&P 500. If the trend of the ratio has been heading higher, that indicates the issue has been outperforming the market. It is worth bearing in mind, of course, is that no security moves in a straight line forever. For more information, have a look at Web sites such as *http://moneycentral.msn.com* and *www.investors.com*.

All in all, despite the fact that many indicators seem to cause confusion nowadays rather than clarifying the situation, it is still important to look at them in their entirety to get at least some sense of how risky the investing environment is. For example, if margin lending has reached extremes, sentiment surveys point to widespread euphoria, aggregate short interest is declining, the Vix index is near long-term lows, and stock prices have been on a tear, that paints a picture suggesting there is a degree of danger associated with being heavily involved in the market. That is not to say shares will go down in the short run, or that the rally cannot continue apace. What it may mean, however, is that if the Federal Reserve decides to hike rates by 50 basis points at the same time that oil prices shoot above $50 a barrel, it may set off a decline that is particularly dramatic and difficult to trade out of. Whether such indicators work as well as they once seemed to or not, they provide a degree of insight that should not be totally ignored.

CHAPTER 10

Global Factors

---

*Global factors and foreign investors are
exerting a growing influence
on share prices.*

Economics and technology have made the world a smaller place than it
used to be. At the same time, the relative standing of many nations is in
flux as the formerly singular dominance of the U.S. empire appears to be
on the wane. Consequently, financial relationships, political developments, and cultural shifts that would have once meant relatively little to
most Americans are beginning to exert a growing influence on domestic
affairs. In addition, the global imbalances that have cropped up in recent
years as a result of various shortsighted decisions and policies have not
only created an economic burden for future generations, they have introduced an element of instability to today's markets that will likely increase
as time goes on. For investors who ignore the effects of this new world
order, the risks of being blindsided by events overseas may turn out to be
dangerously high.

Nowadays it seems just as easy—and requires only a few more digits—to call someone in New Delhi, India, as it does to contact someone in
New York City. In fact, with the efficient global telecommunications
infrastructure that is in place, it is possible for a local call to be automatically routed to a destination on the other side of the planet—with the
caller not necessarily knowing the difference. Even a unique accent might

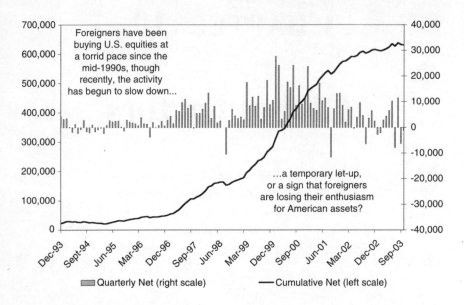

Figure 10.1   Net Foreign Purchases–Sales of U.S. Corporate Stock
(in $ millions) (Source: Bloomberg LP, U.S. Treasury).

not give anything away in the modern multicultural business environment.
It helps, of course, that while much of the world has retained some measure of its native heritage, the longstanding role of the U.S. as military
superpower and economic locomotive has fostered a widespread adoption
of English as a second language—and, perhaps, the first language of business. Together with an extensive worldwide communications network and
a fairly reliable transport framework, this combination allows all sorts of
enterprises to operate relatively easily from far-flung corners of the globe.

There are other forces that have helped to expand the ties that exist
between Americans and those living overseas, too. For many years, persistent images of a consumer-driven economic boom stirred a considerable degree of fascination with and envy about the so-called American
dream. As a result, foreigners have long paid attention to developments
within our borders. For the most part, a comparatively free American
press, the growth of large U.S.-based multinationals with sprawling international operations, the spread of military might around the globe, and
perhaps, a sense of rich-man's arrogance tended to stoke a flow of interest
that moved inordinately outward. What has probably helped to alter that
balance in recent decades, however, has been a substantial increase in
American travel abroad—up 70 percent between 1990 and 2000[1]—as

well as the rapid proliferation of a broad range of global media and information channels. From radio and television to email and the Internet, all have contributed to a dramatic expansion of reach and scope that seems to have spurred growing numbers to stay tuned to what is happening elsewhere.

These various links also underscore a wide assortment of global economic ties that have multiplied in recent decades. Because of differences in geography, population sizes, capital market structures, long-term growth rates, and a host of other factors, most countries have come to depend on neighbors far and wide to survive and thrive. A nation such as Japan, for example, which is chronically short of raw materials but long on technical know-how, has regularly found it necessary to interact with various others to acquire the commodities it needs in exchange for the goods it produces. Even the United States, blessed with abundant resources, a moderately variable climate suited to a host of different activities, a market-driven economy, and other natural advantages, has had to engage in dealings with much of the world throughout its relatively short history. Fifty years ago, the motivation would have been to facilitate demand for American exports; in more recent times, the emphasis has been on sourcing consumer goods, acquiring commodities such as oil, and raising the capital necessary to fund substantial financial imbalances.

Action Point

Gone are the days when U.S. investors could ignore what was going on beyond our shores. In today's investment world, global markets are inextricably linked, and more often than not, trends and events that are affecting overseas trading will ultimately have an effect on domestic share prices. In general, most institutional players tend to keep a close eye on what is happening in key Asian markets such as Japan, Hong Kong, Taiwan, and China, as well as in European centers such as the United Kingdom, Germany, and France. They also pay attention to moves in the currency, precious metals, and global fixed-income markets. For relatively up-to-date information on potentially interesting and important foreign developments, Web sites such as *www.bloomberg.com, www.ft.com*, and *www.economist.com* can be good starting points.

Ironically, part of this evolution has probably been influenced by the capitalist system that many believe has been a major catalyst for sustained growth in past decades. To be sure, the U.S. has also long reaped the rewards associated with having a major global military presence promoting a widespread sense of security, as well as a legal structure that fosters political and economic stability. Nonetheless, despite these seemingly invincible bulwarks, one of the factors that appears to have made America such an economic force to be reckoned with, especially during a period of great technological change, has been a culture that encourages flexibility and adaptability. When U.S. businesses have seen opportunities, they have been quick to capitalize on them. One such example has been the widespread trend towards outsourcing labor-intensive operations to lower-wage economies, which has provided considerable bottom-line benefits to the companies involved. It has also been a boon for American consumers, because it has helped to lower prices for a variety of finished goods. Unfortunately, one result of this shift has been a hollowing out of the domestic manufacturing base.

Interestingly, despite the substantial declines in production capacity and employment—2.5 million of the 3 million jobs lost since January 2001 have been in the manufacturing sector[2]—the U.S. has remained a bastion of relative strength, at least until recently. While there are numerous reasons why, one important contributing factor has been American consumers' willingness to keep spending, even though a significant proportion of the proceeds has ended up in foreign coffers. Indeed, aside from helping to keep the economy moving forward even after the Bubble burst and business investment faltered, this state of affairs has been a boon for overseas exporters. The end result, however, has been to create significant economic imbalances and potentially unstable deficits. One particular example, as seen in Figure 10.2, has been the dramatic widening in the U.S. current account balance, which represents the difference between the value of goods and services coming in and those going out.

Although this indicator has been in the red for some time, reflecting a pattern of chronic debt-financed overconsumption that grew somewhat more pronounced during the go-go years, the scale of the deterioration seems to have become especially noticeable recently, reaching a historically worrisome extreme of around 5 percent of GDP. Clearly, one of the main reasons for this development has been the free-spending ways of the American consumer in the face of relatively subdued growth in personal incomes. What has also added further fuel to the fire, however, has been the aggressive currency management practices of some major global

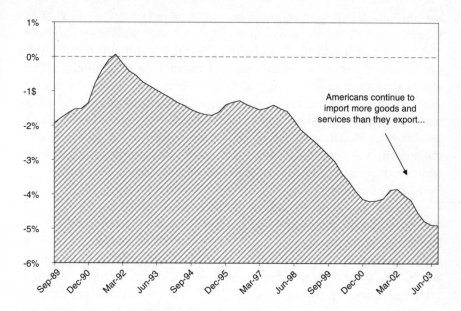

Figure 10.2   U.S. Current Account Balance as a Percentage of Gross Domestic Product (Source: Bloomberg LP, U.S. Bureau of Economic Research).

exporters, such as China, which have kept the U.S. dollar prices of their various manufactured goods at relatively attractive levels.

In simple terms, currency rates are a gauge of value between two countries—or, in the case of the euro, a group of countries. They allow prices in one location to be compared to those in another. In many respects, they are the glue that binds nations together in a diverse international economy. However, they also have various other notions associated with them. For instance, because many government policy tools, programs, and planning processes are often dominated by domestic concerns—for legal or philosophical reasons, or both—foreign exchange rates sometimes act as steam valves that bear the brunt of internal pressures. These might include, for example, aggressive efforts to rejuvenate an ailing economy by boosting the cash in circulation, which would, normally speaking, tend to depress the local currency relative to others because of the increase in supply. The problem is that it can also have an unsettling knock-on effect with respect to other ties that exist between countries.

As a consequence, foreign exchange—also called F/X or forex—rates sometimes serve as lightening rods for all sorts of international tensions and disputes. In addition, because a nation's legal tender is often viewed as a symbol and a measure of its economic well-being, and can also be seen as a reflection of cultural relevance and national pride, this occasionally infuses the local unit of account with a significance that stands apart from purely economic factors. As a result, it may be bought and sold for reasons that have more to do with emotions and chest-pounding nationalism than with logic and financial concerns. The dominant influence and focus of attention, however, is the wide variety of trade, investment, and speculative flows that course through the markets on a regular basis. Still, taken together, these various issues can make for a fairly complicated mix.

Indeed, there any number of conflicts associated with the fact that foreign exchange rates can have multiple meanings and influences. To begin with, from the point of view of exporters, it is beneficial to have a local currency that is weak relative to that of the country or countries where they sell their wares. For example, a rise in the dollar-yen[3] foreign exchange rate—say, from 107.00 to 110.00, which yields three extra yen in return for every greenback—tends to benefit the bottom lines of export-oriented automakers, such as Toyota and Honda. This is because the relative decline of their native currency potentially gives them room to cut the U.S. prices of their vehicles while realizing the same or a higher amount of yen when the proceeds are translated back into that currency. As a result, this can make these manufacturers more competitive in the American market than their Detroit-based counterparts.

For Japanese importers, it works the other way around. A higher greenback will make the price of a commodity that is currently based in dollars, such as oil, more expensive in local currency terms. In other words, using the same rates listed above, the cost of a $30 barrel of the black stuff will rise from 3210 to 3300 yen, even though the dollar price remains unchanged. Arguably, then, the question of which is "better" overall—in this example, a lower yen or a lower dollar—usually depends on two factors: whether a nation is a net importer or exporter and how many politically-sensitive jobs might be affected by an adjustment in the existing parities. Practically speaking, for countries with considerable manufacturing employment and strong export ties to the U.S.—as is the case with Japan and many other Asian nations—the usual answer is a stronger greenback.

There are other players involved, of course. For companies looking to purchase assets overseas, a rise in the local currency relative to the foreign one can bring benefits in the form of lower upfront costs. For example, a 5 percent decline in the euro-dollar rate—say, from 1.2500 to 1.1875—will lower the price of a 1 billion euro acquisition by $62.5 million. Occasionally, in fact, a major swing in the forex market can set off a flurry of cross-border deals, instigated in large part by those based in the country with the strengthening currency. A much more significant group, though, is made up of investors and speculators who look to capitalize on differences in relative interest rates, diversify into other markets, wager on the directional trend of the rate itself, or engage in some combination of all three. Apart from whatever returns they achieve locally, they usually benefit when the currency they own rises relative to the one they do not. While all of this can sound rather confusing, the crux of the matter is that there are many different interests that stand to win or lose when exchange rates move. At the same time, others such as governments may attempt to ensure that parities do not shift too far in the "wrong" direction.

Action Point

One of the keys to success in modern markets is to try and look at the investment universe from a multidimensional perspective. It no longer makes sense, for example, to focus solely on how changes in U.S. interest rates will affect the American economy. In reality, such adjustments may also affect the dollar, overseas stock and bond markets, international trade relationships, and even political sentiment, as existing links are thrown out of kilter. When new information comes to the fore, stand back and look at it with an open mind. To begin with, explore what the facts mean in a literal sense. Then, try to figure out how they might be interpreted by others and what the potential knock-on implications might be. Like playing chess, today's environment requires investors to look at what others may do—many moves ahead.

The approach they use can take many shapes and forms. It may include relatively indirect methods, such as "jawboning" and well-orchestrated propaganda campaigns, or at the other extreme, direct interaction with the market, which is commonly referred to as currency intervention. It may also revolve around manipulation of the money supply, with governments either "printing" more of the local currency or implementing monetary policy measures that adjust the quantity in circulation through purchases and sales of assets such as government-backed debt. On occasion, it may involve overt regulation, featuring such measures as general currency controls, restrictions on convertibility, or laws prohibiting unofficial dealings in foreign exchange. Regardless of the methods chosen, the primary emphasis in recent years has been on maintaining desirable trade relationships and, to a lesser extent, limiting "excessive" volatility.

As it happens, a great deal of the action that has taken place in the forex markets during the past few decades has centered on the dollar. Given the United States' longstanding role as a dominant economic, military, and political power, as well as the widespread acceptance of the greenback as a primary unit of account for all sorts of international transactions, this is not surprising. In some ways, it has made life easier to have a single point of reference. As with the widespread adoption of English as a convenient middle ground for commercial activities, it helps to cut down on the potential confusion cross-border activities might otherwise engender in the absence of an agreed-upon standard. Convenience is not the only issue that matters, of course, but for lack of a better alternative—at least until recently—most of the world seems to have been happy with the status quo.

Nowadays, however, there have been numerous issues cropping up, partly as a result of this broad-based acceptance. For one thing, it has occasionally caused problems in countries where the local currency has been perceived as risky or vulnerable to inflationary pressures. For another, the dollar's function as a store of value and international reserve currency[4] has sometimes clashed with the reality that its primary function is still that of legal tender of the United States. It is also the "product" that exporters receive in exchange for what they sell to U.S. customers, which is not necessarily what they want to end up with. In fact, America's growing dependence on foreign-made goods would, under most other circumstances, tend to put downward pressure on the greenback and stir up a variety of related strains. Despite that, up until the Bubble burst at least, there was a relatively unique alignment of interests. That was because, broadly speaking, the dollar was in a sustained uptrend. This not only benefited exporters to the U.S. but also served as a magnet for overseas capital that helped to bolster asset prices and kept domestic interest rates relatively low.

What essentially happened was, despite a continuing flood of dollars into the marketplace and signs that debt levels were expanding at potentially alarming rates, many outsiders apparently made the conscious decision to hold on to or acquire more greenbacks and invest them here. In other words, rather than losing confidence—a circumstance that might have been expected and has often been the case when other, more fragile nations have seemingly abandoned fiscal prudence—foreigners became even more enthralled. It certainly helped, of course, that many seemed to believe there were few real alternatives, as did the fact that America continued to display a measure of economic vitality and new-era optimism that stood out in contrast to other parts of the world. Whatever the reasons, the momentum seemed to feed on itself and the money came pouring in, as the equity data in Figure 10.1 seems to make clear. That stimulated a significant increase in economic growth during the 1990s and contributed to the feeding frenzy that helped drive financial asset prices through the roof. It also served to fund ongoing U.S. purchases of foreign-made goods, as well as a speculative build-up of excess capacity in a wide range of industries.

It seemed almost a virtuous circle in many ways, creating a vision of neverending prosperity that played no small part in bolstering the widespread euphoria of the era. Eventually, though, the Bubble burst and a hangover phase set in. Although the impact was relatively far-reaching, it did seem to pry open some especially visible chinks in the American armor. It also highlighted substantial financial vulnerabilities that had largely been ignored beforehand. Nonetheless, for a short while at least, the rally in the greenback persisted, helping to attract additional funds from an assortment of trend-chasing overseas operators. To be sure, this continued momentum was helped by continuing strength in the U.S. bond market, itself spurred by anticipation of further rate cuts and expectations that inflation would remain low. It was also given some support by sporadic intervention efforts, as various export-driven nations sought to maintain trade parity with the U.S. in the face of a global economic slowdown. Soon, though, the currency's rate of ascent began to wane, and on the heels of ongoing share price weakness and sluggish macroeconomic conditions, it seemed that some foreigners were beginning to get nervous about the dollar's prospects. Then, during 2002, the greenback started to decline sharply versus many foreign currencies, and that laid the groundwork for occasional jitters in the financial markets ever since.

It is not hard to see why. According to Bill Gross, Managing Director at fund manager PIMCO, foreigners own approximately 13 percent of the U.S. stock market.[5] Although most commentators have generally viewed this interest as an overwhelmingly positive sign, the problem is, as in any situation where sizable positions are free to trade at any time, there is always a possibility that the securities could suddenly come onto the market and seriously disrupt the existing supply-and-demand balance. Over the course of the last few decades, people have not given much thought to such a scenario, because there have been relatively few competing arenas with the depth of liquidity, ease of access, and degree of security necessary to pose any serious threat. Moreover, while the equity exposure is significant, foreign ownership of U.S. debt obligations, especially government-backed securities, is substantially greater in absolute and relative terms.[6] As a result, that interest tends to be somewhat more relevant in this context, and since much of it is held by foreign governments—the constituency least likely to set off any large-scale financial fireworks—many observers have been quick to dismiss fears of a sudden retreat. Nevertheless, as in all markets—whether equities, housing, art, or otherwise—sometimes it only takes a small amount of movement at the margin to shake things up across the board.

Action Point

Although foreign investors have been major investors in American shares in recent years, a significant proportion of their funds have ended up in the fixed income markets—more specifically, U.S. treasury securities, where they reportedly own over a third of the issues outstanding.[7] Consequently, it is worth paying attention to what these players are up to, particularly during the periods before, during, and after regularly scheduled auctions of government bills, notes, and bonds. Chances are, if international operators begin to seriously rethink their outlook with respect to U.S. assets, signs will likely emerge relatively early on in this particular trading arena. *The Wall Street Journal* Credit Markets column and Web sites such as *www.bloomberg.com* frequently offer interesting color on the kinds of activity that dealers are seeing.

That is especially true when the securities involved are marketable and can be offered for sale at fairly short notice. Historically, substantial foreign holdings of such instruments—as opposed to investments in relatively illiquid assets such as real estate—often seem to create a wellspring of potential future instability. That was apparently the case during the 1998 Asian crisis, when a speculative surge of "hot money" flowed into the region beforehand and apparently set the stage for the punishing collapse that followed. Prior to the upheaval, overseas investors had become enamored with the growth prospects of the various Asian Tigers,[8] and that love affair triggered a gold rush that drove equity markets and local currency values to fairly lofty levels. Ultimately, though, the inbound push created an outbound crush that, in many respects, left those nations worse off than before the whole thing got started.

To paraphrase F. Scott Fitzgerald, when it comes to foreign investors, they are often very different from you and me. Of course, the description does not just refer to those who reside in other parts of the globe—in this instance, the term broadly applies to anyone, American or otherwise, who invests funds in markets outside of their own home turf. Nonetheless, aside from the fact that overseas investing involves risks that the domestic variety typically does not, often the attitudes, motivations, emotions, and behavior of those who wander far afield can vary significantly from those exhibited by local operators. History suggests, for example, that many players who get involved in foreign shares, particularly after a noticeable surge, often turn out to be short-term momentum-chasers, as several studies have indicated.[9] This is not entirely illogical, as part of the attraction of looking globally is to try and capture what are perceived to be above-average returns that might not otherwise be available locally. Regardless, what this effectively means is that foreigners can add a destabilizing influence to markets that are already in an excited state.

What can sometimes make matters worse from the point of view of domestic investors is the fact that outsiders typically do not have the same vested interest in the longer-term stability of the markets they play in that the natives do, other than with respect to how it might affect the day-to-day value of their holdings or their ability to cash out when the time is right. Consequently, they are less likely than locals to be sensitive to the negative impact their activities might be having, which, whether inadvertent or not, can have an unsettling impact. Sometimes their detachment from longer-term domestic concerns can foster fallout similar to that of the "tragedy of the commons," which describes a phenomenon where certain individuals take more out of a shared resource than they put back in and end up ruining it for everybody else in the process. Without being exposed to some of the consequences of their actions, foreigners naturally have less incentive to play by the same rules. Hence, they may trample in, draw clumsily from the well, and then disappear in a swirl of dust and disarray.

Apart from that, most global investors have the luxury of arbitrarily picking and choosing their markets, instruments, and timing, further stir-

ring a potential insensitivity to local concerns that domestic money managers often cannot afford to have. Foreign players also tend to be quite
skittish when faced with surprise developments—even those with only
vaguely negative connotations—and occasionally overreact to events that
the natives might easily take in stride. This is not all that surprising,
because it follows from the natural tendency of most people to be somewhat apprehensive when straying far from their home ground. What is
more, when it comes to investing abroad, it is more common to see misunderstandings about day-to-day events and political subtleties, for example, than in similar domestic circumstances, because many cross-border
operators do not have the cultural ties, historical perspectives, or breadth
of understanding of the language that the locals do.

Another issue that can affect the behavior of international investors,
which domestic operators often do not face, is the fact that much of their
understanding about events and circumstances tends to come to them sec-
ondhand—either through the media or local brokers—and hence will
often be colored in the process. There is also the age-old problem of time
and distance, which tends to act as a natural filtering mechanism that can
sometimes distill the rich fabric of life into one-dimensional caricatures.
In addition, newspaper, radio, and television reports about goings-on in
other countries frequently reflect the worst, the most outlandish, or the
most popular aspects, which can foster an unrealistic sense of what local
conditions are really like. For one thing, they may exaggerate certain
aspects, such as the crime rate, and end up creating an image much like
New York City had during the 1970s, when foreign visitors turned up
thinking the place was a war zone. For another, the stories may leave out
relevant details that local residents take for granted, causing outsiders to
make simplistic assumptions about the business and investing climate.

Action Point

The presence of global financial players in business, finance,
and the media often means that popular themes and trends
end up migrating around the globe. This seems to hold
especially   true   in   such   diverse   areas   as   fashion,
entertainment, retailing, travel, and leisure. In addition, it is
frequently the case that what others are eating and drinking,
and how they are going about their daily lives, eventually
impacts what Americans do—and vice versa. Although there
are a host of local magazines and newspapers available on the

Internet—the Journalism Tools section of the *Columbia Journalism Review* Web site at *www.cjr.org* has some useful links, as does *www.journalistexpress.com*—sources such as the foreign editions of *The Wall Street Journal,* available at *http://online.wsj.com,* and *The Economist,* online at *www.economist.com,* often include articles on noteworthy developments overseas.

Taken together, all of these various aspects can paint a picture of what is going on that is more like a matchstick drawing than a Matisse, which can sometimes motivate operators to move in and out of foreign markets with little reason or warning. Language translation and comprehension issues, of course, can also cause confusion, making it difficult for outsiders to get to the bottom of things. Even in those cases where English is the second language—or perhaps the first, as in the United Kingdom—there can be subtle differences in underlying meaning that may have one side thinking it is time to wade in and the other side believing something altogether different. Time zone differences and the natural lags that occur as information crosses borders, even in an age of 24-hour television news coverage, can also cause those on the receiving end to be slightly out of synch with the reality of events on the ground.

What is more, everyone has a view of the world that is shaded to a certain extent by societal and cultural biases, which exist on a variety of levels. These can turn good information into bad as individuals listen with an element of expectation about what they believe they are hearing or what they expect will be said. In some cultures, for example, people may avoid speaking directly about certain topics and will tend to adopt a formal tone in business-related conversations. Consequently, those who are used to a more straightforward approach may end up misinterpreting the responses and wrongly assuming that the other side has something to hide. The same holds true regarding personal interpretations: Some may view things literally, others may search for hidden meaning, and a few will automatically assume the opposite of what is said is what is actually true. Generally speaking, even the possibility of getting minor details wrong can increase the odds that foreign investors might react in an unsettling fashion.

What may also add to the confusion, however—if Richard Nisbett, author of *The Geography of Thought: How Asians and Westerners Think Different...and Why,*[10] is right—is that people from the eastern and western hemispheres may actually be hardwired to see things differently from one another. According to Mr. Nisbett, Westerners tend to view the world in terms of objects and logic, while those from Asia tend to look at it in terms of substances and relationships. There may be other regional issues that play a role in influencing investor behavior as well. In some Eastern cultures, for example, there is no Judeo-Christian ethic that inhibits people from gambling often and gambling big, and this speculative mindset sometimes seems to rub off on those who operate in the share-trading arena. And, somewhat paradoxically, it appears that stock markets in countries where there are considerable social pressures to conform, as well as those where individuals tend to wear their emotions on their sleeves, seem to experience more frequent short-term contagions than have typically been seen in the U.S.

Other disparities may crop up because of historical traditions and regulatory perspectives. Up until the past decade or so, for example, there were considerable differences of opinion about the legality and morality of using inside information to gain a financial advantage. In some countries, attitudes about the subject have historically been more relaxed than here, and whether it was expressly permitted or rules were largely ignored, the practice seemed to be an integral part of the regular wheeling-and-dealing that took place. Moreover, in certain markets, share operators have long invested—speculated, some would argue—almost exclusively on the basis of whispers, rumors, feelings, and themes. That is somewhat contrary to the quantitative approaches that have found favor in the U.S. during past decades, though with the shift to a more speculative approach that seems to be occurring, the divide no longer seems as wide.

Arguably, all of these prospective differences, from those that are more or less specific to overseas investing to those that are associated with cultural distinctions and regional preferences, would probably represent little more than an interesting collection of international investing trivia were it not for the fact that significant financial imbalances and sizable foreign ownership interests have left the United States substantially beholden to outsiders. What has made the situation somewhat trickier in recent years is the fact that many of the developments that have altered the domestic investing landscape seem to have had a similarly pronounced effect on investor behavior and stock market practices around the world—not only with respect to activities taking place at the local level, but in a broader global sense as well.

In many Western European countries, for instance, investors appear to be moving towards a more active investing approach and exhibiting an increased appetite for risk, mirroring the shift that seems to be taking place in the U.S. Along with this evolution has come a similar focus on data points rather than data trends. While there are probably numerous reasons why, it seems a good bet that at least part of it comes down to the increasing influence of large global financial players, on both the sell side and the buy side. Overseas operators are likely imitating what they see taking place as well. Dealing costs—while still mostly above comparable U.S. levels—have also fallen sharply, aided by increased competition and significant advances in technology, which has led to increased turnover, mirroring the trend here. In addition, the global telecommunications infrastructure has probably improved far more in relative terms than what has been seen domestically, creating a fairly dramatic pickup in the flow of information that is sloshing around overseas share-trading arenas.

In terms of our markets, it is worth noting that major foreign operators have not only had the dollars and willingness to invest in the U.S., they have, in many instances, also had access to much of the same dealing technology, broker support, and settlement services that domestic institutional players rely on. Consequently, it is as easy for them to call on the telephone or click with a mouse to execute a U.S. trade as it is for an American operator. This has been helped, of course, by a dramatic change in the ranks of the global investment banking powerhouses, a group that was once made up almost entirely of American firms but which now includes institutions headquartered in cities such as London, Frankfurt, and Zurich with operations that span the globe.

Action Point

There used to be somewhat of a predictable rhythm in the market moves that took place as trading activity shifted from one time zone to the next, but that no longer seems to be the case. Sometimes short-term trends will develop in the U.S. that Asia ignores and European traders look at as a contrarian signal. Alternatively, there have been occasions when the energy from dramatic geopolitical developments that have taken place during the early morning hours has completely dissipated by the time the New York opening bell sounds. Because of intermarket arbitrage and anticipatory trading by large global financial players, share prices do not necessarily follow the domino cascade they once did. The point is, do not assume that strength or weakness in one market will automatically feed through into other share-trading venues.

Generally speaking, not only do many sizable players engage in the same sorts of activities—statistical arbitrage, program trading, short-selling, and others—within various foreign markets as they do here, most view the entire world as their trading arena. Some, for example, will just as readily place a directional bet using an option, future, or exchange-traded fund based on the United Kingdom's benchmark FTSE-100 index as they would with one linked to the S&P 500. Others will think nothing of engaging in spread trades based on historical relationships between, say, the German bellwether DAX future and the NASDAQ 100 future—or perhaps the long bond[11] instead. Even when players have no explicit arbitrage relationship in mind, if a dramatic development takes place on Thanksgiving Day, when all of the U.S. markets are closed, it would not be surprising to see the London-based traders of American investment banks buying or selling Eurostoxx 50[12] futures to hedge their firms' domestic equity exposure.

As it happens, such activities also serve to underscore a growing international interest in trading financial instruments based on bundles of securities. In a world where major competitors in such disparate sectors as oil, autos, and telecommunications may be scattered across a wide range of different countries, it would seem almost inevitable that cross-border thematic trading would turn out to be a popular pursuit. Sometimes traders' strategies have a unifying macroeconomic element, such as those involving the purchase or sale of stocks in "commodity currency" markets like Australia and Canada, for example. Alternatively, the approaches may focus on the shares of countries based in a specific region, such as Asia or Europe, which may comprise an existing ETF or be bundled together as a makeshift derivative. Combined with the large-scale cross-border activities of the global index managers and macro-oriented hedge funds, it is probably safe to say that these activities have reduced at least some of the disparities that can exist between different international markets.

In fact, though history suggests it is not unusual to see major global indices decline in synch during severe bear markets, one side effect of the increased cross-border activity associated with international trading and investing may be a greater correlation between large-capitalization shares listed on exchanges around the world. As Figure 10.3 seems to indicate,

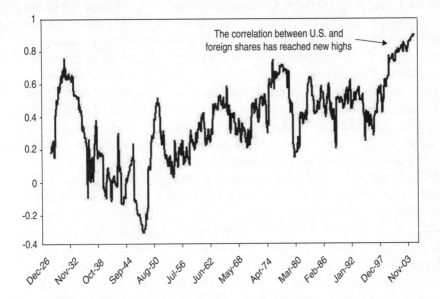

Figure 10.3   Historical Correlation Between U.S. and Non-U.S. Stocks (1928–2003). S&P 500 Index vs. MSCI EAFE Index, 36-Month Moving Windows, Computed Monthly (Source: Zephyr StyleADVISOR, Global Financial Data).

U.S. and foreign stocks are more closely linked in performance terms nowadays than they have been at any time since 1928. While it is likely that expanding information flows, growing trade ties, and parallel shifts in investor behavior may be playing a role, it is probably true, too, that some measure of the convergence has been caused by hedge funds, proprietary trading desks, and others effectively arbitraging the differences in returns from various countries, as well as the deployment of methods that work in one center to a variety of others. Interestingly enough, it may turn out that some of those who invest overseas in order to achieve greater diversification may, in effect, be getting less than they bargained for.

    One of the potential risks associated with this intricate maze of global share-trading activities is the possibility that a significant bet that goes wrong in one market may trigger unexpected selling or short-covering in another, as positions are unwound to meet margin calls or minimum capital requirements. Similarly, given the wide range of asset classes that many modern operators get involved in, it is possible that a dramatic swing in a commodity, bond, or other product could set off a chain reaction response in equities. This may be especially true when it comes to moves in the forex markets. Even when there is no stand-alone exposure, most globally oriented institutions pay as much attention to developments in the currency arena as they do to security selection, asset allocation, and investment overviews. Moreover, whether international operators hedge their forex exposure or not, the decision to buy or sell overseas assets often still depends on a currency view. Arguably, this has probably been the case with respect to at least some foreign purchases of U.S. assets over the past decade, and it raises the prospect that some level of dollar weakness may trigger a widespread desire to exit the greenback—and the associated investments—at the same time.

Although the big-picture elements are clearly important, global influences also seem to be having an impact on day-to-day activities. One development that comes to mind relates to what might be described as time zone compression. In essence, because of the longer hours that some of the more aggressive market operators are putting in, as well as increased 24-hour electronic information, communications, and trading links, a measure of the premarket build-up of overseas order flow that used to occur seems to have disappeared. To give some background, during the past two decades, many of the traditional institutions that invest globally made arrangements to accommodate geographic realities. In some instances, firms utilized a shift system, with traders based at the same location but working at different hours of the day or night. In others, they imitated their global investment banking counterparts and set up shop in key American, Asian, and European market centers.

Nowadays, however, it seems that more operators in more locations are working longer hours to try and capture more of the global action that takes place on any given day. It is not surprising to see some London-based hedge funds and proprietary dealing desks, for example, have staff come in at around 7:00 a.m. or so local time and trade straight through until the New York close, which is at least a 14-hour day. The same sometimes holds true for American-based players who operate in both the domestic and Asian markets. By cutting out some of the natural trading breaks that used to occur, such actions help to eliminate a degree of the prospective buying or selling interest that would typically feed through at the beginning and end of the U.S. session. In some respects, it seems to produce a dissipating effect much like that which occurs at certain times of the year, when a clash of various professional athletic seasons tends to dampen the enthusiasm one might have for any one sport.

What has further blurred the lines between market openings and closings has been the multiple listings of shares on various foreign stock exchanges—though, admittedly, the action that might take place, say, in IBM shares trading in Germany is likely to be relatively light even on the best of days. So has the expanding presence of electronic trading venues, such as ECNs, which, as in the case of Instinet, never really close, at least during the course of a five-day workweek. These developments, together with the significant increase in round-the-clock trading of electronic S&P 500, NASDAQ 100, and Dow Jones Industrials e-mini futures that has occurred in recent years, have not only diminished the prospect of substantial overseas premarket stresses, but have also taken away some of the late-day cutoff pressures that have historically been associated with the U.S. closing bell.

The increased availability of a wide variety of trading vehicles and venues across multiple time zones has also changed the pattern that used to be in effect when activity in each major region of the world was somewhat more segmented. These days, if there is a substantial sector move or a noteworthy development overseas, market participants no longer have to wait for the American markets to open before they can act on—or react to—what is going on. Indeed, what seems to be an increasingly common occurrence is that money will often start flowing into or out of a security or index before the bell rings, and then, within moments of the official opening, some premarket position-takers will suddenly turn profit-takers and stop the move almost dead in its tracks. On a broader scale, this phenomenon sometimes seems in evidence following major geopolitical events overseas, when so many traders jump on board the early-morning action that by the time U.S. session officially gets under way, there is nobody left to keep the trend alive.

It is worth noting, of course, that while the primary emphasis has been on foreign flows into and out of the United States, some domestic investors have long been interested in other equity markets for diversification and performance-boosting reasons, whether through mutual funds, ETFs, ADRs,[13] or direct purchases and sales of local shares. What could be a particularly significant turn of events, however, is if a waning overseas interest in U.S. assets is made worse by an expanding American appetite for cross-border investments. There are signs, in fact, that such a development may be in the offing. Although it may not necessarily represent a sea change, during October 2003, domestic investors bought more foreign equities than foreigners bought U.S. stocks for the first time in five years.[14] Adding further weight to that statistic was the fact that international ETFs saw greater percentage inflows than their domestic counterparts during 2003. Finally, even Warren Buffet, in a bylined article in Fortune, made reference to the fact that the company he oversees, Berkshire Hathaway, had begun buying foreign currencies for the first time ever, on concerns about the United States' deteriorating trade balance.[15] Consequently, this raises the prospect that even a modest foreign retreat could turn into a full-fledged rout if domestic investors really start to join in.

It seems likely that the evolving geopolitical environment may have a substantial impact on U.S. financial markets in the future as well. On the one hand, the continuing prospect of random acts of violence overseas will invariably inject a note of uncertainty into the daily routine, and traders will probably react negatively to any signs that terrorists may be stepping up the pace of their activities. On the other hand, it seems possible that the fallout from the United States' pre-emptive invasion of Iraq may have set the stage for a reaction that has much broader implications down the road. By alienating several longtime allies and giving at least some credence to claims that America is a bully that acts only in its own interests, it may have opened up a chasm that causes foreigners to aggressively reappraise their U.S. exposure. In fact, there are indications in certain parts of the world, such as the Mideast, that governments and private individuals are actively seeking alternative investment havens.

What may facilitate their efforts is a move by countries in various regions to formalize economic and political ties. Following in the footsteps of the European Union agreement and the alignment of the trading interests of U.S., Mexico, and Canada under NAFTA,[16] there seems to be more of a widespread desire to create trade zones where preference is given to those on the inside. One result of this coordination is the formation of marketplaces that are substantial in terms of size and scope, which may represent viable alternatives to that which exists in the United States. In addition, if these regional blocs decide to adopt a single currency, as the Europeans have done, it can provide easy access for large-scale foreign investors. In effect, it gives sizable overseas players who are relatively unenthusiastic dollar holders an opportunity to diversify. While the threat of such a switch remains conjecture at this point, problems may come if the theory turns into a reality. At that point, U.S. investors may need to get their hard hats on.

Action Plan

Although it is a bit of a cliché, the financial world has indeed become a global village, and it is foolhardy for investors to ignore what is going on overseas because they view the American market as their primary focus. Like it or not, at a time when the U.S. economy is dependent on the kindness of strangers to support substantial financial imbalances, it is possible that a coup in the Mideast or an earthquake in Asia might potentially have more impact on the Dow Jones than an unexpected interest rate move by the Federal Reserve. However, because the domestic press often emphasizes a distinctly American-centric point of view, it can make sense to seek out other sources to get a more complete picture of what is taking place outside our borders. As an added bonus, foreign publications often provide an alternative—perhaps, even a more objective—look at what is happening here. For other views, turn to resources such as *www.ft.com*, *www.economist.com*, *http://news.bbc.co.uk*, and the overseas editions of *The Wall Street Journal*.

There is an old saying that goes, "When in Rome, do as the Romans do." In the investment arena, you do not actually have to be based in far-flung locations to adopt that perspective, but forcing yourself to look at the world through others' eyes can often provide useful insights that will add to your overall understanding of the big picture. Aside from that, it is wise to assume that foreigners may not necessarily act and react like domestic players when it comes to the latest data or developments, particularly those that pertain to hot button issues on the macroeconomic and geopolitical fronts. For example, though most Americans admire the dominant role the nation has had on the world political stage, the view of everyone else is much more ambivalent—some resent what the country stands for, while others look forward to continuing American supremacy. Unfortunately, it seems that lately more people are leaning towards the former.

In most countries around the world, politics and economics are firmly linked. Consequently, important issues such as unemployment, trade balances, interest rates, and energy prices can sometimes create enough internal pressure to get government wheels spinning in an unhelpful direction, at least with respect to cross-border relationships. With mounting international conflicts over trade in recent years, accompanied by talk of devaluations, revaluations, duties, embargoes, and "wars," it seems likely that political machinations will increasingly add an unexpected wrinkle to the future investment mix. Sometimes it will be beneficial to U.S. interests, as large overseas exporters promise to direct business to certain American companies to pacify our complaints. The odds are greater, however, that other countries will focus their efforts on penalizing U.S. firms that sell goods in their own markets. To stay informed, pay

attention to reports in national newspapers such as *The New York Times,*
The Wall Street Journal, or *The Washington Post* about any potential trade
disputes that may be in the works.

The world is a much more dangerous place than it used to be, and the
specter of terrorism raises the prospect that random and dramatic events
could cause great harm to life and property. Generally speaking, markets
tend to react sharply when such developments occur, with knee-jerk selling by traders often pushing prices far out of whack. At the risk of sounding callous, it is worth keeping in mind that while the effect on people's
lives can be painfully long-lasting, the markets often shake off these
shocks, staging at least partial recoveries back towards pre-event levels.
In fact, such rebounds have frequently served as catalysts for more sustained turnarounds in markets that have been under pressure for some
period of time. The reality is, these moments can provide a rare opportunity to buy securities at attractive prices. While it would be ghoulish and
repugnant to focus on that possibility, the challenge in today's markets is
to make the most of what can sometimes be very trying times.

Overseas equity investing is not for everyone, but it can represent an
opportunity to diversify into the shares of companies that might be benefiting as their American competitors are faltering. Apart from the challenge of choosing the right stock in the right market, however, there is
almost always a risk associated with adverse currency moves. While certain instruments, such as global ETFs and ADRs, appear to make the process relatively straightforward, bear in mind that if the dollar moves
higher relative to the currency in which the foreign shares are valued, it
will create a drag on the performance of such securities. In fact, it is possible that the stock price could move higher in local terms, but the currency effect could equate to a loss for dollar-based shareholders. The
point to remember is, when you invest overseas, unless you have a way of
hedging the foreign exchange risk, you are effectively betting on both the
local share price and the F/X rate.

PART 3

SURVIVAL OF THE FITTEST

The Jungle of the Future

---

*Developments that will likely influence
tomorrow's markets.*

One of the most significant influences on the stock market over the past decade has been the impact of improving technology and increased information flow. From enhanced communications to better trading systems to refined analytical methods to the phenomenal growth of the Internet, these developments have enabled individuals and institutions to research, analyze, and invest in ways they could not really do before. Up until now, however, the lion's share of the benefit—as has historically been the case—has accrued to those who manage large sums of money—either their own funds or the pooled investments of others. In fact, given the financial and academic resources at their disposal, the economy-of-scale leverage they enjoy, and the close relationships they have with the movers and shakers in the business and financial community, it would have been surprising if they had not been able to maintain at least some measure of their traditional edge over the "little guy" when it comes to identifying and capitalizing on share price disparities.

And yet, despite what appears to be a significant advantage, it seems a good bet that this situation will change in the years ahead, with the differential shrinking in favor of the small investor. Why? Much of it comes down to the disadvantages of size. For, although various parts of the equity market have had numerous inefficiencies wrung out of them—helped by sizeable doses of intellectual firepower and the aggressive efforts of a rapidly expanding hedge fund sector—the primary focus has been on large capitalization issues. This makes sense, of course, given that many modern institutional portfolios tend to be measured in the billions of dollars. Usually when these managers want to invest, what they have to play with seriously limits their options. In fact, even if they want to venture out into less crowded terrain, there is generally not much that they can really do with respect to smaller companies and other less liquid investments. Moreover, with the prospects for consolidation and convergence in the mutual fund and hedge fund industries seemingly assured in the not too distant future, it is not unreasonable to assume that there will be even greater concentrations of pooled funds in the institutional universe than there are now. As a result, what will probably happen is that issues that make the institutional cut, so to speak, will end up being sliced and diced by all sorts of ultracompetitive operators, while those that do not will remain relatively ripe for everyone else to pick over.

What this also suggests, however, is that because many of the obvious mispricings in the weightier issues will be largely arbitraged away, that segment of the market will be increasingly dominated by sector- or theme-driven flows, with stock-specific factors playing a diminishing role. Practically speaking, the emphasis will be even more narrowly focused on overall market direction than it is today, mirroring the essence of what exists in the foreign exchange or bond trading arenas. The exception will be a further escalation in program trading and other forms of mechanized buying and selling that will exploit the narrowest types of anomalies on a continuing basis. The result? More momentum-driven trading, more intraday volatility in the better-known issues, and less opportunity for investors to make money in the shares of large companies using traditional investing approaches. In contrast, those who focus on small-cap stocks could stand to realize substantial rewards from their efforts. For one thing, they will have the opportunity to employ modern tactics and finely tuned methods—and to make use of the most up-to-date knowledge and critical intelligence—to take advantage of inefficiencies that will presumably continue to exist in a diverse universe made up of less widely followed securities. In addition, it is probably fair to say that they will not have to worry about bigger, stronger, and potentially more influential operators coming along and spoiling the party.

Ironically, while these developments will tend, on balance, to eliminate even more inefficiencies than have been eradicated thus far, it is conceivable that they may also put the final nail in the coffin of the Efficient
Market Theory (EMT). This proposition—which essentially argues that
markets are, by definition, correctly priced and tend to be influenced
almost exclusively by rational investors acting in their own best interests—has long been a source of contention between certain academic
interests and experienced professionals who have actively traded shares
on a real-time basis. In the hypothetical world of EMT, anomalies such as
stock market bubbles cannot really exist—or if they do, they are but one
of what appears to be a series of exceptions to the rule. However, like
those who once believed in the emperor's new clothes, it seems that many
former adherents are starting to come around to the idea that the reality of
investing is somewhat different than what they had originally thought. As
it happens, what has helped to alter this perspective is another growing
body of academic research known as Behavioral Finance. This theory rec-
ognizes—correctly so, as many seasoned operators would argue—that
irrationality often plays a significant role in influencing when, how, and
why people buy and sell. Sadly, the shift has also been—and will probably continue to be—supported by the negative experiences of those millions of investors who got caught out by the EMT crowd during the
Bubble years, when the latter group essentially made the case that people
should stay fully invested in stocks "for the long run," regardless of price.

On the plus side, with this greater appreciation of the human factors
that can influence share prices is likely to come an improved understanding of one of the most basic tenets of equity investing. This is one that has
been fairly apparent for many years to those who have a contrarian bent,
and even to those who have merely taken the time to observe what goes
on around them—in nature, in business, and in everyday life. Simply put,
it is the fact that markets tend to overshoot and undershoot, getting dramatically expensive in some instances and exceptionally cheap in others,
because they are influenced by people with biases, emotions, and shortcomings that cause them to act in ways that often defy logic. And, then, as
Figure P3.1 suggests, the markets tend to swing back, like a pendulum,
and revert to their historic long-term averages. As Jeremy Grantham,
Chairman of fund group Grantham, Mayo, Van Otterloo & Company,
noted in January 2003, in the case of 27 different extraordinary moves—
or "classic asset bubbles," as he called these once-every-40-year swings—
involving a full range of instruments from stocks and bonds to currencies

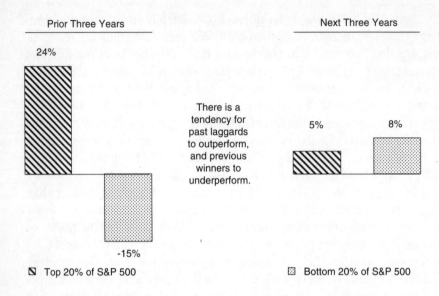

Figure P3.1   Reversion to the Mean? Earnings Growth Rates: 1974–2003
(Rolling Three-Year Periods through June 30, 2003) (Source: Bernstein Investment
Research and Management).

and commodities, "every single one retracted all of the gain [and went] all
the way back to the original trend line."[1].

And lest some make the argument that such reactions are confined to
extraordinary times or unusual macroeconomic circumstances, other
research suggests that is simply not the case. As equities historian David
Schwartz noted, writing in the United Kingdom's *Observer* newspaper,
"Periodic catastrophic declines that destroy years of accumulated profits
are the norm, not the exception," based on his analysis of two centuries of
data from the UK stock market. Adds Schwartz, "History teaches [us] that
virtually every major multi-year advance during the last two centuries
ended with a lengthy period of underperformance."[2] While skeptics might
key in on the fact that the conclusion was not based on an analysis of U.S.
share price trends, the relevance of British finance to the investing world
over the course of the past 200 years would seem to suggest it is not an
observation that should be taken lightly. Interestingly enough, on the back
of this view, one could even make the case that the recent shift towards a
more active trading approach is utterly justified, given the abnormally
high returns that have been seen in the American market over the past two
decades.

Perhaps more alarmingly, the inevitability of a reversion to the mean in the U.S. stock market and the long history of catastrophic declines may also lend credence to fears in some circles that there is an increased risk of a major financial "accident" taking place over the next few years—one which may ultimately affect all investors, large and small. Although there are any number of possible circumstances driving such worries—the widespread acceptance of venturesome behavior; the complexity of instruments and portfolios that depend on significant computational analysis for valuation, monitoring, and assessment; the dispersion of risk through the use of derivatives and other synthetic instruments; the speed with which markets can move and trades can be executed on all sorts of electronic exchanges; and the way that communications about potentially troubling developments can rapidly circulate around the globe—all seem to boost the odds that something may eventually go spectacularly wrong. Although there are supposedly systems and procedures in place that are meant to reduce the possibilities of a systemic reaction, it will be in investors' interests to keep a close eye out for any warning signs that may arise on this particular front.

Finally, while there are other changes that will probably come to pass—expanded regulation on the heels of the recent scandals, increasing disintermediation as individuals and institutions begin to deal directly with one another through the same electronic exchanges, shifting geopolitical fortunes and a continuing decline in America's once singular dominance, and a major restructuring of public and private retirement options—there is one perspective that will likely remain a steady fact of life in the stock market jungle. Just when everyone really starts to get comfortable with the way things are, that will be when circumstances will be set to change once again.

Additional References and Resources

Modern Conditions and Attitudes

Alan Abelson, "Up and Down Wall Street: Q and A: What's The Problem," *Barron's*, Jul. 14, 2003.

David Armstrong, "Short-Seller Rocker Partners Was Mauled by Bull Market," *The Wall Street Journal*, Jan. 23, 2004.

Andrew Bary, "Russian Roulette? Scorning History's Lessons, Investors Again Are Betting Heavily on Tech and Biotech," *Barron's*, Sep. 15, 2003.

Ken Brown, "Stocks March to the Beat of War, Weak Economy," *The Wall Street Journal*, Mar. 31, 2003.

E.S. Browning, "Many Investors Throwing Caution Back to the Wind," *The Wall Street Journal*, Sep. 22, 2003.

E.S. Browning, "Tech-Stock Surge Brings Back a Hint of the Late-1990s Frenzy: Share Rally Runs Well Ahead of Sales and Profit Growth," *The Wall Street Journal*, Aug. 22, 2003.

E.S. Browning, "What Lessons Learned? Markets Echo '99: Skeptics Say Stocks Have Formed An 'Echo Bubble' That Will Pop; But There Are Differences Now," *The Wall Street Journal*, Feb. 2, 2004.

Rebecca Byrne, "Toppy Markets Confound Technical Analysts," *TheStreet.com*, Jan. 8, 2004, http://www.thestreet.com/markets/rebeccabyrne/10135619.html.

Allison Bisbey Colter, "Hedging Trims Some Mutual-Fund Gains: Short-Selling Strategies Take a Toll on Returns as the Market Improves," Mutual Funds Monthly Review: July 2003, *The Wall Street Journal*, Aug. 4, 2003.

Chet Currier, "'Bubble II' in Stocks Is Risk to Be Reckoned With," *Bloomberg*, Jul. 8, 2003.

Bambi Francisco, "Compressing Learning Cycles: Commentary: 2000 Mentality Returns—at Net Speed," *CBS.MarketWatch.com*, Jan. 27, 2004, http://cbs.marketwatch.com/news/story.asp?guid={AE1A1375-7B71-4825-BA05-6D1799AD3491}&siteid=mktw&dist=&archive=true.

Martin Hutchinson, "The Bear's Lair: How News Moves the Markets," *United Press International*, Mar. 10, 2003.

Matt Krantz, "Day Traders Make a Comeback," *USA Today*, Jul. 28, 2003.

Justin Lahart, "Trading Like Lemmings: The Pack-Like Behavior of Stock Traders Has Reached Extremes Not Seen Since 1987," *CNN/Money*, Apr. 3, 2003, http://money.cnn.com/2003/04/03/markets/correlation/.

Maggie Mahar, *Bull! A History of the Boom, 1982-1999*, HarperBusiness, 2003.

Floyd Norris, "Bull Market 2003: The Worse the Company, the Better the Stock," *The New York Times*, Sep. 26, 2003.

Jeff D. Opdyke, "Déjà vu: Buying Stock on Margin is Back in Vogue: Regulators Worry as Investors Pour Borrowed Cash Into Market; Rolling the Dice on High Tech," *The Wall Street Journal*, Sep. 18, 2003.

Jay Palmer, "And Now...Bubbles Within Bubbles," *Barron's*, Dec. 8, 2003.

Michael Santoli, "Hunting Bears: Short Sellers Were Big Losers in the Latest Stock Rally," *Barron's*, Monday, Jul. 9, 2003.

Robert J. Shiller, *Irrational Exuberance*, Princeton University Press, 2000.

Sandra Ward, "Sucker Punch Coming: Jeremy Grantham Says It's Only a Bear-Market Rally," *Barron's*, Nov. 3, 2003.

Gregory Zuckerman, "Speculation Makes a Comeback and OTC Trading Sees a Surge," *The Wall Street Journal*, Oct. 10, 2003.

Hedge Funds and Alternative Investments

Nicole M. Boyson, "Do Hedge Funds Exhibit Performance Persistence? A New Approach," Oct. 2003, http://www.mgmt.purdue.edu/faculty/nboyson/persistence.pdf.

Markus K. Brunnermeier and Stefan Nagel. "Hedge Funds and the Technology Bubble," *Journal of Finance*, forthcoming, http://www.princeton.edu/~markus/research/papers/hedgefunds_bubble.pdf.

Judith Chase, "The State of Hedge Funds," *SIA Research Reports*, Mar. 10, 2003, http://www.sia.com/research/pdf/RsrchRprtVol4-2.pdf.

Ann Davis, "SEC Takes Closer Look At Hedge Funds," *The Wall Street Journal*, Feb. 2, 2004.

Ianthe Jeanne Dugan, "A Small Investor Lives Life on the Hedge: Sick of Stocks, Retired Engineer Joins Rush to Investment Pools; 'The Choices Are Bewildering,'" *The Wall Street Journal*, Apr. 9, 2003.

Dion Friedland and Magnum Funds, "About Hedge Funds," *Hedge Fund Association*, 2001, http://www.thehfa.org/AboutUs.cfm.

Steve Galbraith and Mary Viviano, "Morgan Stanley US Strategy: Tail or Dog—The Pond's Getting Crowded," Apr. 30, 2002.

"Introduction to Hedge Funds," Financial Risk Management, Jun. 2003, http://www.vfmc.vic.gov.au/documents/030911_intro_hedge_funds.pdf.

Joe Kolman, "LTCM Speaks: In a Series of Secretive Roadshows, LTCM Partners Now Admit They Badly Misjudged Market Dynamics and Volatility, Making Common Risk Management Mistakes on a Grand Scale," *Derivatives Strategy.com*, Apr. 1999, http://www.derivativesstrategy.com/magazine/archive/1999/0499fea1.asp.

Gene Koretz, "Economic Trends: Hedge Funds' Long Shadow," *BusinessWeek*, Jul. 16, 2001.

Roger Lowenstein, *When Genius Failed*, Random House, 2001.

Maha Khan Phillips, "Alternatives: Hedge Funds Still Failing At Risk Management," *Global Investor*, Nov. 2002.

"Spotlight on Hedge Funds," U.S. Securities and Exchange Commission, http://www.sec.gov/spotlight/hedgefunds.htm.

Daniel Strachman, "Managed Futures: Back in Vogue," *Futures Industry Magazine*, May/June 2003.

Richard Teitelbaum, "Wall Street Refugees," *Bloomberg Markets*, Nov. 2003.

David Wells, Robert Clow, and Elizabeth Rigby, "Hustling for the Hedge Funds' Dollar," *Financial Times*, Jul. 10, 2003.

Global Influences

Andrew S. Adelson and Seth Masters, "Are U.S. and Foreign Equities Separate Asset Classes?" *Institute for Fiduciary Education*, 2002, http://ifecorp.com/Papers-PDFs/Masters602.PDF.

Michael Brennan and Henry Cao, "International Portfolio Investment Flows," *Journal of Finance* 52, 1851–80.

Deborah Brewster, "Global Investing: US Investors Take Wider World View," *Financial Times*, Oct. 6, 2003.

Warren E. Buffett, "America's Growing Trade Deficit Is Selling the Nation Out From Under Us. Here's a Way to Fix the Problem— And We Need to Do It Now," *Fortune*, Oct. 26, 2003.

"Dancing in Step," *The Economist*, Mar. 22, 2001.

William H. Gross, "Investment Outlook, The Grand Scheme of Things," PIMCO, Jan. 2003, http://www.pimco.com/LeftNav/Late+Breaking+Commentary/IO/2003/IO_01_2003.htm.

Woochan Kim and Shang-Jin Wei, "Foreign Portfolio Investors Before and During a Crisis," CID Working Papers 6, Center for International Development at Harvard University, 1999.

Aaron Lucchetti, Greg Ip, and Phillip Day, "A Global Journal Report: U.S. Push for Weaker Dollar Rattles Markets Around Globe," *The Wall Street Journal*, Sep. 23, 2003.

Joel Millman, Phillip Day, Jason Singer, Michael R. Sesit, and Michael M. Phillips, "Foreign Cash Flow Is Vital to U.S.—But Will It Last?" *The Wall Street Journal*, Jan. 15, 2004.

Peter Navarro, *If It's Raining in Brazil, Buy Starbucks: The Investor's Guide to Profiting from News and Other Market-Moving Events*, McGraw-Hill Trade, 2001.

Richard Nisbett, *The Geography of Thought: How Asians and Westerners Think Differently...and Why*, Free Press, 2003.

Floyd Norris, "Foreigners May Not Have Liked the War, but They Financed It," *The New York Times*, Sep. 12, 2003.

Didier Sornette and Wei-Xing Zhou, "Evidence of Fueling of the 2000 New Economy Bubble by Foreign Capital Inflow: Implications for the Future of the US Economy and its Stock Market," Jun. 19, 2003, http://arxiv.org/PS_cache/cond-mat/pdf/0306/0306496.pdf.

"U.S. Investors Take a Wider World View," *The Financial Times*, October 6, 2003.

Information and Analysis

Alex Berenson, *The Number*, Random House, 2003.

Ken Brown, "As Analysis Gets Cut, More Firms Are Going Unheard on the Street," *The Wall Street Journal*, Oct. 27, 2003.

Ken Brown, "Wall Street Plays Numbers Game with Earnings, Despite Reforms," *The Wall Street Journal*, Jul. 22, 2003.

Louis K.C. Chan, Jason Karceski, and Josef Lakonishok, "Analysts' Conflict of Interest and Biases in Earnings Forecasts," Feb. 2003, http://www.afajof.org/Pdf/2004program/UPDF/P303_Asset_Pricing.pdf.

Lynn Cowan, "Pressure on Analysts Remains Despite Rise in Sell Ratings," *Dow Jones News Service*, Apr. 29, 2003.

Bill Fleckenstein, "Contrarian Chronicles: The Street Still Plays Games With Investors," *MSN Money*, Jul. 28, 2003, http://moneycentral.msn.com/content/P56519.asp.

James K. Glassman, "Another P for Your Pod: Take P/S Ratios as Seriously as You Take P/Es," *National Review Online*, Oct. 2, 2003, http://www.nationalreview.com/nrof_glassman/glassman200310020809.asp.

Ron Lazer, "The Increased Importance of Earnings Announcements after Regulation FD: Evidence from Revisions of Analysts' Forecasts and Pre-Announcements," Preliminary Draft, Jan. 2004, http://www.rotman.utoronto.ca/accounting/lazer.pdf.

Neal Lipschutz, "Point of View: Selective Disclosure Still Doing Damage," *Dow Jones News Service*, Sep. 15, 2003.

"Market Commentary: Distorted Values," Comstock Partners, Inc., Feb. 5, 2004, http://www.comstockfunds.com/index.cfm/act/newsletter.cfm/CFID/5410450/CFTOKEN/11523150/category/market%20commentary/menuitemid/29/MenuGroup/Home/NewsLetter ID/1069/startrow/7.htm.

"Market Commentary: Exclusion of 'One-Time' Charges Still a Problem," Comstock Partners, Inc., Feb. 3, 2004, http://www.comstock funds.com/index.cfm/act/newsletter.cfm/category/market%20 commentary/menuitemid/29/MenuGroup/Home/NewsLetterID/ 1067/startrow/4.htm.

Gretchen Morgenson, "New Math Aside, Earnings Still Reign," *The New York Times*, Feb. 1, 2004.

John R. Nofsinger and Kenneth A. Kim, *Infectious Greed: Restoring Confidence in America's Companies,* Financial Times Prentice Hall, 2003.

Andy Puckett and Marc L. Lipson, "Who Trades on Analysts' Recommendations?" Midwest Finance Association 53rd Annual Meeting, Mar. 18–20, 2004, http://www.mfa-2004.com/papers/7065830385 ap.pdf.

Susan Pulliam, "Street Sleuth: Return Of the Online Hype," *The Wall Street Journal*, Jan. 12, 2004.

Lauren R. Rublin, "The Whole Truth: A Value Manager Profits By Looking Through The Numbers and Running Against The Crowd," *Barron's*, Nov. 17, 2003.

Anna Scherbina, "Analyst Disagreement, Forecast Bias, and Stock Returns," Sep. 2003, https://wpweb2k.gsia.cmu.edu/wfa/wfasecure/upload/779578_dispersiontitlepage.pdf.

Ellen E. Schultz and Theo Francis, "GM, Others Boost Their Earnings By Pouring Billions Into Pensions," *The Wall Street Journal*, Dec. 4, 2003.

Shawn Young, "Talking Up 'Net Debt' Allows Some Firms to Take a Load Off," *The Wall Street Journal*, Jul. 28, 2003.

Institutional Behavior and Investor Psychology

Timothy R. Burch and Bhaskaran Swaminathan, "Are Institutions Momentum Traders?" Nov. 2001, http://ssrn.com/abstract= 291643.

Edward Chancellor, *Devil Take the Hindmost: A History of Financial Speculation*, Farrar Straus & Giroux, 1999.

Víctor M. Eguíluz and Martín G. Zimmermann, "Transmission of Information and Herd Behavior: An Application to Financial Markets," *Phys. Rev. Lett.* 85, 5659, Dec. 23, 2000.

Josh M. Griffin, Jeffrey H. Harris, and Selim Topaloglu, "The Dynamics of Institutional and Individual Trading," *Journal of Finance*, Dec. 2003.

Mark Grinblatt and Matti Keloharju, "The Investment Behavior and Performance of Various Investor Types: A Study of Finland's Unique Data Set," *Journal of Financial Economics* 55, 43–67.

"Herding Psychology and Financial Markets," The Socionomics Institute, 2003, http://www.socionomics.org/what_is/what_is_herding _psychology.aspx.

David Hirshleifer and Siew Hong Teoh, "Herd Behavior and Cascading in Capital Markets: A Review and Synthesis," Dec. 19, 2001.

"Investment Perspectives: Exploiting the Effects of Emotions on the Capital Markets," Bernstein Investment Management & Research, Oct. 8, 2003, http://www.bernstein.com/Public/story.aspx?cid= 1252&pid=0&nid=184.

Bruce I. Jacobs, "Momentum Trading: The New Alchemy," *Journal of Investing*, Winter 2000.

"John J. Wheeler on Institutional Order Routing," *The Trader Bulletin*, Jul. 3, 2003, http://www.traderbulletin.com/stories/storyReader $770.

Charles Mackay, *Extraordinary Popular Delusions and the Madness of Crowds* (Reprint Edition), Three Rivers Press, 1995.

John R. Nofsinger, *Investment Madness: How Psychology Affects Your Investing...and What to Do About It*, Financial Times Prentice Hall, 2001.

John R. Nofsinger and Richard W. Sias, "Herding and Feedback Trading by Institutional and Individual Investors," *Journal of Finance* 54, 2263–2295.

Robert R. Prechter, Jr., "Unconscious Herding Behavior as the Psychological Basis of Financial Market Trends and Patterns," *The Journal of Psychology and Financial Markets*, 2001, Vol. 2, No. 3, 120–125.

Jeffrey Rothfeder, "Case Study: NASDAQ," *CIO Insight*, Jun. 16, 2003, http://www.cioinsight.com/article2/0,3959,1459034,00.asp.

Richard W. Sias, "The Behavior of Institutional Investors: Tests for Herding, Stealth Trading, and Momentum Trading," Mar. 9, 2001, http://www.panagora.com/research/2001crowell/2001cp_36.pdf.

Marcia Vickers, "The Most Powerful Trader on Wall Street You've Never Heard Of: Meet Steve Cohen. Even His Enemies Admit He's the Best Stock Trader Around, Routinely Trouncing the Market with His $4 Billion Hedge Fund. Just How Does He Do it?" *BusinessWeek*, Jul. 21, 2003.

Bill Virgin, "Investors Will Happily Delude Themselves," *Seattle Post-Intelligencer*, Jun. 26, 2003.

Seasonal and Cyclical Factors

E.S. Browning, "Investors Take Cycles for a Spin," *The Wall Street Journal*, Jan. 26, 2004.

E.S. Browning, "Investors Wonder Whether Stocks Will Be Naughty or Nice," *The Wall Street Journal*, Nov. 17, 2003.

Yale Hirsch, *Stock Trader's Almanac 2004*, Jeffrey A. Hirsch (Editor), John Wiley & Sons, 2003.

David Hirshleifer and Tyler Shumway, "Good Day Sunshine: Stock Returns and the Weather," Aug. 17, 2001, http://www.cob.ohio-state.edu/fin/dice/papers/2001/2001-3.pdf.

"International Banking and Financial Market Developments," *BIS Quarterly Review*, Jun. 2003, http://www.bis.org/publ/qtrpdf/r_qt0306.pdf.

Mark Kamstra, Lisa Kramer, and Maurice Levi, "Winter Blues: A SAD Stock Market Cycle," *American Economic Review*, Mar. 2003.

Angeline M. Lavin, "An Empirical Investigation of the Persistence of Stock and Bond Return Seasonality," *Journal of Applied Business Research*, Vol. 16, No. 2, Spring 2000.

W. Marquering, "Seasonal Predictability of Stock Market Returns," Tijdschrift voor Economie en Management, Vol. 47, 2002, http://web.eur.nl/fbk/dep/dep5/faculty/wmarquering/seasonal.

Ian McDonald, "Mutual Funds Grateful for Automatic Pilots," *The Wall Street Journal*, Jul. 8, 2003.

Glenn N. Pettengill and John R. Wingender, Jr., "Short-Sellers, Put Options and the Monday Effect: Another Look (Extended Abstract)," Midwest Finance Association Annual Meeting, Mar. 18–24, 2004, http://www.mfa-2004.com/papers/jwmfa04.doc.

Stephen Roach, "Global Economic Forum: The Latest Views of Morgan Stanley Economists: Global: Macro Passion," Nov. 17, 2003, http://www.morganstanley.com/GEFdata/digests/20031117-mon.html#anchor0.

Mike Robbins, "Strategies: How to Pick the Right Stock for the Season," *MSN Money*, Dec. 16, 1998, http://moneycentral.msn.com/articles/invest/strat/2893.asp.

Heydon Traub, "Bear Hibernation: A Method Behind Calendar Myth," *Boston Business Journal*, Nov. 21, 2003, http://www.bizjournals.com/boston/stories/2003/11/24/editorial5.html.

Tom Walker, "Statistics Tell Seasonal Story of Stock Market," *Laredo Morning Times Business Journal*, Aug. 11, 2003, http://www.lmtonline.com/lmtbusiness/archive/081103/jrnl2.pdf.

Derivatives, Leverage and Volatility

Antony Currie, "Harvesting Value from Volatility," *Euromoney*, Jun. 2003.

Robert H. Dugger, "Remarks to the Economic Outlook Roundtable 2004: Financial Leverage and the U.S. Economic Outlook for 2004 and Beyond," Federal Deposit Insurance Corporation, Dec. 12, 2003.

Kenneth L. Fisher, "Volatility, the Good Kind: The Bear Market Made It Fashionable to Say Stocks Might be Flat for Ten Years or More. It Has Never Happened that Stocks Lie Flat for a Decade," *Forbes*, Jun. 23, 2003.

Yuka Hayashi, "Investors Find More Use for a Tool: Exchange-Traded Funds, With Varied Exposures, Are Gaining in Popularity," *The Wall Street Journal*, Jul. 17, 2003.

Tom Kohn, "Derivatives Market Grows 20% to $170 Tln, BIS says" *Bloomberg*, Nov. 12, 2003.

Justin Lahart, "Watch the VIX: Wall Street's Favorite Sentiment Reading May be Giving a False Signal," *CNN/Money*, Jan. 26, 2004, http://money.cnn.com/2004/01/26/commentary/bidask/bidask/.

Ian McDonald, "Complainers Are Culprits When It Comes to Volatility," *The Wall Street Journal*, Jul. 7, 2003.

Michael Santoli, "Back to the Futures: Pre-Trading Readings Foretell Stock Market's Opening Tone, But Beware the '10 a.m. Turnaround,'" *Barron's*, Jan. 19, 2004.

Kopin Tan, "Cruising in Convertibles: For Many, They're the Vehicle of Choice," *Barron's*, Jul. 7, 2003.

Aaron L. Task, "E-Minis Cause Some Major Worry," *TheStreet.com*, Jul. 28, 2003, http://www.thestreet.com/markets/aarontaskfree/10103840.html.

Markets and Trading

Elroy Dimson, Paul Marsh, and Mike Staunton, "Irrational Optimism," *Financial Analysts Journal*, Vol. 60, No. 1, pp. 15-25, Jan./Feb. 2004.

Thomas G. Donlan, "A Fool and His Money: Staking One's Fortunes on Efficient Markets Isn't Wise" *Barron's*, Feb. 16, 2004.

Robert D. Edwards and John Magee, *Technical Analysis of Stock Trends*, W.H.C. Bassetti (Editor), Saint Lucie Press, 2001.

Jeremy Grantham, "Special Topic: Ivory Towers," Grantham, Mayo, Van Otterloo & Co. LLC, Jan. 2003.

"In Search of Those Elusive Returns," *The Economist*, Mar. 20, 2003.

Charles M. Jones, "A Century of Stock Market Liquidity and Trading Costs," May 2002, http://www.columbia.edu/~cj88/papers/century.pdf.

Owen A. Lamont and Jeremy C. Stein, "Aggregate Short Interest and Market Valuations," Dec. 2000, http://mba.yale.edu/pdf/aggshortinterest.pdf.

Edwin Lefèvre and Market Place Books, *Reminiscences of a Stock Operator*, John Wiley & Sons, 1994.

Jon D. Markman, *Swing Trading: Power Strategies to Cut Risk and Boost Profits*, John Wiley & Sons, 2003.

John J. Murphy, *Technical Analysis of the Financial Markets*, Prentice Hall Press, 1999.

Peter Navarro, *When the Markets Move, Will You be Ready?* McGraw-Hill Trade, 2003.

Philip Russel and Ben Branch, "Penny Stocks of Bankrupt Firms: Are They Really a Bargain?" 2001, http://www.westga.edu/~bquest/2001/penny.htm.

Michael Santoli, "Silver Lining: Grasso's Exit from the NYSE May Portend Lower Costs for Investors," *Barron's*, Sep. 22, 2003.

David Schwartz, "Revealed: The Great Stock Market Swindle," *The Observer*, Jul. 13, 2003.

Deborah Solomon and Kate Kelly, "NYSE May Revise Best-Price Rule," *The Wall Street Journal*, Feb. 3, 2004.

Deborah Solomon and Kate Kelly, "Wide SEC Review May Revamp Structure of U.S. Stock Markets: As Upstart Trading Venues Proliferate, Donaldson sees "Stresses and Strains," *The Wall Street Journal*, Sep. 19, 2003.

Endnotes

Part 1

1. Bulls are those who believe prices—of individual securities or the overall market—are headed higher, while bears are those who look for lower prices. Dogs are securities that have performed poorly in comparison to others. Dinosaurs are certain companies in mature industries. Spiders are a phonetic representation of SPDRs (Standard & Poor's Depositary Receipts), American Stock Exchange–listed securities designed to track moves in the well-known market index. Sharks are aggressive market operators who capitalize on the naiveté of less-experienced investors.

2. Broadly describing the widespread shift towards—and enthusiasm for—electronic commerce on the Internet, this expression literally refers to the ".com' appendage found on the end of the addresses of most commercially oriented Web sites.

3. This term was made famous by Alan Greenspan, long-serving Chairman of the Federal Reserve Board of Governors, during a 1996 speech that questioned whether investors had unduly boosted share values without regard to any of the potential downside risks. It was later the subject (and title) of a popular business book by Robert J. Shiller.

4. Block trades are transactions of 10,000 shares or more.

5. This is calculated by multiplying the market price of a stock by the total number of shares outstanding.

6. Joshua D. Coval, David A. Hirshleifer, and Tyler G. Shumway, "Can Individual Investors Beat the Market?" Harvard NOM Working Paper No. 02-45, Jan. 6, 2003, http://ssrn.com/abstract=364000.

7. The Securities and Exchange Commission ordered this in response to pressure from the U.S. Justice Department.

8. ECNs are "virtual" marketplaces where buyers and sellers can display, match, and execute orders. CNs are order-matching systems designed to help buy-side institutions efficiently balance offsetting supply and demand needs.

9. Mandated by Congress and ordered by the SEC in August 2000, the change from fractional increments to cents helped to narrow the spread between "bids" (what "displayed" buyers are prepared to pay) and "offers" (what sellers are willing to accept), effectively reducing trading costs.

10. Energetic options trading reportedly took place in Holland during the Tulipmania of the 1600s, while Chinese rice dealers are known to have hedged their exposure with futures in the eighteenth century.

11. This change was stoked in large measure by the explosive growth of "cash-poor" TMT start-ups and the enthusiastic granting of incentive stock options by a wide variety of publicly traded corporations.

12. Starting in 2001, the Federal Reserve embarked on an aggressive course of monetary stimulus, featuring multiple cuts in short-term interest rates, intended to keep the faltering U.S. economy afloat.

13. As an interesting aside, one recent study provides additional support for previous research showing greater risk-taking behavior among young managers. See Nicole M. Boyson, "Do Hedge Funds Exhibit Performance Persistence? A New Approach," Oct. 2003, http://www.mgmt.purdue.edu/faculty/nboyson/persistence.pdf.

14. Jack Willoughby, "Happy Trails: Stocks Are Heading Higher, Portfolio Managers Say," *Barron's*, Oct. 27, 2003.

15. Markus K. Brunnermeier and Stefan Nagel, "Hedge Funds and the Technology Bubble," *Journal of Finance*, forthcoming, http://www.princeton.edu/~markus/research/papers/hedgefunds_bubble.pdf.

16. Amid suggestions by "futurists" such as Alvin Toffler that the limits on human processing power may have already been reached.

17. Through "fund of funds" or pooled investment programs and other means.

18. Sales-traders are specialized sales representatives who have traditionally provided trading and advisory support directly to buy-side equity dealing desks.

19. Market-makers are sell-side traders who have authority to make prices and commit resources to buy and sell securities with their firm's clients and other authorized counterparties.

20. This classic market theory revolves around the idea that an imprudent purchaser will eventually be able to offload a questionable investment on another foolish buyer at a higher price.

21. They had only been allowed to do this because of rule changes triggered by the Taxpayer Relief Act of 1997.

22. Chaos Theory is a method of analyzing complex systems first developed during the 1960s.

23. Regulation Fair Disclosure was put into effect by the SEC in October, 2000.

24. The Sarbanes-Oxley Act of 2002 was enacted by Congress in January of that year.

Part 2

Chapter 1

1. Specialists are exchange-designated market-makers who are obligated to buy or sell shares as necessary to maintain an "orderly" market in those securities.

2. Some lower-priced securities or exchange-traded funds were denominated in sixteenths or even thirty-seconds. After 2000, some of the more actively traded issues were priced with the lower order fractions.

3. These are mechanisms that trigger a message or warning when a security trades in the market at a predetermined price.

4. Some strategies rely on trading only a certain proportion of the underlying securities, usually determined through statistical analysis.

5. The messaging feature offered by Bloomberg LP does allow unread messages sent to other subscribers to be retracted.

6. These are electronically traded futures contracts, typically with lower value denominations than those bought and sold on the floor of the commodities exchanges. Each Chicago Board of Trade–listed Dow Jones e-mini is worth $5 times the value of the index, or approximately $45,000 at July 2003 prices.

7. Stop-losses are buy or sell orders that become active when a security or commodity trades in the market at or through a predetermined price.

Chapter 2

1. Monetary policy refers to actions taken by a central bank to control interest rates and the money supply, often to ward off inflation or currency woes. Fiscal policy refers to government spending decisions and the impact they have on the overall economy.

2. Y2K is shorthand for the year 2000. It also referred to the technology-inspired fear that some older computer programs would not function properly when the first two digits of the calendar year switched from 19 to 20 at the turn of the century.

3. Initial Public Offerings are SEC-registered shares sold by a company and offered to the public for the first time.

4. The yield on the safest possible investment, this is often based on the returns available from three-month U.S. government treasury bills.

5. This describes when the actual or estimated price of a security or securities is recorded to determine the value of an outstanding position or portfolio.

6. These are fixed income securities that can be exchanged for other related securities during some predetermined period at an established price—usually, but not always, at the option of the holder.

7. Although futures, options, LEAPS (Long-Term Equity Anticipation securities, a form of long-dated, exchange-listed option), and warrants (another type of long-term option) can have maturity dates that stretch out a year or more into the future, most equity-related activity tends to be centered on securities that expire in three months or less.

8. ETFs, or index shares, are depositary receipts representing ownership of baskets of individual stocks which track indices but trade like shares. Some popular examples include the Dow Jones Industrial Average index shares, known as "Diamonds," which have the quote symbol "DIA"; the S&P 500 ETFs, referred to as "Spiders," which have the symbol "SPY"; and, the NASDAQ 100 index shares—based on the market-weighted measure of the 100 largest constituents of the NAS-DAQ Stock Market Index—known as "Qubes," which goes by the symbol "QQQ."

9. Indications of Interest are a specialized form of electronic broadcast messaging designed to uncover natural pools of liquidity that can help balance short-term supply and demand needs.

10. Whisper numbers are informal but up-to-the-minute consensus views of forthcoming earnings reports and economic statistics. For more information, check out Web sites such as *www.whispernumber.com.*

Chapter 3

1. A floor broker is a member of an exchange who executes orders on behalf of others.
2. For example, the New York Stock Exchange's SuperDOT (Super Direct Order Turnaround) electronic routing system accepts limit (fixed price) orders for up to 99,999 shares and market orders for up to 30,099 shares.
3. Perhaps one of the wildest examples of one person's influence over share prices is that of New Jersey teenager Jonathan Lebed, who rose to fame when he settled with the SEC in 2000 over stock manipulation charges without admitting or denying guilt. On January 7, 2004, he reportedly recommended a stock called Renegade Venture Corp. which managed to surge 8.2 percent before closing down 14 percent on 10 times average daily volume. See Susan Pullman, "Street Sleuth: Return of the Online Hype." *The Wall Street Journal*, Jan. 12, 2004.
4. This formed the basis of the $1.4 billion Global Settlement agreement involving 10 major brokerage firms, the stock exchanges, the SEC, and various state securities regulators. There were also numerous investor lawsuits.
5. These rules are mandated by the Sarbanes-Oxley Act of 2002 and the Global Settlement accord.
6. Resistance refers to a level that represents at least a short-term barrier to further increases in the price of a security or commodity. The corresponding opposite is known as "support."
7. Tape-watchers are market participants who focus on and analyze the continuous record of share transactions reported by the various exchanges for clues about investor interest and potential future price moves.
8. Technical analysis is an analytical method that studies factors such as price and volume to determine supply and demand conditions and potential future price moves.
9. The translation, for those who are interested, goes as follows: The original questioner A, most likely an institutional investor or trader, is asking what the current market price of Coca-Cola shares is. The respondent B, who could be a floor broker on the New York Stock Exchange or sales-trader, responds first with the buying interest that is

being indicated on the floor. In this case, the bid is 20 (e.g., $48.20), which would typically represent the digits to the right of the decimal point, and the amount is most likely 14,000 (though it could be 1,400 in a high-priced or thinly traded issue). The displayed selling interest is 24, and the amount on offer is 3,000 shares. A then requests that B try to sell 14,000 at 20. B comes back and indicates that only 12,000 shares were completed at that level and that another lower offer had come into the market at 11. A decides to cut the price on the 2,000 shares remaining to 8, making that the most competitive offer. Eventually, another buyer steps in and B reports that A sold the balance of the order at that price.

Chapter 4

1. A label first used by former U.S. Vice President Al Gore to describe a high-speed communications network designed to carry voice, data, video, and other information around the world, it is sometimes used as a synonym for the modern Internet.
2. Specialist-salespeople are representatives who focus on a specific product, sector, geographical region, or client base.
3. This form of indirect response was made famous when Richard Nixon was U.S. President.
4. The FOMC is the policy-making arm of the Federal Reserve Bank.
5. Beta measures the risk of a security relative to the market as a whole. Beta-adjusted means that positions are weighted accordingly, with the more volatile securities having a proportionally greater impact on net market exposure than their less volatile counterparts.
6. Andy Puckett and Marc L. Lipson, "Who Trades on Analysts' Recommendations?" Midwest Finance Association 53rd Annual Meeting, Mar. 18–20, 2004, http://www.mfa-2004.com/papers/7065830385ap.pdf.

Chapter 5

1. This is a good-faith deposit, marked-to-market or adjusted daily, that is designed to ensure that contractual obligations are honored.
2. Benchmarking is targeting a specified market barometer or standard as a baseline measure of performance.
3. With the relatively recent introduction of single-stock futures, a more accurate description might be "Quadruple Witching."

4. This is the process by which an option premium naturally shrinks as the time remaining to expiration decreases.

5. Federal Regulations T and U, mandated by the Securities Exchange Act of 1934.

6. Rule 10a-1 and 10a-2 under the Securities Exchange Act of 1934; SEC Rule 105 of Regulation M; NASD Rule 3350.

7. The computerized trading system established by the NASD, NASDAQ was originally an acronym for National Association of Securities Dealers Automated Quotation system.

8. According to the New York Stock Exchange definition, program trading includes a wide range of portfolio-trading strategies involving the purchase or sale of a basket of at least 15 stocks with a total value of $1 million or more.

9. One such is the NYSE Collar (Rule 80A).

10. These are orders executed at the best available price at or near the close of trading.

Chapter 6

1. For an interesting academic overview, based on stock market returns from Belgium, Germany, the Netherlands, UK and U.S., see W. Marquering, "Seasonal Predictability of Stock Market Returns," *Tijdschrift voor Economie en Management,* Vol. 47, 2002, http://web.eur.nl/fbk/dep/dep5/faculty/wmarquering/seasonal.

2. *Stock Trader's Almanac* is produced annually by Yale Hirsch and Jeffrey A. Hirsch, and published by John Wiley & Sons, Inc.

3. Heydon Traub, "Bear Hibernation: A Method Behind Calendar Myth," *Boston Business Journal,* Nov. 21, 2003, http://www.bizjournals.com/boston/stories/2003/11/24/editorial5.html.

4. These plans are so named because they are found in Section 401(k) of the Internal Revenue Code.

5. See Traub above.

6. Window-dressing is the euphemism that describes the deceptive practice of buying and selling certain shares to create a favorable portfolio snapshot at the end of a quarter or year.

7. A $1.00 change in the price of any share in the index has an equivalent effect on the value of the benchmark.

8. Stephen Roach, "Global: Macro Passion," *Global Economic Forum: The Latest Views of Morgan Stanley Economists*, Nov. 17, 2003, http://www.morganstanley.com/GEFdata/digests/20031117-mon.html#anchor0.

9. There are other theories as to why the shift may have occurred. These include the introduction of put options and the growth of institutional investors, though the latter would presumably lend support to the view that investors' attempts to capitalize on anomalies ends up changing them. See Glenn N. Pettengill and John R. Wingender, Jr., "Short-Sellers, Put Options and the Monday Effect: Another Look (Extended Abstract)," Midwest Finance Association Annual Meeting, Mar. 18–24, 2004, http://www.mfa-2004.com/papers/jwmfa04.doc.

10. "International Banking and Financial Market Developments," *BIS Quarterly Review*, Jun. 2003, http://www.bis.org/publ/qtrpdf/r_qt0306.pdf.

11. Ken Brown, "Stocks March to the Beat of War, Weak Economy," *The Wall Street Journal,* Mar. 31, 2003.

Chapter 7

1. Jeffrey Rothfeder, "Case Study: NASDAQ," *CIO Insight,* Jun. 16, 2003, http://www.cioinsight.com/article2/0,3959,1459034,00.asp.

2. For an interesting overview, see Richard W. Sias, "The Behavior of Institutional Investors: Tests for Herding, Stealth Trading, and Momentum Trading," Mar. 9, 2001, http://www.panagora.com/research/2001crowell/2001cp_36.pdf.

3. Some traders have been known to skirt the rules and engage in "naked" short-selling—in other words, they do not make any arrangements to borrow the stock in advance. Regulators have been exploring ways to prohibit the practice.

4. Floyd Norris, "Bull Market 2003: The Worse the Company, the Better the Stock," *The New York Times,* Sep. 26, 2003.

Chapter 8

1. The price earnings ratio is the price divided by earnings per share (EPS).

2. Benjamin Graham and David Dodd are the authors of a classic book on value investing called *Security Analysis*.

3. This is a figurative, and often physical, separation between those on the investment banking side of the equity business and those performing secondary research, sales, and trading functions, intended to prevent the illegal use of inside information.

4. Lynn Cowan, "Pressure on Analysts Remains Despite Rise in Sell Ratings," *Dow Jones News Service,* Apr. 29, 2003.

5. Ibid.

6. GAAP is Generally Accepted Accounting Principles, mandated by the Financial Accounting Standards Board.

7. Sometime between the fourth quarter of 2001 and the end of 2002, companies were required to begin reassessing the value of their intangible assets on an annual basis and to write them down to their present value. This represented a substantial modification from previous treatment, and was mandated by an accounting rule change known as FASB 142.

8. Ken Brown, "Wall Street Plays Numbers Game with Earnings, Despite Reforms," *The Wall Street Journal*, Jul. 22, 2003.

9. "Baby Bells" was the name given to the Regional Bell Operating Companies created in the wake of the break-up of AT&T in 1984.

10. Shawn Young, "Talking Up 'Net Debt' Allows Some Firms to Take a Load Off," *The Wall Street Journal*, Jul. 28, 2003.

11. Ellen E. Schultz and Theo Francis, "GM, Others Boost Their Earnings by Pouring Billions into Pensions," *The Wall Street Journal,* Dec. 4, 2003.

12. Gretchen Morgenson, "New Math Aside, Earnings Still Reign," *The New York Times*, Feb. 1, 2004.

Chapter 9

1. Robert D. Edwards and John Magee, *Technical Analysis of Stock Trends.* W.H.C. Bassetti (ed.). Saint Lucie Press, 2001.

2. Daniel Strachman, "Managed Futures: Back in Vogue," *Futures Industry Magazine,* May/Jun. 2003.

3. For more information about surveys from: Investors Intelligence, see *www.investorsintelligence.com;* Market Vane, see *www.marketvane.net*; Consensus, see *www.consensus-inc.com*; and American Association of Individual Investors, see *www.aaii.com.*

4. The Vix index was formerly based on the S&P 100 index, also known as the OEX. Another similar indicator that some operators look at is the Vxn index, which is based on the NASDAQ 100 index.

Chapter 10

1. "U.S. International Travel and Transportation Trends: Overseas Travel Trends," Bureau of Transportation Statistics, U.S. Department of Transportation, http://www.bts.gov/publications/us_international _travel_and_transportation_trends/overtrends.html.

2. Steve Holland, "Bush Vows to Help Restore Lost Manufacturing Jobs," *Forbes.com,* Sep. 1, 2003, http://images.forbes.com/work/newswire/ 2003/09/01/rtr1070410.html.

3. This is an example of the dollar-oriented currency convention used by foreign exchange traders, which usually, though not always, refers to the ratio of the foreign unit to the greenback.

4. Dollars are often held as reserves by foreign central banks to provide a measure of diversified backing for local currencies.

5. William H. Gross, "Investment Outlook: The Grand Scheme of Things," PIMCO, Jan. 2003, http://www.pimco.com/LeftNav/ Late+Breaking+Commentary/IO/2003/IO_01_2003.htm.

6. According to Gross, "Foreigners now hold over $7 trillion of U.S. assets and they will not take kindly to a devaluing of their investments. 13% of the U.S. stock market, 35% of the U.S. Treasury market, 23% of the U.S. corporate bond market, and 14% direct ownership in U.S. companies are now in the hands of foreign investors." More recent Treasury Department data, in fact, suggests the proportion of U.S. government securities that foreigners own exceeds 40 percent.

7. Ibid.

8. "Asian Tigers" is the name given to the economies of Taiwan, Hong Kong, South Korea, and Singapore—and sometimes others in the region—used as a catch-all phrase to highlight the phenomenal economic growth many experienced in the latter part of the twentieth century.

9. Michael Brennan and Henry Cao, 1997, International Portfolio Investment Flows, *Journal of Finance* 52, 1851–1880. Woochan Kim & Shang-Jin Wei, 1999. "Foreign Portfolio Investors Before and During a Crisis," CID Working Papers 6, Center for International Development at Harvard University. Mark Grinblatt and Matti Keloharju, 2000, "The Investment Behavior and Performance of Various Investor Types: A Study of Finland's Unique Data Set," *Journal of Financial Economics* 55, 43–67.

10. Richard Nisbett. *The Geography of Thought: How Asians and Westerners Think Differently...and Why.* Free Press, 2003.

11. "Long bond" is a popular name for the U.S. 30-year Treasury bond.

12. This is a benchmark measure comprised of the shares of the 50 largest European companies.
13. ADRs is short for American Depositary Receipts, which are certificates representing a depositary interest in a foreign security that are traded like ordinary U.S. shares.
14. "U.S. Investors Take a Wider World View," *The Financial Times,* Oct. 6, 2003.
15. Warren E. Buffet, "America's Growing Trade Deficit Is Selling the Nation Out From Under Us. Here's a Way to Fix the Problem—And We Need to Do It Now," *Fortune,* Oct. 26, 2003.
16. NAFTA is the North American Free Trade Agreement.

Part 3

1. Jeremy Grantham, "Special Topic: Ivory Towers," Grantham, Mayo, Van Otterloo & Co. LLC, Jan. 2003.
2. David Schwartz, "Revealed: The Great Stock Market Swindle," *The Observer,* Jul. 13, 2003.

Index

informIT

www.informit.com

YOUR GUIDE TO IT REFERENCE

Articles

Keep your edge with thousands of free articles, in-depth
features, interviews, and IT reference recommendations –
all written by experts you know and trust.

Online Books

Answers in an instant from **InformIT Online Book's** 600+
fully searchable on line books. Sign up now and get your
first 14 days **free**.

POWERED BY

Safari

Catalog

Review online sample chapters, author biographies and
customer rankings and choose exactly the right book from
a selection of over 5,000 titles.

Investment Fables

The world is full of investment stories: "Buy companies trading below book value, and you can't lose." "Buy stocks that are already going up." "Buy stocks with low P/Es." "Stick with quality companies and you'll do fine." "Buy after bad news." "Buy after good news." "Follow the insiders." "Do whatever Warren Buffett's doing." You've heard 'em all — but which ones hold up to critical examination? Do any of them? In this book, one of the world's leading investment researchers identifies 14 widely touted "investment stories," and the psychological reasons that make each story so compelling. Then he runs the numbers — objectively.

© 2004, 576 pp., ISBN 0131403125, $29.95

"This is a magnificent, creative, scholarly— indeed a noble—book and one that should be in every investment library and on every practitioner's desk. Like a good doctor, the author diagnoses a serious illness, and then provides a prescription for how to alleviate it."

Victor Niederhoffer, Chief Speculator, Manchester Investments

Aswath Damodaran

Investment Fables

Exposing the Myths of "Can't Miss" Investment Strategies

Stock Profits

Traditional methods of analyzing and picking stocks aren't enough anymore. The key reason: some companies now systematically distort the operating results that investors depend upon for accurate analysis. In *Stock Profits: Getting to the Core*, Michael C. Thomsett offers a new approach to fundamental analysis that reveals exactly what's real — and what isn't. Thomsett shows how to strip away misleading data that distorts a company's true "core earnings," growth curves, and business realities. You'll learn powerful new ways to manage market risk by assessing a stock's fundamental volatility. Next, Thomsett shows how to apply all five elements of success in today's market: investigation, regulation, communication, planning and discipline. Whether you're already using fundamental analysis, technical analysis, or a dartboard, *Stock Profits* can help you achieve higher, more consistent return.

© 2005, 288 pp., ISBN 0131435272, $24.95

New Fundamentals for a New Age

STOCK PROFITS

Getting to the Core

Michael C. Thomsett

For more information on our business titles, visit www.ft-ph.com